THE
UNWELCOME
IMMIGRANT

Stuart Creighton Miller

THE UNWELCOME IMMIGRANT

The American Image
of the Chinese,
1785-1882

UNIVERSITY OF CALIFORNIA PRESS

BERKELEY AND LOS ANGELES   1969

University of California Press
Berkeley and Los Angeles, California
Copyright © 1969, by
The Regents of the University of California
Library of Congress Catalog Card Number: 76-81763
Printed in the United States of America

TO
THE CHINESE-AMERICAN COMMUNITY
AND ITS TRANSCENDING DIGNITY

Foreword

The only immigrants barred by law and by name from entering the United States in the nineteenth century, except for Africans, were the Chinese. Traditionally, the American aversion for non-whites has been offered as the explanation for the exclusion law of 1882. Recently, this interpretation has been ably contested by Dr. Gunther Barth. Barth has argued that the hostility to the Chinese, especially in California which has borne the major blame for the exclusionist legislation, was due to their peculiarity as unfree sojourners who by their presence threatened the assumptions of a society committed to freedom and a cohesive nationalism and insistent that all newcomers sink their roots in American soil and accept its terms.

Professor Stuart C. Miller now contributes an entirely new dimension to our perception of the problem. In this exhaustively researched study, Miller demonstrates that anti-Chinese attitudes were national and not at all merely regional, that they antedated the coming of the coolie migration by at least a generation, that they reflected a clash of extremely contrasting cultures and values, and finally that events and developments of the mid-century and after only seemed to vindicate these predispositions. American opinion makers, both in China and at home, as Miller makes clear, invariably portray the Chinese as uniquely enslaved to an idolatrous ancient tradition, politically servile, morally depraved, and loathsomely diseased. China was viewed as singularly impervious to nineteenth-century ideals of progress, liberty, and civilization to which an emergent modern America was fervently committed. No less a representative American than Ralph Waldo Emerson was absolutely convinced of the irredeemable backwardness of the Chinese. By contrast, the Japanese were much admired for swiftly modernizing Japan, neatly emulating American values and aspirations.

This book, a valuable contribution to the history of Chinese-American relations and to American social and intellectual history, also has major implications for an understanding of the encounters between disparate cultures and peoples throughout the modern world. In an era when change has contested tradition within and across national and continental boundaries, the disequilibrium among nations and races has generated both positive and negative attitudes, images, and stereotypes of no mean consequence. The confrontation between Chinese, the most ancient of contemporary peoples, and Americans, the most spirited of the world's modern nations, provides us with a classic paradigm that obliquely illuminates a world in flux.

MOSES RISCHIN

Preface

This study began as an investigation of the yellow peril fears in American society at the end of the nineteenth century. As I pursued the roots of these fears, however, the original intent of my work became obscured by more fundamental questions about the tacit and expressed assumptions in American historiography concerning American attitudes toward the Chinese in the eastern United States before 1882. In order to limit my research on the yellow peril concept, I had relied on the accepted historical interpretation that Americans esteemed the Chinese up to the Opium War, if not later, and that easterners looked favorably upon Chinese immigration before 1882. As I continued to uncover evidence that seriously challenged these assumptions, however, I decided to abandon my original quest of the yellow peril in order to trace systematically the evolution of the unfavorable image of the Chinese in nineteenth-century America and to examine the role of this image in the national decision to exclude the Chinese from the melting pot.

During the years of research on this problem, I received invaluable stimulation and encouragement from Professor Frederick D. Kershner, whose own work on Australian immigration and general interest in the historical processes of acculturation and assimilation provided me with important insights into the materials with which I was working. I am also indebted to professors Robert D. Cross, C. Martin Wilbur, Alice W. Spieseke, and Moses Rischin who read this work at various stages of its development and commented on it from the perspective of each one's special interest.

Generous assistance from librarians at many institutions greatly lightened the task of research. I particularly remember the staffs at the Essex Institute, whose warm response to my research needs contrasted sharply with a very cold Salem winter, and the New York Historical Society, whose unstinting aid made more bearable a hot New York summer. I am also grateful to the librarians at the historical societies of Massachusetts, Rhode Island, and Pennsylvania; the Library of Congress, Library Company of Philadelphia,

Peabody Museum, Mariner's Museum, American Antiquarian Society, Boston Athenaeum, Tamiment Institute, Irish Historical Society, and New York Public Library; and the university libraries of Harvard, Yale, Brown, Union Theological Seminary, Columbia, and Berkeley. I am deeply grateful to Professor M. Searle Bates of the Missionary Research Library, who was so generous of his valuable time in helping me organize the missionary sources. Frequently, I met librarians who, as descendants of old China hands themselves, took a special interest in my study well beyond the call of professional duty.

For the more mundane but no less crucial clerical assistance necessary to ready this manuscript for publication, I relied heavily on Mrs. Edith Hunter who marshaled the efforts of a number of assistants, the most dedicated of whom was Gordon Thompson. I am also indebted to the faculty at San Francisco State College for having awarded me a research leave in 1968 in order to complete this manuscript.

And last only in a chronological sense, my wife Naomi spent long hours checking bibliographical data, editing and proofreading while meeting the needs of two small children and renovating a tired, old house in Sausalito. For this Herculean effort I will never be able to find words adequate to express my gratitude.

S.C.M.

Contents

PART ONE

*The Inside Dopesters
and
China's Image*

The Asiatic cannot go on with our
population and make a homogene-
ous element. The idea . . . comparing European immigration with an
immigration that has no regard to
family, that does not recognize the
relation of husband and wife, that
does not observe the tie of parent
and child, that does not have in the
slightest degree the ennobling and
civilizing influences of the hearth-
stone and the fireside.

Senator James G. Blaine, Rep. of
Maine, *Congressional Record*, 45th
Cong., 3rd Sess., Feb. 14, 1879,
p. 1301.

I

The California Conspiracy and Chinese Exclusion

The Chinese Exclusion Act of 1882 has earned a special place in American history. It was the first departure from our official policy of open, laissez-faire immigration to be made on ethnocultural grounds. Likewise, it was the nation's first step on the pathway that led ultimately to the controversial quota legislation of the 1920s. Less obviously, the decision for exclusion sharply challenged the comfortably vague presumptions that prevailed as to the melting-pot nature of American nationality. That a watershed event of such importance has received only limited monographic coverage is hard to believe. Yet Mary Roberts Coolidge's pioneer study of Chinese immigration to America, written in 1909, remains the standard account of Chinese exclusion today, more than half a century after its first appearance. Only recently Gunther Barth has called our attention to this condition and has challenged some of Mrs. Coolidge's conclusions.[1]

3

It was the dictum of Mrs. Coolidge, and subsequent works have followed her views closely, that the initial American response to Chinese immigration was a favorable one; as representatives of an old and respected civilization the Chinese were welcome additions to the melting pot. She believed that because of special circumstances existing in Californian mining communities—the high incidence of settlers from the South, the absence of a core of settled citizens and any real social structure, oversettlement, and the exhaustion of alluvial gold deposits—a strident xenophobia was directed against the Chinese after initial attacks on French, Australian, and Chilian miners. Governor John Bigler's "violent race prejudices and political ambitions" fanned the flames of resentment, but the issue was not politically viable in California before 1869 or 1870. Indeed, anti-Chinese restrictions legislated by various mining localities were invariably struck down by state courts.[2]

Not until a commercial depression in 1869, coincident with the completion of the transcontinental railroad, filled San Francisco with unemployed and disappointed men was anti-Chinese sentiment organized on a statewide level, Mrs. Coolidge maintained. The even division of voting strength between the two major parties in California, together with prevailing labor unrest, made it expedient to respond to the demands of the sinophobes. Between 1870 and 1876 a number of restrictive measures were passed by the state legislature, only to be invalidated by the U.S. Supreme Court. Thus the anti-Chinese movement was forced to turn from Sacramento to Washington for satisfaction. Ironically, the same conditions that had given the sinophobes so much influence in California in 1870 unexpectedly began to operate at the national level in 1876. That is, evenly divided political parties, reflected in the close presidential elections of 1876 and 1880, plus a general depression and labor unrest, as exemplified in the strikes of 1877, forced both major parties to make concessions to this peculiar prejudice of California and the West Coast. Two restrictive measures passed by Congress ran into presidential vetoes, however, before success was attained in 1882.

The essence of this California thesis has been stated clearly by Mary Coolidge herself in her concluding reflection on the Chinese Exclusion Act: "The clamor of an alien class [Irish] in a single state—taken up by politicians for their own ends—was sufficient to change the policy of a nation and to commit the United States to a race discrimination at variance with our own professed theories of government, and so irrevocably that it has become an established tradition." [3]

That some leading sinophobes resided in the East was never denied by Coolidge and Sandmeyer, but this circumstance was dismissed as a consequence of personal ambition and political expediency. Ben Butler and James G. Blaine burned with presidential fever, and their tirades against the Chinese were designed not for local consumption but for the western delegations to the next nominating convention. An anticoolie demonstration in New York in 1870 was provoked, Sandmeyer explained, "by Henry George's strong article in the *New York Tribune* and by the shipping of Chinese to North Adams, Massachusetts, to break a strike of St. Crispins." [4] The fact that Sandmeyer cited George's article ahead of a concrete and focal incident symbolizes the tendency of writers of this school to find the hidden hand of a Californian behind any anti-Chinese sentiment manifested in the East before 1882. Sinophobia was a sectional disease, they insisted; and not until the effects of the exclusion laws themselves, coupled with Californian propaganda, the rise of powerful unions, and the arrival of a significant number of Chinese on the East Coast, was the entire nation infected.[5] Essentially, it is this interpretation that has found its way, with occasional refinements, into the major survey treatments of immigration; although the authors usually dismiss the Chinese in a page or two, being much more concerned with the numerically greater trans-Atlantic influx.

The support given to the California thesis has been formidable, almost universal. It was first articulated by contemporary eastern opponents of the exclusion laws and iterated by historians Richmond Mayo-Smith and Prescott Hall well before the Coolidge book. From Henry Pratt Fairchild to Marion Bennett, it has been reendorsed by historians many times.[6] Marcus Hansen gave it enthusiastic approval, concluding that Americans were well pleased with the arrival of Chinese workers in the East in 1870. Tales of the grandeur of distant Cathay had been firmly planted in the New England mind by seafaring ancestors so that farmers recounted "the wonders of Chinese agriculture." [7]

Carl Wittke and Lawrence Brown gave somewhat greater attention to the role of organized labor and the Irish in helping to nationalize the issue of Chinese exclusion. Wittke in particular noted the existence of sinophobic sentiment in the pages of the *Cincinnati Inquirer* in 1870.[8] But if such a citation was intended to indicate that anti-Chinese feeling outside California was significant at this time, it was left entirely to the reader's inference.

Carey McWilliams made a southern–western alliance an open corollary of the California thesis. The "Southern Bourbons," he

reasoned, quickly saw the relationship between California's demands and their own racism. "Once the federal government sur-
rendered to the South [1876], it was logically compelled to ap-
pease California on the subject of 'coolie labor,'" McWilliams
concluded.[9] Oscar Handlin added the racist thinking of Gobineau
and certain nineteenth-century ethnologists, which apparently had
its main effect upon the western and southern sections of the country.[10] It is difficult to escape the inference in these works that
racism was absent in the Northeast and Midwest before 1882, at
least in so far as the Chinese were concerned. John Higham, in an
incidental reference to the Chinese, was still more explicit in this
regional emphasis: "At the turn of the century . . . the Anglo-
Saxon idea of American nationality was so widely popularized that
the racial egoisms of South and West could easily permeate a nationalism ideologically adapted to receive them." [11]

Appealing as this California-oriented interpretation of the exclusion acts may be, it does have the quality of making the tail
seem to wag the dog. The alleged willingness to bid for anti-
Chinese votes is not paralleled by a similar willingness to bid for
anti-Negro or anti-Mexican votes in close balance-of-power situations elsewhere in American history. Why was one section able to
impose its prejudice on the rest of the nation in 1882 when the
South was unable to accomplish such a result several decades
earlier? Maldwyn Jones has provided a clue: "That Congress
proved sympathetic was due to the rivalry of the national political
parties for western votes *and to the almost complete absence of opposition to the measure.*" [12] The second half of Jones's statement
opens the door for a closer examination of eastern attitudes toward
the Chinese before 1882.

There is a further point to be made here. Two historians recently have questioned the assumption that sinophobia in California originated among the rabble, with leadership from irresponsi-
ble and ambitious politicians. Leonard Pitt contends that it was
much more a "respectable middle class" phenomenon, related to
that package of fears known as nativism.[13] Earlier, John Higham
had insisted that there was no relationship between the anti-
Chinese movement in the Far West and "other anti-foreign
phobias": "Although the basic Chinese exclusion law was enacted
in 1882, the year of the first general immigration law, the Congress
that passed the two measures sensed no connection between them.
. . . The two issues seemed so different that foreign-born whites
felt no embarrassment in leading the anti-Chinese crusade, while

San Francisco's most bitterly anti-European nativists held entirely aloof from the war on the Oriental." [14] But California sinophobia certainly began as an attack on other foreign elements; and while it differed from the East Coast variety of nativism in that it left the Irish alone and even attacked the Anglo-Saxon Australian miners, it can be considered as a form of nativism instituted by respectable elements in the community. "A running debate among Americans over the nature of their growing society was always in the background of the encounter . . . ," Gunther Barth observes of the Chinese issue in California.[15]

Barth placed particular stress on the fear of slavery as well as general cultural anxiety in explaining the middle-class hostility toward the Chinese.[16] This had not altogether escaped the notice of Mrs. Coolidge, who concluded that it was unfortunate that the Chinese had arrived in the middle of the slavery controversy.[17] "Public opinion, as represented in the press, tended to identify Chinese labor with Negro slavery in the south, a slavery not of law, but of condition and custom," wrote Sandmeyer.[18] To associate sinophobia with antislavery agitation was therefore not new, although the stress on its importance certainly was. Since the center of antislavery sentiment was undoubtedly in the East and not the West, just as the core of fears and anxieties over the cultural threat of large-scale immigration was in the East, further support is available for an investigation of American attitudes toward the Chinese from an eastern perspective prior to the exclusion law of 1882.

An inquiry of this sort must begin with pre-1850 origins. The Chinese did not arrive on American shores in an opinion vacuum. Americans had been trading with the Chinese since 1785 and enthusiastically supporting Protestant missionaries there since 1807. Missions to Peking by the English, Dutch, and Russians and especially the Anglo-Chinese War in 1840 had greatly heightened American consciousness of China. To understand fully the national decision to exclude the Chinese in 1882, it is essential to contruct a historical image of these people in the American mind and to examine the interrelationships between that image and subsequent events in both China and the United States. For example, the California thesis isolates 1870 as a crucial year in the organization of the anti-Chinese forces on the West Coast. The summer of that year witnessed the first "spectacular demonstrations" in San Francisco, Sandmeyer reported.[19] But other events during that same summer served as a catalyst in hardening eastern

attitudes against Chinese immigration as well: The first Chinese
workers arrived in North Adams, Massachusetts, and Belleville,
New Jersey; the United States Senate refused to grant the right of
naturalization to Chinese immigrants; massacres of Christian missionaries took place in China; and finally Chinese "coolies" in
Peru staged a bloody uprising—all of which received sensational
treatment in the eastern press.

It would be an error, however, to tie mechanically such events
to the American decision to exclude the Chinese in 1882. Obviously the interaction of these events on an older image is crucial.
The human mind does not see an object or situation and then define what it has observed. Rather, it brings to any situation or
object a definition and then sees what it has already defined. "In
. . . the confusion of the outer world," Walter Lippmann states,
"we pick out what our culture has already defined for us, and we
tend to perceive that which we have picked out in the form stereotyped for us by our culture." [20] There is, of course, great economy in such a process. We are bombarded with far too many
stimuli to see everything freshly and in great detail, but must perceive in categories, types, generalities, or stereotypes. Indeed, such
attitudes, categories, and stereotypes make up a cognitive map in
the human mind which is a powerful determinant of public opinion. Essentially, this more stable, less conscious, less rational, and
more generalized substrata of public opinion is what the historian
frequently calls a "climate of opinion" or "image." [21]

Such cognitive pictures are constantly being added to or modified over generations. But the human mind is not a tidy filing system, so new percepts rarely replace older contradictory ones but
are simply filed away side by side. As experience reenforces the
newer percepts an image emerges that dominates but does not
totally displace older ones. Hence, Harold Isaacs of the Massachusetts Institute of Technology was able to produce strange contra-
dictions when in 1958 he asked a sampling of Americans to associate freely with such words as *China* and *Asia*. The result was a kind
of psychological pastiche with counterthemes of hostility and affection, admiration and contempt, nostalgia and fear. The overall
effect was essentially favorable. The Chinese were "good, kind,
highly civilized, vigorous, industrious, persevering, courageous,
loyal, wise" in the minds of these subjects. "It takes a second,
sharper look at the kaleidoscope screen," Isaacs cautioned, "to see
more shadowy places where the less attractive images of the
Chinese lurk, and where attitudes of dislike, antipathy, and
hostility are to be found." [22]

While the dichotomy revealed in the Isaacs study might be interpreted by a philosopher in terms of Western man's proclivity for dualism in all his thinking, it can also be accounted for historically in terms of the conflicting propaganda about the Chinese to which Isaacs's interviewees had been subjected during their lifetimes. The older members of his sample passed through their most impressionable years during the journalistic heyday of interest in the yellow peril, tong wars, and subterranean opium dens in the Chinatowns of San Francisco, New York, and Boston.[23] They read about daring and bloodcurdling forays three stories down into the bowels of the earth by fearless female missionaries in order to rescue white slave girls held by Chinese "opium fiends." [24] Perhaps they vicariously toured San Francisco's notorious Chinatown on the pages of the *Chautauquan* amidst "wild-eyed hatchet men," lepers, and "infectious diseases that germinate in the filth of that malodorous quarter," with its thoughtful warning that the "meek, inoffensive, non-resistant Chinaman whom the enthusiasts have pictured, exists chiefly in the imagination and in the decorations on tea-chests. . . . But the night is wearing on," the reader was cautioned, "and we must get us hence. The dark figure that passed us but a moment since, slipping so stealthily into the shadow of yonder alley, is a highbinder." [25]

With the development of movies, these subjects may have watched with terror Lon Chaney's portrayals of a murderous highbinder and the evil "Mr. Wu." Or perhaps they merely examined the poster advertising Boris Karloff's performance as the sinister "Dr. Fu Manchu" which promised "menace in every twitch of his finger, . . . terror in each split second of his slanted eyes." [26]

In the mid-1930s these interviewees experienced a revolutionary manipulation of their conception of the Chinese. Vehicles for the new image were the books of Pearl Buck and Lin Yutang; Paul Muni's portrayal of the simple, honest, virtuous, and stoic peasant in Hollywood's version of *The Good Earth;* and the wise "Charlie Chan," whose Confucian wisdom was employed in catching criminals rather than in concocting mysterious poisons for a white hero. As China became our wartime ally, a conception of heroic Chinese, special friends of the United States, emerged from books, movies, and official propaganda. Today the success of the Chinese communists threatens to begin a new phase in this historic cycle of opinion.

Isaacs argues, however, that the themes he abstracted were part of a culturally based conception that transcended the life span of any interviewee. More precisely, American culture has conceptual-

ized China and the Chinese in sharply contrasting ways over the
past two centuries. Isaacs characterized these periods in terms of
dominant American attitudes toward the Chinese as follows:

1. The Age of Respect (eighteenth century)
2. The Age of Contempt (1840–1905)
3. The Age of Benevolence (1905–1937)
4. The Age of Admiration (1937–1944)
5. The Age of Disenchantment (1944–1949)
6. The Age of Hostility (1949–   ) [27]

Thus, Isaacs reasoned, the paternalistic attitudes he uncovered
among contemporaries might be related to the "old China hands";
the feelings of contempt to the Boxer Rebellion or even the
Tientsin Massacre; and the fears could be traced to Boris Karloff
or perhaps even to the yellow hordes of Genghis Khan. All of the
characteristic attitudes in the six historical periods specified above
played a part in the formation of the present Chinese image in the
American mind. Isaacs is not suggesting a kind of Jungian inher-
ited, collective subconscious. The historical sources of these attitudes have been kept alive in contemporary literature, textbooks,
and movies.[28]

If the Isaacs theory is valid, then similar studies at various periods in the twentieth century should have also produced these
assortments of conflicting attitudes, albeit with a different cumula-
tive stereotype as an end product. That is, a study before 1937
should have a more unfavorable total effect than one conducted
during the next decade. In working on racial steroetypes, David
Katz and Kenneth Braley found greater agreement among their
subjects over the adjectives applied to Negroes and Chinese than
for any other ethnic groups. Terms chosen for the Chinese formed
strange oxymorons, so that the Chinese were "deceitful" and "absolutely trustworthy" in the same sentence.[29] In this 1933 study the
unfavorable image was more pronounced than in Isaacs' investigation, though not so much as in Bruno Lasker's 1929 study with
children.[30] But in all these studies the intermixing of conflicting
themes was characteristic. Indeed, a less sophisticated but mark-
edly similar study was conducted in three New York City public
schools in 1850. Several classes were asked to write down what they
knew about China. While most of the students recorded the type
of information they would have garnered from a geography lesson, such as the large population, location, and commercial products, about a dozen made evaluative comments on the Chinese.
Five students thought the Chinese uncivilized, while one de-

scribed them as highly civilized, and another as overcivilized. Six thought that they were "peculiar" and "treacherous," were addicted to opium, and dined on "rats, dogs and vermin." Three others considered them clever, industrious, and intelligent people.[31]

Historically it is possible to order western perceptions of China into two basic images. On the one hand there is the favorable image of the China of ancient greatness and hoary wisdom: the China of Confucius, Father Ricci, Leibniz, Voltaire, Anson Burlingame, Lin Yutang, and Madame Chiang Kai-shek. In sharp contrast, there is a second basic image of a stagnating, perverse, semi-civilized breeding ground for swarming inhuman hordes: the China of Daniel Defoe, Lord Anson, John Quincy Adams, Denis Kearney, Sax Rohmer, and Mao Tze-tung. The purpose of this study is to demonstrate how an unfavorable image of China evolved and dominated American thinking during the nineteenth century and how it ultimately affected the American reaction to Chinese immigration.

Presumably the roots of American attitudes toward the Orient are located in our European heritage. The European conception of China prior to the period of this study has been adequately examined by a number of scholars. The most succinct treatments are William Appleton's *A Cycle of Cathay* (1959) and Raymond Dawson's *The Chinese Chameleon* (1967); but the most comprehensive promises to be Donald Lach's *Asia in the Making of Europe,* the first volumes of which appeared in 1965.[32]

Appleton identified three distinct phases in the development of an image of China in the European mind before 1800.[33] From Marco Polo to the *The Travels of Sir John Mandeville* in the sixteenth century there was a wondering, exotic never-never-land image, followed by a more realistic phase in which the assets and liabilities of Chinese civilization were carefully weighed. Then during the second half of the seventeenth century, Jesuit missionaries began to idealize Chinese government, law, and Confucian philosophy. The works of Fathers Louis Le Comte, Jean Baptiste Du Halde, Joseph Mailla, Jean Amiot, and Jean Baptiste Grosier, published between 1697 and 1788, are typical of this idealistic third phase and are important here only in that they continued to be influential in nineteenth-century America. The great Chinese sage was elevated to the rank of Christian prophet by these Jesuit admirers, who characterized his philosophical system as "the science of princes." Collections of Confucian works bore such titles as

Sinarum Scientia Politico-Moralis.[34] This was the age of reason and of absolutism in the West, and the Chinese social system offered an attractive model to European philosophers. During the eighteenth century, Chinese society was equally attractive to physiocrats, deists, and iconoclasts. Of the diversity of China's panegyrists in eighteenth-century Europe, Paul Honigsheim wrote, "The Jesuits had extolled the high standard of the Chinese ethics. Primarily because of this, China became admired as the land of order, morality and diligence by Gallicans, Deists, materialists, Mercantilists and their adversaries, the physiocrats, by the moderate Montesquieu, the radical Diderot and most of all Voltaire." [35]

But Appleton warns that the excitement over China and the Sage was always more subdued in England than on the continent, Sir William Temple's paeans to the Chinese notwithstanding.[36] China's reputation also declined more rapidly in England than elsewhere during the second half of the eighteenth century. Patriots and clerics began to smell treason and heresy in the remarks of sinophiles: "A *free thinker* can easily assume all shapes. . . . He is sometimes seen in the guise of a Chinese, talking notably of Confucius: Anon he is a Turk, and lavishing his praises on Mohammed: Next, perhaps, he is a Magian. . . . His business is to play the opinions of mankind upon one another with an eye to their common destruction, and to erect upon their ruins a monument to *universal scepticism.*" [37]

The vitriolic criticism of the Chinese launched by Daniel Defoe and Lord Anson, abetted by such literary lions as Johnson, Addison, Chesterfield, and Swift, endorsed by scholars like Bolingbroke and Adam Smith, and supported on the continent by de Pauw, de Guignes, de Mairan, and Condorcet, thoroughly impugned the earlier idealized image of China.[38] By the end of the eighteenth century Appleton's third phase, the idealistic approach to China, was clearly over. Samuel Johnson, who had once planned some Chinese stories, now dismissed the Chinese as "barbarous" and, in answer to Boswell's objections, explained that they had no alphabet and no arts, only pottery.[39]

In answer to these critics, Father Amiot, one of the great Jesuit sinologues, angrily retorted in 1780, "To say that the Chinese are a barbarous, gross and ignorant people without genius, laws, sciences, arts or industry—that they are descendants of the Scythians, and received their first civilization in the twelfth century from the

Mogul Tartars, who conquered their country . . . is an absurdity of the grossest kind." [40]

Presumably the sentiments of the American colonial opinion maker should have paralleled those of his European, or at least his English, counterpart. But this does not appear to have been true in the case of China. An exhaustive search of the lists of books in private libraries in colonial America has failed to turn up more than a handful of works on China.[41] Louis Wright called the second Richard Henry Lee "the best scholar in Virginia during the early eighteenth century"; but although heavily steeped in the classics, Lee apparently ignored China.[42] The same lacuna exists in the Carter library [43] and in the collection of John Smith, whom Frederick Tolles called "one of the most literate of the Quaker merchants." [44] Conspicuously absent from Lawrence Wroth's hypothetical library of a fictitious mid-eighteenth-century gentleman was any mention of China or Confucius.[45] Only among the thousands of volumes collected by James Logan, a colonial bibliophile who described his mania for collecting books as a "disease," can one find the works of Confucius in evidence, alongside two copies of the Koran.[46] Among the 6,000 volumes that Jefferson sold to Congress in 1815 to replace the library burned by the British were the works of Le Comte, Du Halde, and Grosier on China; but it is clear that these were purchased by Jefferson in Paris after 1783.[47]

The absence of specific works on China in these private collections does not indicate necessarily that colonial opinion makers were ignorant of the Celestial Empire, although it does reflect a lack of strong interest. Works by Lord Anson, Captain Dampier, Matthew Hale, Daniel Defoe, and Oliver Goldsmith on their bookshelves did touch on China, as did also such favorite English periodicals as the *Monthly Review* and the *Gentleman's Magazine*.[48] Comments and notes by Hamilton and John Adams and even colonials of cosmopolitan tastes like Jefferson and Franklin, however, indicate that they stumbled on the subject of China late in their careers and found it a new and relatively unstructured topic. For example, John Adams scribbled in his notes taken during the debate over the Articles of Confederation: "China is not larger than one of our Colonies. How populous." He acknowledged as his source for this bit of information another colonial cosmopolite, Dr. Benjamin Rush.[49] The notes on China that Hamilton recorded in his paymaster's book during the Revolution could only have been written by someone who had discovered China for the first time.[50] Jefferson's comments on Pierre Poivre's travel book in 1789 and his comments on Chinese *flora* made after 1783 indicate that this was also a relatively new area of interest for him.[51] All of Franklin's comments on China and his sketch of its system of central heating, with a few suggestions for improvement, of course, were made in 1784, at which time he confided to a friend that he was "fond of reading about China," and should have liked to visit the county if he were younger.[52] In a somewhat excited tone, Madison requested Jefferson to purchase in Paris the recently published travel in China by a "Mons. Amelot." Madison probably had in mind Father Amiot, whose travel collection had then been available for over a decade.[53] George Washington in 1785 expressed great surprise to learn that the Chinese were not white, although he had known that they were "droll in shape and appearance." [54]

The colonial press reflected the same lack of interest in China. A careful examination of twenty-eight American periodicals in the colonial period uncovered less than two dozen references to China, exclusive of advertisements for tea or porcelain. The exploits of Commodore Anson in Canton in 1742 provoked a review of Du Halde's famous work in an American magazine nine years after its initial publication.[55] The *Boston News-Letter* in 1749 published a lengthy article on the "celebrated Chinese Emperor Kambe," who never existed.[56] Occasionally a colonial editor would exploit the remoteness of China to direct some criticism at the English monarch. At least one gets the impression that the alleged advice to a Chinese emperor that he cut his court expenses and get rid of indolent flatterers, which commanded so much space in two colonial magazines, had more to do with London than Peking.[57] Even religious news of China failed to provoke the interest of these editors. Certainly they were less than enthusiastic over reports of successful missionary efforts in China on behalf of Rome.[58]

This innocent, unstructured perception of China in the American mind of 1785 has significance in terms of modern communication theory. The less that is known on a given topic, the easier it is for an opinion maker to influence his audience.[59] Once the China trade triggered American interest in that part of the globe, the important opinion makers were the traders, missionaries, and diplomats, whose influence on the development of an American image of the Chinese was greatly enhanced by virtue of having been in China. Kurt Lewin conceptualized the role of such individuals as "gatekeepers" or what Herbert Hyman calls "inside dopesters," whose monopoly on a type of experience or a source of information makes them more effective in shaping public opinion on related topics. Thus, Part I of this study focuses on those three categories of "inside dopesters" who were able to etch their views of the Chinese on the American cognitive map with little or no competition from older images of these people.

Once events in China attained worldwide significance and received wide coverage in the American press, the events themselves helped to influence American images of the Chinese.[60] Conveniently, the first of these events, the Opium War, 1839–1842, coincided with the evolvement of a mass medium in the United States.

Finally, the arrival of Chinese in California provoked editorial fears across the nation, fears that can only be explained in terms of the unfavorable image of these people that preceded them to American shores. The presence of the Chinese on the West Coast reenforced many of the negative stereotypes of them, which in turn interacted with other anxieties affecting nineteenth-century American society. The Chinese arrived in the middle of the slavery controversy, when modern racist theory was being developed and when Americans were becoming more conscious of antisepsis and germs. This stimulated editorial fears of "coolie-ism," of alien genes and germs, all of which more adequately explain the national decision to exclude the Chinese immigrants than does a California conspiracy.

The closer contemplation we condescend to bestow, the more disgustful is that booby nation. The Chinese Empire enjoys precisely a Mummy's reputation, that of having preserved to a hair for 3 or 4,000 years the ugliest features in the world. I have no gift to see a meaning in the venerable vegetation of this extraordinary (nation) people. They are tools for other nations to use. Even miserable Africa can say I have hewn the wood and drawn the water to promote the civilization of other lands. But China, reverend dullness! hoary ideot!, all she can say at the convocation of nations must be—"I made the tea."

An 1824 entry in *The Journal & Miscellaneous Notebooks of Ralph Waldo Emerson,* ed. William H. Gillman, *et al.* (Cambridge, 1961), II, 224.

2

The American Trader's Image, 1785-1840

A persistent assumption in American historiography dealing with Sino-American relations is the belief that Americans held Chinese civilization in high esteem during the early years of the China trade, roughly from 1785 to 1840. In the introduction to a study of contemporary American images of China, Harold Isaacs characterized this period as one of "respect" followed by an "age of contempt" from 1840 to 1906.[1] Given the treatment of Sino-American relations by American historians, it is difficult to imagine Isaacs coming to any other conclusion. The pioneer works on the subject by Kenneth Latourette and Tyler Dennett conceived of the period before 1840 as one during which American opinion of China was one of "respect and admiration." The Celestial Empire "inspired something of awe and even of envy" in America, Latourette asserted.[2] This interpretation has been iterated by

George H. Danton, Foster Rhea Dulles, and Thomas A. Bailey and appears in a good many histories of American diplomacy.[3]

The first Anglo-Chinese conflict in 1840 dramatically destroyed the esteem enjoyed by the "Middle Kingdom," according to Latourette: "A sudden revulsion of feeling took place and from being respected and admired, China's utter collapse before the British arms and her unwillingness to receive Western intercourse and ideals led to a feeling of contempt. . . . Contrasting their old ideas of her greatness with their sudden discovery of her weakness, the impression spread through America and Europe that China was decadent, dying, fallen greatly from her glorious past." [4]

Other scholars have been reluctant to accept such a dramatic explanation for this reversal of opinion. Danton, for example, attributed the change to the influence of the Protestant missionary, whose reports after 1840 painted China in darker tones in order to explain his failure at proselytizing or to elicit greater support from his audiences in the West.[5] S. Y. Teng, on the other hand, attributed China's loss of esteem in the West to the latter's industrialization which rendered China increasingly backward in the eyes of the Westerner.[6] Rose Hum Lee identified Chinese immigration as the effective instrument in vitiating China's respectable image in the United States.[7] However plausible such interpretations appear to be in contrast to Latourette's focus on a single event, all these scholars viewed the middle of the nineteenth century as a kind of turning point, before which China was admired and respected in the United States if not generally in the West.

The evidence on which so universal an assumption rests is neither clear nor convincing. Dennett, for example, merely cited the reminiscence of a single trader in China to document his contention that Americans greatly esteemed the Chinese. How Dennett arrived at the conclusion that William Hunter's *The "Fan Kwae" at Canton Before Treaty Days, 1825–1844,* "embodies the prevailing spirit of the Americans toward the Chinese," as he contended, was never spelled out.[8] Thomas A. Bailey mentioned "the quiet educational process" that acquainted Americans with China's great civilization during the first half century of the China trade, but he neither illustrated nor explained such a process. Presumably he was referring to the reports of traders, missionaries, and diplomats, as well as to comments on China in the mass media, the content of which, one infers, was favorable. Bailey also noted that "the exhibition of a Chinese girl with bound feet in a New York theatre, and the establishment of an excellent Chinese museum in

Philadelphia [Nathan Dunn's collection put together by the trader W. W. Wood of that city in 1839], contributed to the public knowledge of the middle kingdom." [9]

These scholars have also relied on a variety of logical arguments in lieu of specific evidence to support the assumption that Americans admired the Chinese before 1840. The Yankee trader was "free of the racial prejudice which already marked British dealings with the people of the Orient," which permitted him closer contacts with Chinese merchants and resulted in a higher estimation of Chinese culture.[10] Others deduced that a common fear of British aggression drove the Chinese and Americans together, creating "bonds of affection and mutual respect" between them.[11] A third and much more unusual argument advanced by Danton asserted that Americans perceived in China a social system not wholly unlike their own. Local democracy and autonomy in Chinese villages and clans had a decidedly Jeffersonian flavor; and the examination system, which offered opportunity for advancement to the lowest peasant, created a social mobility unrivaled anywhere except in America. The absence of aristocratic or caste restrictions in China was not wasted upon American traders who saw in the Celestial Empire a possible ally against Europe's closed social system, or so goes Danton's argument.[12]

However appealing or logical such assertions may be, it must be emphasized that little, if any, evidence has been systematically mustered to support them. Hunter's book could also be utilized to argue that American traders were contemptuous of the Chinese. While Hunter did express a profound respect for the Celestial Empire, he also voiced some dismay over the attitudes of his compatriots in Canton. The only way to deal with the Chinese, one American advised Hunter, was "to knock them down . . . they are only tea and rice." [13] That Hunter's respect for the Chinese was not necessarily representative of the American community in Canton is implicit in much of his commentary. It is also possible to reason that the continual frustration associated with the trade strained American relations with the Chinese and solidified the Western community in Canton in the face of official harassment.

From the very beginning of the trade in 1785, America's expectations were romantically unreal or exaggerated. Traders and editors anticipated great wealth in the trade, which they believed Americans would eventually dominate. For some, this would be a natural result of our abundant supply of ginseng or pelts, which would permit us to solve the vexing problem of balancing the trade that was faced by other Western nations. For others more mystically inclined, fate had to bind together the youngest nation with the oldest one. Only artificial intervention could block our commercial destiny in China. "Thank God the intrigues of a Christian court do not influence the wise decrees of the eastern world," one such commercial prophet concluded.[14]

John King Fairbank observed that "American commercial interest in China has always had a large admixture of imagination and hope." [15] One might also add to this the other side of the coin, despair, for the rewards of the trade never lived up to such unrealistic expectations. Until 1840 it never amounted to more than 6 percent of our total foreign trade in any single year and, after that date, less than 2 percent per annum.[16] The trade was also subject to sharp fluctuations. By 1790, inflated hopes had motivated the business community of every city of any significance on the Atlantic, from Salem to Norfolk, to send at least one ship to Canton; and the trade became so crowded that Salem, one of the first to send ships to China, abandoned it altogether between 1790 and 1798. Jefferson's embargo terminated the next commercial cycle in the China trade; and after the War of 1812, the tonnage from the Celestial Empire grew slowly over the next decade. By 1830, however, one of Boston's wealthiest firms reported that it was barely able to make the interest on the money that it had invested in the China trade.[17] The failure of this venture to evolve satisfactorily for Americans was rendered even more vexing by the assistance it received from state and federal governments in the form of delayed tea duties and taxes on Chinese goods shipped to the United States in foreign bottoms. Tyler Dennett called such aid "almost incredible" in view of the actual value of the trade,[18] and it can only be explained in terms of America's romantic hopes for this commercial activity.

Balancing the trade was even more exasperating than the problem of the fluctuating price of tea. Between 1785 and 1840, close to 70 percent of our exports to China took the form of specie,[19] a condition that sent American skippers scurrying all over the globe in a desperate search for nonspecie items for the Chinese market. Seal and otter pelts were sought from the Aleutians to the Antarctic, or suitable products were obtained by skilful bartering in several ports on the outward voyage. Often the need to balance the trade involved dour Yankee skippers in some rather bizarre pursuits, such as cutting down sandalwood on Pacific islands to be burned at heathen rites in Chinese temples or gathering and cur-ing snails on deserted atolls with special wood according to the elaborate methods prescribed by the whimsical Chinese palate. Not only did such activities involve the natural risks of typhoons, hostile islanders, and coral infections, but if an insufficiently fragrant species of sandalwood was cut or if the snails were poorly selected or cured in a fashion unacceptable to the culinary standards of the Cantonese, such botcheries had to be hastily jettisoned to avoid the added indignity of paying duties on a worthless cargo.[20]

Under such conditions it would be expected that American traders would grumble frequently over China's peculiar tastes or rail against a government that placed so many restrictions on their activities. Such complaints cropped up early in the trade. In 1791, Thomas Randall, trader and vice-consul, complained to Alexander Hamilton over the discrepancy between the image of China in America and the reality faced by traders in Canton: "It is needless to a gentleman of your historical information to make any remarks on the representation given by writers, on the government of China, as they must be merely speculative, and would not in the least elucidate those points of information, which you wish to consider, . . . but it may be necessary to detail to you, how the merchants from this country trading to Canton, actually feel and suffer under the operations of the Chinese government. . . ." In support of his case Randall cited the fraudulent behavior of Chinese merchants, harassment by the mandarins, prevalence of false promises, and unjust execution of a gunner from H.M.S. *Lady Hughes* by the Chinese authorities. Finally, he remarked, "the Chinese are considered by most persons who have seen them, as very contemptible, however importantly they think of themselves. . . ."[21]

Such comments cast doubt on the validity of the friendly trader concept which is so crucial to the belief that Americans admired and respected the Chinese before the Opium War. One is able to gather an impressive array of statements similar in nature to that of Randall by culling through the records left by Americans who journeyed to China prior to 1840. Yet the views of the traders on China recorded in travel books, diaries, journals, letters, and logs, much of which has been preserved by historical societies along the northeastern seaboard, have been largely ignored by the historians who have generalized about American opinions of China during this period.[22]

Rather than string together random remarks which contradict

the belief that American traders esteemed the Chinese, a sample of fifty traders with experience in China before 1840 was selected to test more systematically the basic historical interpretation of a favorable trader image and the logical arguments on which that interpretation rests. I had first planned to distribute this sample temporally over the fifty-five years involved and geographically among the various American cities and towns along the Atlantic seaboard that sent ships to China. I soon discovered, however, that fifty traders would just about exhaust the available sources. In other words, the sample was selected by the passage of time rather than by the individual scholar, a type of sample to which the historian is often restricted.

First, the premises that the Yankee trader at this time was free of racism, was anglophobic enough to produce a close alliance with the Chinese against their mutual enemy, the British, and perceived in the Chinese social system evidence of local democracy and social mobility were tested against the records comprising the sample. Then, in order to test the deduction that such conditions led to American respect for the Chinese and admiration of their culture, persistent themes mentioned by more than ten traders, or 20 percent of the sample, were abstracted from these records in order to construct an American trader image of China before 1840. Finally, an evaluation of each trader in the sample in terms of a basically favorable or unfavorable estimation of Chinese society was attempted. While slightly more than half the sample defied such a simple, dichotomous classification, the remainder fit into one of the two categories easily enough to provide us with a quantitative test, however crude, of the validity of the basic historical interpretation under question here.

The assumption that American traders were free of racial prejudices before 1840 is well supported by these records. Only two members of the sample were interested in the racial characteristics of the Chinese, one of whom, William Waln, was obviously committed to an environmental explanation of racial differences. Indeed, he was puzzled over the fact that Chinese, Hottentots, and American Indians all were cruel in their treatment of the female in spite of vast climatic differences in the environments of these three groups.[23] Erasmus Doolittle made a feeble attempt to relate the Chinese, Turks, and Hottentots both physically and behaviorally in a manner that hints of a more modern racist conception.[24] But Doolittle consistently attributed what he considered despicable behavior in China to its despotic form of government rather than to natural or genetic determinants. This was generally true throughout the sample; and Peter Dobell, one of China's severest critics in this group, continually cautioned his readers that the notorious behavior of the Chinese was "due to the nature and conduct of government rather than to the character of the people." [25]

The comments of the traders are also studded with friendly references to particular hong merchants. Bryant Tilden of Salem left a detailed account of a feast at the home of his friend, Paunkeiqua, whom he thought "worthy of being considered a true 'Celestial' gentleman of the Chinese empire—or any other country." [26] This same hong merchant was made an honarary member of the Massachusetts Agricultural Society in 1819.[27] Sullivan Dorr, Thomas Ward, and T. H. Perkins also expressed very warm feelings for individual Chinese. E. C. Carrington received dictated messages from Cheonqua and "Sam Sin Friend" long after his return to Rhode Island.[28]

What weakens the argument that the absence of racism permitted closer Sino-American ties is that a cursory glance at the records left by English traders fails to substantiate the charge of British racism and turns up friendly references to the very same hong merchants. Moreover, a closer examination of the evidence in the sample makes one wonder about the serious language barrier to Sino-American friendships on what a sociologist would call a primary level. Communication between Americans and these hong merchants was restricted to pidgin English, which involved such fantastic metaphors and clumsy structure that any attempt to convey more than the most rudimentary information necessary to a commercial transaction was rendered quite ludicrous. "I now chin chin the sky and wish you may catch too much profit" was all that Cheonqua could say in a letter to Carrington in 1816.[29] Paunkeiqua's attempt at a theological discussion with Tilden was so awkward, preposterous, and barely intelligible that the Salem trader could only respond with a "yes sir." This agreement overjoyed Paunkeiqua who exclaimed, "Ayah! My flinde, now no more occasion for make talke talke dat Josh pidgin [religious subject]. Tluly now my can see you long my tinke [think] all same same." [30]

It is also questionable that the relationships with the hong merchants were necessarily reflective of American attitudes toward the Chinese in general. That these merchants were something of an exception to the rule in China can be safely inferred from the remarks of the majority of the traders. Finally, the evidence seems to indicate that no one replaced these famous hong merchants as they died off. At least the names of individual Chinese merchants appear less frequently in the testimony of traders after 1830. Hunter, who could not sing China's praises loudly enough, failed to single out any particular Chinese as especially friendly; while Peter Auber of the East India Company and Augustine Heard of Russell and Company testified that by 1832 even the last two survivors of the famous hong merchants, the venerable Houqua and Mouqua, were no longer so trusted by the Western community in Canton.[31]

A more startling conclusion is suggested by these records, however. Rather than the hostility presumed to exist between the American and British communities in Canton, the records suggest a pattern of friendly, cooperative, and intimate relations between these two national groups. Only three traders, Isaac Bull, Ebenezer Townsend, and W. W. Wood expressed any anglophobia; and significantly, in view of the hypothesis that a mutual distrust of the English drew Americans and Chinese together, these same three traders were equally hostile to the Chinese. Wood, in fact, likened the Chinese Empire to the East India Company for its tyrannical and unjust practices.[32] Conversely, those traders in the sample who did admire the Chinese demonstrated no pattern of anglophobia. On the contrary, they were without exception very chummy with the English in Canton. For example, William Hunter, who Dennett singled out as the typical sinophilic American in China, continually sang paeans to the "unbounded hospitality" extended to Americans by the British whose generosity and warmth, he testified, approached that of "parental care."[33] True, Major Samuel Shaw, the first American consul in China, reported that Americans and British in Canton "can barely treat each other with civility."[34] But this was in 1785, at the very beginning of the trade, and it is corroborated nowhere else in the sample. On the other hand there is ample evidence to support Silas Holbrook's description: "The two nationals lived together as brothers. English physicians daily visited our deck without fee or other reward than the satisfaction of doing a good deed." Holbrook even insisted that this spirit transcended the War of 1812: "Notwithstanding the war between the two nations, there was no hostility between the Americans and English in Canton."[35]

Far more impressive than such deliberate testimonials of Anglo-American friendship in Canton, however, are the many unconscious ones in the descriptions of co-recreation in the form of boating or card-playing; the constant American use of the library and

religious and medical facilities in the English factory; Anglo-
American forays into the city of Canton to present a joint petition
to Chinese officials or to peek into Chinese houses, a type of voy-
eurism they called sightseeing. The names of certain English
traders, such as Plowden, Marjoribanks, Davis, Auber, and Pier-
son, or of the English missionaries Morrison and Milne appear so
frequently in these records that it is difficult to realize that they
were not Americans. This alliance sometimes transcended class
barriers. At least the Marquis of Ely extended invitations to American captains to dine with him aboard his ship.[36] The two groups
even exchanged occasional economic aid, talk of fierce competition
between the two countries over the China trade in the American
press notwithstanding.[37] Americans who arrived in Canton for
the first time often received useful advice about duties, "chops,"
and the "cumshaw" ceremony from the British; and when the English were ordered out of Canton on several occasions, Americans
filled the orders of their Anglo-Saxon cousins waiting in Macao.[38]
As George W. Heard, Jr., explained it years later, "There was
plenty of jealousy of trade, but in spite of this, a great deal of
kindness and good feeling. Out of their [English] offices, the residents were always 'hail fellow, well met.' "[39]

Significantly, there was much more grumbling about the Dutch
and Portuguese. Five traders who called at Batavia en route to
China were critical of their Dutch hosts and nine traders expressed
contempt for the Portuguese at Macao, where the governor flagrantly discriminated against Americans and even refused them
refuge for several years, when foreigners had to vacate Canton between trading seasons. In times of special harassment by Chinese
officials, however, national rivalries among the Westerners were
usually suspended. Dennett described "a certain solidarity of public opinion . . . which imposed upon each individual trader the
obligation to accept the decisions of the majority."[40] But within
this common Western front, the shared language and culture in a
foreign land bound the Anglo-American community in Canton together more tightly. By 1825 the heavy involvement of these two
nationals in the illegal opium trade cemented their tacit entente
in China.[41] The close affinity between the two was not lost on the
Chinese, who labeled Americans "second chop Englishmen."[42]

Finally, the American perception of some resemblance in China
to their own social system, hypothesized by Danton, finds absolutely no support in the records left by traders. On the contrary,
criticism of China's despotism, vindictive system of law, and social

injustice are the most dominant themes in evidence. Despotism
was to the trader what paganism was to the Protestant missionary.
That is, all of China's flaws were seen as a function of this single
defect, the "impure source from whence the black stream of vice
flows to infect the whole nation." [43] In the eyes of these traders,
China was a huge pecking order in which each official terrorized
those under him, which resulted in cowardice, corruption, venality, and deceit. "Their government is admirably well adapted to
make them hypocrites and knaves," explained Erasmus Doolittle,
who most succinctly summed up the trader view of China's political system when he described it as "a representative despotism,
where you may see the 'image of authority' better than in a cur
barking at a beggar." [44]

The government was, of course, the first Chinese institution
with which the trader came into contact, for the customs official
came on board as soon as the anchor was dropped. The "ceremony
of the cumshaw" ensued in which the celestial official was permitted to purchase some Western items such as "sing songs" (cuckoo
clocks) at a fraction of their market value. Even then, the official's
instructions to bill him for the clocks were invariably ignored by
the Chinese comprador. The trader stoically accepted this bit of
extortion which he must have faced in other ports. Indeed, he was
often amused at the lengths to which the Chinese official would go
to conceal the true nature of the transaction. But it is apparent that
these traders, particularly the early ones in the sample, lost some
respect for a government that turned its officials into what Nathaniel Appleton called "beggars." [45]

But the trader's contact with the government generally went beyond bribing a customs official. Many learned of governmental
abuses through Chinese servants or from the hong merchants.
Shaw described how one poor soul was put into the stocks simply
for neglecting to carry his "chop" or pass into the foreign factories
one day. Even then he had to bribe a mandarin to secure his release.[46] Others described public tortures and punishments, "the
variety and ingenuity" of which are "little creditable to a people
which boasts of so high degree of civilization, and many of them
are unequaled among the most barbarous nations." [47]

Western brushes with Chinese law between 1785 and 1840 gave
these traders an opportunity to see Chinese justice in action. Just
when Americans inaugurated their commercial relations with
China, the Celestial government insisted on executing a seaman
from H.M.S. *Lady Hughes* for neglecting to draw his charge before

a salute, which resulted in the death of a Chinese national.[48] Later, in 1821, an Italian seaman serving aboard the *Emily* out of Baltimore was charged with the death of a Chinese boatwoman to whom he had thrown a crock to be filled with the fruit that she was peddling. Americans refused to release seaman Terranova to Chinese authorities, and the hong merchants worked out a compromise by arranging a hearing on board the *Emily* which gave Americans their first glimpse of a Chinese court in action. In their eyes the presiding official was obviously prejudiced and Terranova was railroaded. The American consul, Samuel Snow berated the hong merchants present: "You know in your own hearts you are so servile a set that you dare not open your mouths in opposition to anything however flagrant and unjust on the part of the mandarin." [49] Such a travesty of justice did the Americans consider this hearing that they refused to surrender Terranova to the Chinese. But they finally capitulated in the face of Chinese threats of economic reprisals, in spite of the support offered by the British community for a showdown with the Celestials. No American even bothered to attend Terranova's trial in Canton. "A few noble Englishmen" tried but were "driven back" by Chinese mobs outside the courthouse, Holbrook reported, admonishing his countrymen with a "Shame. Shame. Shame." [50]

But long before the Terranova trial, Shaw noted in his journal: "Notwithstanding the encomiums which are generally bestowed upon the excellence of the Chinese government, it may be questioned whether there is a more oppressive one to be found in any civilized nation on earth." [51] Thirty-five traders in the sample who followed Shaw to China answered his implied question with a resounding "no." It was axiomatic to this group that the basis of Chinese law was a primitive retribution that did not distinguish between murder, manslaughter, and even accidental death, and that China was essentially ruled by the cudgel. Even China's chief defendant in the sample, Amasa Delano, conceded to her numerous critics that there was "only one law in China, which will be condemned by the people of countries where there is more freedom enjoyed." [52]

Other critical themes besides that of despotism are clearly discernible in the records left by these traders. The most persistent ones dealt with Chinese "peculiarities," dishonesty, xenophobia, vices, cowardice, technological and military backwardness, and the static condition of Chinese society. There are also favorable comments on crafts, agriculture, large population, and Confucius. But the latter themes were not mentioned by a significant enough portion of the sample to balance those on the debit side. Surprisingly, only seven traders mentioned China's fabled agricultural system, and two of these, Wood and Dobell, criticized its lack of scientific principles and reliance on "dogged labor." [53] Nine traders praised the craftsmanship of the Chinese, although one of them insisted that these skills were not indigenous but were borrowed from the Japanese. Confucius was admired by seven traders, including the hypercritical Dobell, who ranked the Sage with Solon as "one of the great moral law givers," although he hastily added that the Chinese were incapable of fully grasping Confucian wisdom.[54] Wood and Roberts stood alone in their view that the wisdom of Confucius was little more than a collection of banalities and trite aphorisms.[55] Twelve traders admired China's huge population, and among her many critics there was evidence of some uneasiness over this feature since a large population was prima facie evidence of a high degree of civilization at this time. Only W.S.W. Ruschenberger, a surgeon who accompanied the New Hampshire trader Edmund Roberts to China on a mission for President Jackson, argued that China's large population was the root of all evil in that country. Excessive population, he stated, had made the Chinese "the most vile, the most cowardly and submissive of slaves" and had led to "baseness and extinction of every moral virtue." [56] To China's critics in the sample of traders, however, it was her despotic government that had produced these conditions and not her large population. Since Ruschenberger was very active in American intellectual circles, his conclusions may have been influenced by Malthusian theory.

In view of the antics required of American skippers to balance the trade with China, it is not surprising that a dominant theme developed by the traders was that the Chinese were a very "peculiar" people. These records are replete with descriptions of bizarre tastes and habits ranging from astonishment that one would make medicines of the horn of a rhinoceros or soup from a bird's nest, to stronger condemnations of the alleged Chinese propensity for eating dogs, cats, and rats. Even those traders more favorably disposed to the Chinese expressed anxiety over dishes proffered by their Celestial friends, and the anonymous verse of one trader elicited the laughter of his compatriots each time it was repeated:

> Mingqua, his host, pressed on each dish
> With polished Chinese grace;
> And much, Ming thought, he relished them,
> At every ugly face!

At last he swore he'd eat no more,
   'Twas written in his looks;
For, "Zounds!" said he, "the devil here
   Sends both the meats and the cooks!"

But, covers changed, he brightened up,
   And thought himself in luck
When close before him, what he saw
   Looked something like a duck!

Still cautious grown, but, to be sure,
   His brain he set to rack;
At length he turned to one behind
   And, pointing, cried: "Quack, Quack."

The Chinese gravely shook his head,
   Next made a reverend bow;
And then expressed what dish it was
   By uttering, "Bow-wow-wow!" [57]

Only William Hunter denied that the Chinese ate "roast or boiled puppy." [58] Two traders admitted tasting dog inadvertently, and nine others testified that they had seen such delicacies offered for sale in Cantonese butcher shops. Nothing was more firmly implanted in the American cognitive map of China than these culinary aberrations.

The peculiar Chinese tastes were by no means confined to gastronomy. The habits of footbinding, queer theatricals, and weird music all enhanced the impression of eccentricity. Wood described in detail their "ridiculous or disgracefully obscene" theatre, and labeled the music a "mass of detestible discord," a "musique infernal." [59] One trader likened a Chinese band to "ten Jackasses braying, five brazier's pounding on the copper boiler of a steamboat, thirty bag-pipers and a sexton to pull a cracked bell." [60] Virtually every aspect of Chinese life was used to illustrate and lampoon the Chinese propensity for doing everything backward: wearing white for mourning, purchasing a coffin while still alive, dressing women in pants and men in skirts, shaking hands with oneself in greeting a friend, writing up and down the page, eating sweets first and soup last, etc.

But such "a lamentable disregard of fitness and proportion" [61] in everything the Chinaman did, in the eyes of the ethnocentric trader, evoked laughter rather than any sustained indignation. Doolittle was in the minority when he hinted that there was something basically evil about a society in which "rats are fattened for epicures and a pheasant sold at the same price as a cat." [62] He was closer to the mood of the majority of his colleagues a few pages later when he was able to simply laugh at this "peculiar creature": "The first impulse of an American, when he sees for the first time a Chinese, is to laugh at him. His dress, if judged by our standards, is ridiculous, and in a Mandarin, a stately gravity sets it off for a double derision. His trousers are a couple of meal bags . . . , his shoes are huge machines, turned up at the toe, his cap is fantastic and his head is shaven except on the crown, whence there hangs down a tuft of hair as long as a spaniel's tail." [63]

One historian warned that the type of information about China supplied by these traders was designed to thrill rather than instruct American audiences. "We must be on constant guard against exaggerating the knowledge of Chinese culture acquired by New Englanders. Their interest in China was, in the main, hardly more than an interest in the exotic, a fantastic striving to escape the drabness and dry routine of their daily round of existence," cautioned Professor Ping Chia Kuo. [64] One old resident of Salem recalled some "real whoppers" about the Celestials told to him in his youth by sailors and sea captains in "the tradition of Sir John Mandeville." [65] The East India Marine Society of Salem, an important agency for diffusing knowledge of China in the United States before 1840, tended to collect in its museum "strange and curious objects," Kuo notes, "most of which still signify 'Chinese culture' in American eyes!" [66] William Bently recorded how members of this society dressed themselves in the bizarre costumes of China in order to amuse the audiences at their annual meetings. [67] In reading some of the newspapers and magazines of the time, one could easily get the impression that the firecracker was China's greatest contribution to civilization, and that pidgin English was the style in which Celestials generally expressed themselves. While there is considerable truth to Kuo's assertion, the records comprising the sample also reveal some very serious commentary as well. And more important, even the exotic and frivolous content was not flattering to the Chinese. It portrayed him as a ludicrous specimen of the human race and was not designed to evoke the admiration and respect for Chinese culture attributed to American traders during this period.

While the perceived gastronomical or musical absurdities of the Chinese offended American stomachs and ears rather than their moral sensitivities, the allegedly universal dishonesty in China mentioned by thirty-seven members of the sample was a more serious matter. Nine traders described utterly fantastic swindles, from being sold wooden hams, covered with real fat and painted so cleverly that often the victim did not discover the fraud until he attempted to cook it, to rare birds and flowers created by painting feathers or securing petals to stems with tiny pegs or glue. In the latter cases, a sudden rainstorm generally led to a dramatic denouement, leaving the hapless owner with a very ordinary sparrow or holding worthless stems.[68] One wonders how such ruses could have been very profitable considering the effort they must have required, and their frequency shakes one's faith in the reputation of these Yankee traders for shrewdness.

There were more mundane swindles, of course, such as padding the bottom of tea chests with ordinary leaves. John Boit warned that even the hong merchants felt bound only to the quantitative aspects of a bargain and might switch the quality of the goods at any time. As for the lesser Chinese peddlers, they were worse than the Indians at home and "the greatest villians in the Universe," Boit declared.[69] The usually friendly Perkins reasoned that the function of the long sleeves worn by Celestial gentlemen was to hide stolen articles! [70] Even Delano conceded the charge of dishonesty in his defense of the Chinese, although he insisted that it was restricted to the Canton region where it had been learned from Western traders.[71] Only Hunter and John Murray Forbes defended the Chinese on this score. "I never saw in any country such a high average of fair dealing," Forbes testified.[72] Hunter insisted that all Chinese, big and small merchants, officials, clerks, and workers were "honorable and reliable in all their dealings." [73] Such eddies of protest, however, were lost in a sea of testimony on Chinese swindles.

Surprisingly, these traders again expressed little moral indignation over this alleged Chinese trait. This may have been a function of the trader's expectation to encounter such cheating. "The knavery of the Chinese" was already "proverbial" in 1785, according to Shaw.[74] But there was even a soupçon of admiration for the diabolical cleverness behind some of the frauds. "Barrington men never picked a pocket with such ingenuity," Townsend confessed. It was in some ways an agreeable challenge to their Yankee wits: "A man should have his eye teeth cut to come to Canton," Townsend counseled.[75] An American had "to be up very early to get to the windward of a Chinaman," Daniel Arnold cautioned.[76]

"They *will* cheat you if they can, therefore your business is to see *that they shall not*," Boit resolved.[77]

Thirty of these traders were aware of the pejorative meaning of the term "fanqui" with which the Chinese addressed them. It quickly joined such terms as "chop" and "cumshaw" in the lexicon of the trade. Most traders translated it into "foreign devil" or "outside barbarian." Captain Fanning thought that it meant "Christian" but he also described how boys frequently accompanied the epithet with a shower of stones.[78] Only Hunter adamantly insisted that "fanqui" simply ment "red hair'd" after the first Dutch traders, while the Chinese referred to themselves as "black hair'd." [79] But even Delano admitted to its hostile intent, although he argued that its use was confined to the Canton region. Northern Chinese were too polite to address foreigners in such a manner, he asserted.[80]

Paradoxically, these traders never exhibited any anger over the epithet and frequently referred to themselves as "fanqui," at first in jest and then quite casually. Convinced of China's inferiority, they laughed at this further evidence of her supercilious pretensions. The term was placed in a category with those Chinese maps depicting a vast "Middle Kingdom" covering most of the earth's surface; or with the bombastic edicts from the emperor declaring all other monarchs to be his vassals; or warnings that he would create terrible diseases in the West by stopping their supply of tea and rhubarb. The traders could not take such bumptious claims seriously, and rather than reject the title "fanqui" they willingly accepted it with the same sardonic laughter with which they greeted every aspect of these "peculiar people." [81] If they had felt sincere respect for China, they would probably have found such xenophobic arrogance more irksome.

Vice, as determined by the criteria of Christian morality, was another major theme. Reports of Chinese vices did not depend on the arrival of the Protestant missionary, for the trader noted the existence of idolatry, gambling, and prostitution on "flower boats" and occasionally mentioned polygamy and infanticide. But the trader did not dwell on these vices and was less pharisaical in reporting them than was the average missionary. "With respect to their religion, suffice it to say, that the most seemingly extravagant accounts of their idolatry and superstition . . . may be safely credited," Shaw noted with a stoic acceptance that was typical of the trader group.[82] Such practices were to be expected in a pagan country, and the trader came to deal in tea, not in souls. Rather than indignation, the trader occasionally made fun of Chinese religious practices and Fanning delighted in teasing his servant about "Josh" or pointing out a small aperture at the base of an idol through which the sly priests took the food left for the spirits of his ancestors.[83]

Indeed, the traders appeared to be much more outraged by the Chinese propensity for gambling. "This vice prevails among people of every rank in society," Wood explained. "Children play at gambling games. People game for purchases."[84] Stories of the suffering that followed in the wake of this vice were almost as ubiquitous in the sample as the tales of Chinese swindles. For Major Shaw the report that the Chinese even gambled with Josh, by throwing sticks in the air before his image to see how they would land, was more shocking than the idolatry involved.[85] "Nothing lowered the Chinese so much" in the eyes of the traders as this propensity for gambling, Benjamin Goodhue testified.[86] Thomas Perkins observed that even overseas in Batavia the Chinese were "inveterate gamblers."[87] To Peter Dobell this was the best evidence of the general "venality" and the "moral debasement" of these people.[88]

Oddly enough, these traders, of Puritan stock for the most part, failed to manifest any serious concern over the potentially more explosive issues of polygamy and infanticide. To be sure, the opportunities to witness domestic arrangements in China were limited, but it is doubtful that the public executions they described were ever directly observed either—at least not before 1840. The six traders who did mention polygamy and infanticide among China's vices—Delano, Doolittle, Waln, Wood, Dobell, and Roberts—could be identified as part of the more literate segment of the sample on the basis of vocabulary, historical knowledge, and references to other books on China which reflected a wide reading experience if not an extensive formal education. In fact all of them felt it necessary to cite other writers when mentioning infanticide. "It has been asserted by writers, and possibly may be believed by some people, that the Chinese women are in the habit of drowning a certain portion, say one third of their female offspring in the rivers," Delano complained.[89] He also dismissed the charge of polygamy, arguing that it was not common.[90] While such disavowals were consistent with Delano's role in the sample as China's chief apologist, the other five traders were hypercritical of the Chinese and yet made no attempt to capitalize on these alleged practices beyond reporting them. Doolittle even attempted to mitigate the charges, in a rare display of cosmopolitanism, when he reminded his readers that the poor in Europe attempted to get rid of unwanted offspring and that aristocrats everywhere took a second woman, whether as wife or mistress.[91]

The same low-key treatment was given the "flower boats" and the use of opium in China. They were mentioned, but it was left to the Protestant missionary to scold the Chinese about these vices. The trader's heavy involvement in opium smuggling would explain his reticence on this topic, but his failure to become incensed over Chinese vices in general was consistent with his lack of indignation in discussing all facets of Chinese culture.

The easy defeat of the Chinese at the hands of the British in 1840 could not have come as much of a surprise to these traders. Twenty-six of them mentioned the military ineptitude of the Chinese, ranging from observations of obsolete weapons and mounted cannon that could not be elevated, depressed, or trained, to hearty laughter over soldiers dressed in petticoats, armed with fans, and relying on gongs to frighten the enemy in battle. Even the friendly Hunter was unable to suppress a chuckle over the Chinese efforts to convert a purchased Western vessel into a Celestial man-of-war. Huge eyes were immediately painted on the bow to aid in navigation and in sighting the enemy. Then days were spent analyzing the "scuttlebutt," which the Chinese believed to be "a great machine of war." Finally the "insignia of invincibility" were hoisted from every yardarm, depicting dragons swallowing the moon and announcing thunder and lightning. The commander of all this "destructive paraphernalia, with the peacock's feather in his cap, a large silk umbrella over his head, seated himself comfortably in a bamboo chair, smoking his pipe," Hunter reported with amusement.[92]

Very early in the nineteenth century Fanning, Delano, Appleton, Holbrook, and Doolittle predicted that a coalition of European nations would probably topple the Celestial Empire. By 1830, Wood insisted that any Western maritime power could do it alone. Seven other traders, however, argued that China could make up in sheer numbers what she lacked in military skill and individual courage. But the widely diffused ridicule of China's military efforts that one finds in the records left by these traders indicates that as a group they must have been adequately prepared for the debacle that actually took place in 1840.

If these Americans viewed the martial impotence of the Chinese as quaint rather than contemptible, they felt more strongly about cowardice. Even the fabled Great Wall in the north was reduced to a symbol of Chinese pusillanimity, "a labor of cowardice inviting attack because it displayed fear," Doolittle declared.[93] Half the sample mentioned this alleged character deficiency in China, and the widespread contempt that it engendered occasionally led to lawlessness on the part of the traders in Canton. Five members of the sample described how they dispersed armed Chinese sentries with their walking sticks, although some braggadocio may have been involved here. Wood explained that to keep them out of his way it was necessary to cuff and kick the Chinese soldiers whom he described as "loathsome, disease ridden, miserable wretches" whose "silly grunts and menaces mean nothing and are to be disregarded." [94] A British trader, C. Toogood Downing, described one Anglo-American assault on a Chinese sentry and reported: "These pigtailed sons of Mars have quietly submitted to being pushed aside by more determined opponents, and have contented themselves with silently grounding their arms, whilst they stared after the intruders with speechless astonishment. . . ." [95] But such a civilized reaction only reenforced the American image of the Chinese as rank cowards.

China's technological and scientific backwardness was mentioned by nineteen traders. However, its reputation for having invented gunpowder, the compass, inoculation, and printing presented something of a problem to these members of the sample. Nine of them simply acknowledged these past achievements, which made the superstitious nature of contemporary Chinese science something of a paradox for them. The others discounted such historical contributions by pointing out that the Chinese never used gunpowder for anything but firecrackers until introduced to guns from the West, and that Celestial sailors were still "coasters," terrified of losing sight of land in spite of the compass invented by their ancestors. Indeed, Waln, Dobell and Doolittle insisted that, since the scientific rationale behind these innovations was never fully understood by the Chinese, they were accidents rather than true discoveries. "The Chinese for ages practiced inoculation for the smallpox; the matter is put on a piece of cotton and thrust up the nostril, and if the patient lives, he was born under a lucky star to which he is as much indebted as to his doctor," Doolittle explained.[96] Wood alone denied China credit for any of these inventions, which were, he claimed, imported from the West via India and then predated to satisfy the needs of Chinese vanity.[97]

Possessing a value system that equated change with progress, fourteen traders in the sample reported with some disgust that Chinese society was totally static. "The Chinese are a peculiar people in this respect," Fanning wrote, "and tenaciously adhere to old customs and forms." [98] In pidgin English this Chinese perversity was known as "ol'o custom," which one commercial guide to the trade, published in 1834, defined as "an excuse for every fault." [99] It also became a key term in the China trader's esoteric vocabulary. The Chinese were actually "hostile to all improvement," Townsend testified, concluding, "If the world were like the Chinese, we should yet have worn fig-leaves." [100]

In attempting to evaluate each trader in the sample as either friendly toward the Chinese and admiring of their culture or hostile and contemptuous, I sought statements that would leave the reader with little doubt about the individual's position. For example, Delano's statement that "China is first for greatness, riches and grandeur of any country ever known" [101] clearly places him well inside the friendly camp. On the other hand, it is no more difficult to classify Roberts as unfavorably disposed to the Chinese when he wrote, "The Chinese of the present day are grossly superstitious, . . . most depraved and vicious: gambling is universal . . . ; they use pernicious drugs, . . . are gross gluttons. . . . The most horrid tortures are used to force confession and the judges are noted for being grossly corrupt; the variety and ingenuity displayed in prolonging the tortures of miserable criminals . . . can only be conceived by a people refined in cruelty, bloodthirsty, and inhuman." [102]

Only six traders—Delano, Tilden, Ward, Hunter, Dorr, and Nye—can be easily classified as being favorably disposed toward China, although Gideon Nye's admiration might more accurately be labeled nostalgia. "The very name of China—the distant Cathay—was at that day pregnant with the romance of history, and suggested imaginative dreams of that vast shore washed by the farthest sea," Nye wrote of his youth in the China trade.[103] T. H. Perkins was a seventh but marginal member of this group. In contrast, eleven traders—Randall, Doolittle, Holbrook, Wilcocks, Townsend, Bull, Peter Snow, Samuel Snow, Wood, Dobell, and Roberts—were contemptuous of the Chinese. Five more traders held Chinese culture in low enough esteem to be marginal members of this group: Fanning, Boit, Charles Forbes, Olyphant, and Waln. The remaining twenty-seven members of the sample defied an easy classification, although eighteen of these were sufficiently

critical of the Chinese to conclude that it would be impossible to
consider them among China's admirers.

To put the matter plainly, the evidence left by these Americans
in the China trade before 1840 does not support the hypothesis
that this group admired, respected, and esteemed the Chinese and
their culture. Indeed, these records point in the opposite direction; and one is forced to conclude that the majority of Americans
who journeyed to China before 1840 regarded the Chinese as ri-
diculously clad, superstitious ridden, dishonest, crafty, cruel, and
marginal members of the human race who lacked the courage, intelligence, skill, and will to do anything about the oppressive
despotism under which they lived or the stagnating social conditions that surrounded them. Few detractors in the sample even
took the Chinese seriously enough to become indignant over their
perceived behavior, but were content to derisively dismiss them
with a supercilious guffaw and go about their business of acquiring tea for the American market.

Compared with the other categories of "inside dopesters" who
diffused knowledge about China among Americans, the traders
were, on the whole, less literate. They certainly left fewer formal
records than the European diplomats who staffed missions to
China before 1840 or the Protestant missionaries, who not only
produced numerous books on China but had a press of their own
in the United States. "The duty of a sailor is too hard, and his deficiency in general knowledge too great to enable him to describe
even his own wanderings," Silas Holbrook apologized.[104]

It would be a serious mistake, however, to take lightly the influence of the traders in developing an American image of the Chinese. Holbrook's self-admitted deficiency had not deterred him
from commenting on China frequently in a series of letters to the
New England Galaxy and the *Boston Courier*. While his modest
protest that the "sailor's journal is but a logbook, filled with the
courses of the winds and aspects of the skies" [105] was generally
true, fortunately many a Yankee skipper managed to squeeze between the navigational and commercial transactions a good deal of
descriptive material and evaluative judgments on China. Those
that were richer in such information were sometimes published or
were serialized in newspapers and magazines. A small number of
these traders produced books on China, and those of Dobell and
Wood in 1830 were very well received.[106]

But the trader influence on American attitudes toward China
should not be measured by public utterances alone. These sea-

farers also communicated their experiences and opinions privately to friends, neighbors, and business associates orally and in letters, a highly personalized means of communication considered by modern theorists of public opinion to be the type most effective in terms of altering or shaping opinions.[107] One citizen of Salem recalled how "youths and old men thrilled to stories of savage Indians, of Owhyee chiefs draped in capes of multicolored plumage, of Tripolitan pirates and of unfathomable Chinese merchants, which, in the telling lost no flavor." [108] If these tales reached only youths and old men, their significance might be sharply discounted. But most of these traders and sea captains, as well as some members of the crews on the ships that went to Canton, were scions of prominent mercantile families and became the influential bankers and important merchants of the next generation.[109] As such, their judgments of the Chinese reached wider and more significant circles which included important opinion makers. Not infrequently newspaper editors quoted them, and the indefatigable Dr. Benjamin Rush, a commentator on almost every subject, relied heavily on his personal contacts with traders in Philadelphia for information on China.[110]

The final test of the efficacy of trader influence on the American image of the Chinese must be in the changes one finds in the content of American magazines, newspapers, and school textbooks between 1785 and 1840. Before this is attempted, however, it is necessary to examine the communication of two other inside dopesters who reported on China to American audiences: the professional diplomat and the Protestant missionary.

Nothing has ever been more exaggerated than the state of civilization and social advancement among the Chinese. . . . The administration of public affairs, is such as would disgrace any country on the globe, and the code of laws which is expressed in such high flown metaphors, and boasts such wonderful wisdom in its doctrines, serves, in truth, but as a cloak to hide injustice and oppression.

American Quarterly Review (Phila.), IX (1830), 60.

3

The Diplomatic Image, 1785-1840

Of the three major sources from which the pre-1840 American image of China was drawn, the diplomats differed from both the traders and missionaries in several important respects. Most striking was the fact that all of the diplomat-authors, except for two at the very close of the fifty-five-year period, were European. In a sense they represent a continuation of that American dependence on transatlantic sources of opinion which was an inheritance from the long colonial experience. As inside dopesters, these diplomats could also claim to have seen substantial parts of the interior of China, an experience not open to traders and missionaries before the Opium War. To this was added the weight of government sanction as the official embodiment of "great power" policy and wisdom. For the most part these authors were also aristocrats with extensive education and superior social status, factors by no means lost on American observers. As far as American editors were concerned, ten books on China that were by-products of European embassies to that nation were more important than the accounts of the less literate and prestigious traders. Scarcely an article written on China before 1850 failed to cite at least one of these diplomatic memoirs for authority. Bibliographies and recommended reading lists on the subject of China continued to cite many of them throughout most of the nineteenth century.

These ten works were written by Aeneas Anderson, Sir George Staunton, Sir John Barrow, André Van Braam-Houckgeest, John M'Leod, Sir Henry Ellis, Sir John Davis, George Timkowski, Edmond Roberts, and W. S. W. Ruschenberger. The first three authors were members of Lord Macartney's mission in 1792; Van Braam assisted the Dutch envoy, Isaac Titsingh, in 1794; while M'Leod, Ellis, and Davis went to China with the Amherst mission in 1816, Timkowski with a Russian one in 1821, and the last two with an American mission to Asia for President Jackson in 1832.

In 1791 England dispatched an embassy to Peking under Earl Macartney, a seasoned diplomat with experience in Ireland, the West Indies, and Russia, with instructions to secure trading privileges in additional Chinese ports, a reduction in duties, permission to teach Christianity in China, and the establishment of a permanent British embassy or warehouse in the Celestial capital. The last goal may well have been the most challenging, since the Chinese, from time immemorial, had greeted ambassadors as representatives of imperial vassals who came to Peking to deposit tributary gifts and then depart.[1] Macartney was, in fact, proclaimed by Chinese banners to be such a tribute bearer. The English ambassador ignored this indignity, but refused to perform the kowtow unless a Chinese official of equal rank duplicated the gesture before a portrait of George III. Finally a compromise permitted the ambassador to bow low on one knee as he would before his own sovereign. Then the Chinese postponed action on his proposals through the summer, at the end of which they abruptly denied all of the English requests and packed the embassy off to Canton.[2]

Three important works, in terms of influence on American opinion, came out of this mission. Aeneas Anderson, whose status with the embassy is unclear, rushed into print with the first narrative. He presented himself as the chief mate of the *Lion* and part of the military contingent that accompanied the embassy to Peking.[3] However, Macartney wrote to Lord Grenville: "You will please observe the said Aeneas Anderson was a servant in the livery attending upon the Embassy, and, of course, you will judge of its [Anderson's work] authenticity and what sort of materials it was likely to be composed of." [4]

Anderson declared that his intention in writing the book was "to correct the erroneous accounts of Abbé Grosier."[5] Most of the works critical of China in the eighteenth century began in this manner. Each new author seemed to think that his was the first attempt to strip China of the ill-deserved glory bestowed upon her by the Jesuit missionaries. By 1795 this was a well-worn gambit, except that Anderson was no critic. On the contrary, he sought to refute every popular charge against China and showed irritation at the concessions made by Grosier to the increasing number of sinophobes. For example, Grosier had admitted that gruesome tortures and executions were commonplace in China.[6] Yet Anderson testified that he had interviewed scores of Chinese up to seventy years of age and failed to uncover one who had witnessed such an execution.[7]

One by one Anderson discussed each popular belief about China and then demolished it. Far from being an oppressive despotism, the Celestial government was the "epitome of good sense," from which England could learn a great deal about keeping "the more obnoxious classes" under control. Even footbinding was a myth, insisted Anderson. He swore that all Chinese females had normal feet; and contrary to the report that women were kept locked up in China by jealous males, he had been free to communicate with any of them. There were far fewer idols in evidence than believed, and none were as hideous as described by travelers. The streets were "clean and elegant" and the people "attractive and healthy" with hardly a one marked by smallpox. Everywhere the Chinese were truthful and honest, except in Canton where they had been contaminated by Western influence. Indeed, Anderson warned, the Western misconceptions of the Chinese had caused the embassy trouble on at least one occasion. When a British soldier was caught buying native liquor against regulations, it was decided that a public lashing would impress their Chinese hosts. Instead, the latter were horrified at the inhumanity of such a punishment for a trivial offense, or so Anderson claimed.[8]

The roads and canals in China offered mute testimony that the Chinese were as scientifically advanced as the West, Anderson continued. In fact, the refusal of the mandarins to examine the mechanical and optical instruments brought from England as gifts merely showed that the Chinese had nothing to learn from Europeans in this area. Suggestions forwarded by other members of the embassy that the refusal was attributable rather to ignorance and obstinacy were typical of European "prejudice" against the Chinese, in the judgment of Anderson. Only in ship construction were the Chinese behind Westerners, and this was not due to "mechanical ignorance" as much as to "their prejudice in favor of long established habits." Anderson was singularly impressed by the skill with which a Chinese doctor diagnosed a stricken member of the British embassy.[9]

Nothing revealed Anderson's partiality for the Chinese so much as his praise for the "martial appearance" of the soldiers of the imperial guard. He was particularly impressed by the skilful manner in which a Chinese soldier could draw a sword from behind his back with either hand. Not once did he criticize the continued reliance on the sword and other outdated weaponry such as the halberds, lances, sabres, and matchlocks which he described in some detail. "In short," Anderson wrote, "everyone of these military divisions was distinguished by their dress and arms. . . . I never saw a finer display of a military parade." [10] Lord Macartney labeled Anderson's narrative "a mere bookseller's job to gratify the public curiosity." [11] It also appeared to be a deliberate attempt to restore some of China's eroded prestige in Europe.

A second book reached the market ahead of Sir George Staunton's official version of Macartney's embassy, this one by William Winterbotham in 1795. The following year an American edition of Winterbotham's work was published in Philadelphia with huge advertisements in the *Aurora* promising to provide the reader with "a pretty correct opinion of that Nation, in many instances the most astonishing of any recorded in the pages of history." [12] Winterbotham's treatment of China was more friendly than his promise "to strip the accounts of the visionary missionaries of their visions" would indicate.[13] He seemed chiefly concerned with attacking Lord Macartney and the conduct of the embassy in China. But the almost total failure of American magazine editors to cite Winterbotham's work and its absence from most reading lists and bibliographies in the nineteenth century deprive it of importance to this study. Winterbotham was not a member of Macartney's embassy, and the poor response to his work corroborates the value of the inside dopester status.

Sir George Staunton's official narrative of the embassy finally appeared in 1797. It is virtually impossible to separate Staunton's view of China from that of his superior, since the book was "Taken Chiefly from the Papers of His Excellency the Earl of Macartney" as the full title asserted.[14] Both diplomats had ambivalent attitudes toward China. They made no attempt to dismiss the popular charges against the Chinese in the fashion of Anderson. On the contrary, ample attention was paid to the military impotence of the Chinese, their scientific and technological crudity, lack of cleanliness, practice of infanticide, and official arrogance. Staunton interpreted the refusal of the mandarins to examine the mechanical gifts as an attempt to hide from these "conquerors of India" the full extent of their technological backwardness. If so, the effort was wasted on Staunton, who asserted that the Chinese had not made any real scientific gains since "the first rude notions entertained among mankind that the whole earth was one flat surface." [15]

The same medical incident that had so impressed Anderson earned Staunton's scorn: The doctor played foolishly upon the pulse at various parts of the patient's body, "as if upon the keys of a harpsichord." Staunton concluded that the Chinese physician was unaware of the consistency of blood pressure throughout the body. Indeed, Chinese medicine was so backward, Staunton asserted, that blood-letting was still unknown in the Celestial Empire.[16]

Staunton and Macartney not only acknowledged the practice of infanticide but helped to document it further. The ambassador noted in his journal that a French missionary of Peking in secret testimony had "confirmed . . . that it is a common practice among the poor to expose their children." [17] Staunton carefully detailed this process and estimated the annual number of victims at two thousand female infants.[18]

In spite of all this, Macartney and Staunton admired China's efficiently run despotism and retained a good deal of nostalgia for the older China of Marco Polo and the Jesuit missionaries. Staunton recalled his youthful sentiments upon reading Du Halde and conceded that his final impression of Chinese society was pleasing.[19] "However meanly we must think of the taste and delicacy of the Court of China . . . ," Macartney wrote, "it must be confessed there was something grand and imposing in the general effect." To Macartney this effect was essentially "a calm dignity, that sober pomp of Asiatic greatness which European refinements have not attained." [20]

But in many other ways Macartney and Staunton found the Chinese court to be astonishingly crude. Underneath their elaborate robes, Macartney asserted, Chinese courtiers never change their underwear, and they "spit about the rooms without mercy, blow their noses in their fingers and wipe them with their sleeves or upon anything near them," a practice he called "universal" in China. Such behavior, thought the two senior members of the mission, was ample evidence that the Chinese were becoming "semi-barbarous." At this stage, they argued with obvious regret, nothing could save China from continued rapid decline. A single statement in Macartney's journal best summarizes the verdict that these two diplomats brought back to England: "The Empire of China is an old, crazy, first-rate Man of War, which a fortunate succession of able and vigilant officers have contrived to keep afloat for these hundred and fifty years past, and to overawe their neighbors merely by her bulk and appearance. . . . She may, perhaps, not sink outright; she may drift some time as a wreck, and will then be dashed to pieces on the shore; but she can never be rebuilt on the old bottom." [21]

Professor William Appleton has declared that Staunton's work was "the last of consequence to appear" from members of Macartney's embassy, thereby cutting out Sir John Barrow's *Travels in China* which appeared in 1803. Indeed, Appleton relegated the latter work to a footnote in which he dismissed it as "notoriously inaccurate." [22] One wonders why it should have been thought any more inaccurate than the account of Anderson, who never explained how he interviewed all those Chinese or communicated with their women without knowing the language.[23] However, for the purposes of this study, accuracy is of less importance than popularity and influence in the United States. The significant difference between Anderson and Barrow was that the former was an unabashed sinophile and the latter an exceptionally vigorous—one hesitates to say vicious—sinophobe. In a sense, both books were out of place at the end of the eighteenth century. If Anderson's work was a throwback to the late seventeenth century, Barrow's book fits more readily into the nineteenth. For this reason, the latter became increasingly popular after 1830; and it is virtually impossible to locate a bibliography or reading list of books on China between 1830 and 1850 that failed to cite Barrow's work, whereas Anderson's account appeared only occasionally. In terms of the frequency with which American journalists referred to these diplomatic sources, Anderson's report was totally eclipsed by the Staunton and Barrow memoirs. Fifty-eight years after its first publication, Barrow's *Travels* was still identified by one English sinophile as the crucial work in "bolstering up prejudices and preconceived notions about the Chinese." [24]

Barrow's reputation added to the importance of his volume.

Contemporaries thought very highly of him. Staunton praised his
intelligence and described him as "conversant in astronomy, mechanics, and every other branch dependent upon the mathemat-
ics." [25] Thirty years later, Sir John Davis pronounced Barrow an
"excellent observer," although Davis's view of China was considerably less critical than was Barrow's.[26] Barrow's reputation rested
on more than testimonials, however. He also published tomes on
South Africa (1801), the Arctic (1818), Holland (1831), and
Pitcairn Island (1832), as well as biographies of Peter the Great,
admirals Anson and Howe, and an autobiography. Barrow was,
moreover, an Oxford graduate and fellow of the Royal Society.

One would have to go back to de Pauw to find a critic of China
as implacable as Barrow. Not only did Barrow repeat all the old
charges, but he added several new ones. The government was so
oppressive, Barrow charged, that the Chinese had to be considered
slaves; this explained why they had no sense of honor, lied,
cheated, and displayed abject cowardice without shame. "A slave,
in fact, cannot be dishonoured." In some ways Barrow approached
the modern racist position, although well short of twentieth-
century extremes. He provided his reader with elaborate drawings
to demonstrate the close physical relationship between the Chinese and the Hottentots. He went on to testify, having been in
Africa, that these two peoples were identical in voice, manner of
speaking, and temperament. "A Hottentot who attended me in
travelling over Southern Africa was so very like a Chinese servant
I had in Canton, both in person, features, manners, and tone of
voice, that almost always inadvertently, I called him by the name
of the latter," he testified. Aware that this comparison would raise
eyebrows among his readers, he assured them that it was not made
loosely and that the "mental qualities" of the two groups were also identical. "The aptitude of a Hottentot in acquiring and
combining ideas is not less than of a Chinese; and their powers of
imitation are equally as great, allowance being made for the difference of education." Later, he implied that the famed Linneaus
had considered the Chinese "among the monsters in nature, *Homo
monstrosus, macrocephalus, capite conico, Chinensis.*" But Barrow thought the conical shaped head only common enough among
the Tartars, and not the Chinese, to warrant such a classification.[27]

The technique of citing a critic more harsh than himself and, in
the ostensible interest of fair play, refusing to go quite so far was
one that Barrow employed frequently. In discussing infanticide,

for example, he accepted de Pauw's contention that stray dogs and swine frequently devoured abandoned infants before the official cart arrived to make scheduled pickups. He endorsed an estimate of infant victims of twenty-four daily and nine thousand yearly in the city of Peking alone. But Barrow was "not credulous enough" to accept Torreen's charge that the exposed children were eaten by the Chinese for medicinal purposes.[28]

Essentially Barrow regarded China as a nation of great paradoxes. Although first in size and population, she was near the bottom in military power. Civilized before the Greeks, she was now scarcely civilized at all. Her boast of filial piety was unconvincing in the light of the exposure of infants. In this vein, he continued, "the strict morality and ceremonious conduct of the people are followed by a list of the most gross debaucheries; the virtues and the philosophy of the learned are explained by their ignorance and their vices; if in one page they speak of the excessive fertility of the country, and the amazing extension of agriculture, in the next, thousands are seen perishing by want; and whilst they extol with admiration the progress they have made in the arts and sciences, . . . without the aid of foreigners they can neither cast a cannon nor calculate an eclipse." Although Barrow never made this theory of paradoxes explicit, it was implied in his discussion of each Chinese institution. Even the national character he described as "a strange compound of pride and meanness, of affected gravity and real frivolousness, of refined civility and gross indelicacy." [29]

This paradoxical quality in Chinese civilization also helped Barrow to explain the sharply contrasting picture of China painted by the Jesuits. They had stressed only favorable aspects, whereas Barrow contended that his objective was "to draw a faithful picture, neither attempting to palliate their vices, nor exaggerate their virtues." Barrow saw his own work as providing the balance that would "enable the reader to settle in his own mind" the true nature of Chinese civilization.[30]

Barrow's heavy use of statistical tables and diagrams must have been impressive to his audience. In discussing China's population and food supply he provided an array of illustrations and documents, and even included musical scores to demonstrate China's alleged inferiority in this field. But underneath his quasi-scientific approach was a good deal of ethnocentricity; he was totally unable to appreciate that the Chinese might have a defensible perspective of their own. Their theatre was measured with a European yardstick and condemned as "so very puerile, or so gross and vulgar,

that the tricks and puppet-shows which are occasionally exhibited
in the common fair . . . of England, may be considered as comparatively polished, interesting and rational." Chinese entertain-
ment by itself, he argued, should make Europeans wonder about
the "supposed state of civilization" in China.[31]

This same ethnocentrism was discernible in Barrow's comments
on Catholics, Jews, Moslems, and the French. Indeed, it was only
in such moments that Barrow inadvertently complimented the behavior of the Chinese. In discussing footbinding, for instance, he
explained that the Chinese would "consider as egregiously absurd,
the custom of circumcision," which Barrow thought related to a
practice universal among savage tribes of "maiming or lopping off
some part of the body." In describing the filthy habits of the Chinese, he emphasized that the French were little different—the
members of the Chinese court spit on the floors while the French
spit on the walls, and the Chinese had longer sleeves to use as a
combination handkerchief and napkin than did Barrow's Gallic
neighbors in Europe. In his discussion of superstition, the Chinese
came off better than the Roman Catholics: "Surely it is not more
repugnant to reason, nor less consonant with human feelings, to
offer grateful gifts to the manes of deceased parents and friends,
than to fall down before the Virgin Mary and the thousand saints
whom caprice or cabal have foisted into their calendar, and of
whose history and actions even their votaries are totally ignorant."
The one thing that Barrow seemed to admire in China was her religious toleration, along with Confucius, whose philosophy, he
opined, was too sublime to be preserved in purity among the Chinese.[32]

Following close on the heels of Macartney, Isaac Titsingh in
1794 led a Dutch mission to Peking. Apparently Cantonese officials and merchants were eager to produce a more docile European
embassy, lest Peking contemplate closing off the trade altogether
after its experience with Macartney.[33] The members of the Dutch
embassy readily complied with all the demands of Chinese proto-
col only to face additional humiliating requests that the kowtow
be performed before the prime minister, before pieces of cloth
upon which the emperor's name was printed, and finally before
the refuse from the emperor's plate. To Barrow this was ample
proof that Macartney had acted wisely in refusing to perform the
gesture at all.[34]

But Staunton argued that the West continually underestimated
Peking's system of intelligence. Not only were Chinese officials

aware of Holland's relative weakness, but they also recognized that
Titsingh's embassy had only a quasi-official status, being more representative of the Dutch East India Company than it was of the
government of Holland.[35] It is even possible, though unlikely,
that the Chinese may have known that the government of Holland
no longer existed by the time Titsingh reached Peking. At any
rate, the Dutch envoys were treated much more considerately on
their return journey to Canton after what C. L. Boxer called a
"grossly discourteous" reception. Except for Titsingh, the experience was pleasant enough to mitigate some of the bitterness felt by
members of the mission.[36]

Only two books grew out of this embassy. Joseph de Guignes,
son of a famous sinologue and official interpreter for the mission,
published *Voyage à Pekin* in 1808. As this memoir was not translated into English, it was virtually ignored in the United States.
Van Braam-Houckgeest, second in command of the embassy, and a
naturalized citizen of the United States, published a two-volume
account in Philadelphia in 1797. Part of this edition was captured
en route to England by the French, who then published a "pirate"
edition in Paris in 1798. Still another edition was published in
London that same year.[37]

Van Braam returned to his adopted country after the mission,
and built a home that still stands on the banks of the Delaware in
Bristol, twenty miles from Philadelphia. There he maintained an
Oriental atmosphere with one Malay and five Chinese servants
and Chinese furniture, sculpture, porcelain, lacquerware, and
even a pagoda-like cupola on his house. Named "China's Retreat,"
it was a popular rendezvous for the elite of Philadelphia as well as
for celebrated French émigrés, according to several historians.[38]

Under such circumstances one would expect Van Braam's book
to have provoked a popular response in the United States. Although well received, particularly by Philadelphia publications, it
never approached the influence of the Staunton book, published
in the same year, or Barrow's work that followed five years later.
Probably it should be ranked ahead of the Anderson account,
however, in terms of influence on American opinion.

It is difficult to generalize about Van Braam's chronicle. The
general position taken was not far from that of Staunton. Van
Braam's numerous criticisms of China were continually softened
by his obvious nostalgia for old Cathay. Evidently his long residence in Canton as a Dutch merchant had not dimmed his faith in
a fabulous capital and a sumptuously equipped palace. He ex-

pressed great disappointment when his experience did not substantiate "the brilliant accounts that the Missionaries [Jesuits]
have sent to Europe of this capital." [39] Yet his enthusiasm and his
romantic expectations seemed to be dampened rather than extin-
guished by his adventure.

Frequently Van Braam's criticisms were nullified by ensuing
remarks and descriptions. For example, he stated his agreement
with the general estimate of the "primitive" level of Chinese scientific knowledge. Nevertheless, he lavished extensive praise on such
items as Chinese bridge construction, the system of central heating
in houses, an ingenious sowing machine, and a clever soldering
mechanism.[40] Thus, he made it difficult for the reader to accept
his original low estimate of Chinese technology without serious
reservations.

Van Braam also warned continuously that the Chinese should
be judged by their own standards and tastes rather than those of
Europe. Even when the author was presented with gnawed bones
from the emperor's dinner plate as a token of honor and favor,
Van Braam explained that the emperor was "no doubt ignorant"
of how disgusting this would be to a European. In another instance, Van Braam expressed profound shock at discovering political graft and corruption in the imperial household itself. But the
Dutch diplomat quickly regained his composure and urbanely
soliloquized: "But where is there a place in the universe inaccessi-
ble to corruption?" After lengthy descriptions of the military in-
competence of the Chinese, the harsh humiliations to which the
women of China were subjected, and the many peculiar manners
and customs of the people, Van Braam concluded, "As far as the
opposition of manners allows me to judge, . . . the Chinese live
very happily in their way. And if that be the case, what have they
more to desire? Why should they wish to discover things . . . ? " [41]

Van Braam was a cultural relativist long before that term was
coined, and one must agree with C. L. Boxer's conclusion that he
"came to have a sincere affection for the [Chinese] people and customs that was rare indeed amongst his European contemporaries." [42] Only in his attack on the *"coulis,"* whom he called "the
very refuse of the Chinese nation," did Van Braam lose his sense of
affection and his cosmopolitan composure.[43]

After the Napoleonic wars, Britain sent another mission to China,
under Lord Amherst, once again attempting to establish a permanent embassy in Peking, open up ports for trading, and in general
wring further commercial concessions from the Chinese. But Am-

herst was even less successful than his predecessor, Lord Macartney. Negotiations over the kowtow ceremony were short and not
sweet. Amherst flatly refused to make any such obeisance, although the Chinese officials insisted that Macartney had performed the ritual. As a result, Amherst was immediately dismissed
from Peking without having seen the emperor at all. The embassy's official historian, Sir Henry Ellis, called the Chinese action
"unparalleled insolence," [44] and his account was studded with
such adjectives as "outrageous" and "mortifying" to describe the
behavior of the mandarins.

Like Macartney and Titsingh before him, Amherst left all public expositions of the mission to other members of his staff. Supple-
menting the official Ellis account, personal narratives were published by Clarke Abel, a trader who accompanied the embassy;
John M'Leod, the surgeon; Basil Hall, a naval captain; and
George T. Staunton, son of Macartney's second in command.
Staunton's work was "for private circulation only" and reached
such a limited audience that it has no value for this study.[45] Captain Hall's book dealt almost entirely with a side trip to Korea,
and his scanty references to China proper make it hardly relevant
to the concerns of this inquiry.[46]

Abel's was the most friendly report to come out of the Amherst
mission. It was his position that the Chinese were much maligned
in the West, although he conceded that certain situations obtained
that were shocking from a strictly European viewpoint. But other
alleged evils, he contended, existed only in the minds of Western
reporters. For example, he denied that infanticide existed at all.
Throughout his volume, Abel constantly expressed admiration for
the order that China had established over a vast region by means
of her despotic form of government and her efficient network of
roads and canals. His attitude toward China's antiquity approached a state of reverential awe at times.[47] Abel's book ex-
emplifies the continued viability of the older, more favorable view
which still existed alongside the rapidly growing hostile sentiment.

As for Doctor John M'Leod, his commentary was bitterly hostile
to China. In 1816, M'Leod had been aboard the Amherst mission's
naval escort vessel *Alceste,* when it was refused a safe anchorage at
Canton after returning from a rough voyage to Korea and Formosa. Incensed over what M'Leod described as "a good many
gratuitous insults," Captain Murray Maxwell, in the style of Lord
Anson almost eighty years earlier, simply "took" a safe anchorage.
In the process he fired upon one fort and sank several war junks,

killing a number of Chinese. Whereupon M'Leod recorded an instantaneous change on the part of the Chinese officials, who effusively and obsequiously apologized for the "mistake" and showed themselves eager to dismiss the matter as "some saluting" by gunners with bad aim. To the author, the lesson was abundantly clear that the Chinese would respond only to force. "Half-measures," he advised, "seem to be a bad system in any dealings, but more especially with uncivilized people for they are apt to attribute forbearance to fear, and acquire, under that impression, fresh courage." In place of "the kotowing ceremony" M'Leod recommended that future missions to China utilize another type of "head thumping," involving Chinese heads! M'Leod acknowledged that Anson had proffered similar advice to the West unavailingly much earlier. "The forbearance and mistaken lenity of the greater civilized powers," he warned, "have emboldened these savages, not only to consider as barbarians all Europeans, but actually to treat them as such." [48]

M'Leod's work had two other significant aspects. Until the Protestant missionaries arrived in force, he was the only author to question China's civilized status openly and seriously. Barrow had done so only by implication. Always on the threshold of civilization, China had never quite reached the inner sanctum; according to M'Leod, "The Chinese . . . afford a melancholy example of the perverseness of human nature; exhibiting a people who have had for some two thousand years a dawn of civilization, which, from the operation of the most narrow-minded principles, has never brightened into day. But for the presumptuous folly of supposing themselves at the summit of perfection, and the absurd tyranny of fettering the human understanding by forbidding all innovation and improvement, China might and ought to have been at the present hour the greatest nation of the world." [49]

Later on, the Protestant missionaries were to question China's civilized status because she lacked the revealed word of God. But M'Leod reached the same conclusion because the Chinese lacked the Western conception of progress that valued commerce and constant innovation. Condemnation of China's static condition and orientation to the past became increasingly prevalent as the nineteenth century wore on, particularly among American traders. The leading apologists for Chinese civilization, such as Van Braam, Staunton, and Abel, were now traditionalists who admired China's emphasis on hoary customs and instinctively sympathized with her aristocratic, strictly governed society. Ironically, in the eighteenth century it had been the innovators, such as Voltaire, Leibniz, and William Temple, who had generally admired China.

Another significant feature of M'Leod's book was that he, like Barrow, seemed to adumbrate a modern racist position. In discussing the sinophiles of Europe, he divided them into two groups. One "very distinct class of encomiasts . . . of the true antediluvian school" admired the Chinese "solely on account of their unvarying habits, and tenacious adherence to their ancient customs." Such men deemed "anything antique desireable, however primitive." A second group of sinophiles attributed Chinese "suspicious meanness, knavery, silly pride and other ill qualities, to their depraved mode of government." These men were foolish enough to believe that by changing the government, the Chinese "would be a gay, civil, industrious and honest people. . . . Perhaps there may be a good deal of truth" to this, M'Leod conceded, "and it is . . . unfortunate that some change does not take place in a system which produces effects so injurious to the reputation of mankind." But, he carefully warned, that "character" had "deeper roots," and it was entirely likely that China's government was the product of a "natural defect" in her people.[50] Here M'Leod not only anticipated the germ theory of culture, but inferred that anyone who did not view China in these terms was a sinophile.

The last and most important work on China produced by the Amherst mission was the journal of Sir Henry Ellis. In frequency of citation by American magazine editors prior to the Opium War, it was outstripped only by the Barrow and Staunton reports. One such editor attributed its wide and favorable reception to the reputation of the author, "handsome illustrations," and a reasonably low price.[51] In Ellis' journal the sinophobes discovered a trump card that powerfully corroborated Barrow's view of China. One American reviewer twitted the "many" persons who had "felt Barrow's book was the result of resentment due to the unceremonious treatment of the Macartney mission." He reminded them that he, on the contrary, had not only agreed with Barrow but had charged him with being "too lenient" in judging the Chinese. Throughout his review he rejoiced that both he and Barrow now had been vindicated by the Ellis journal.[52]

Ellis himself quoted Barrow's work frequently and testified of the leaders of the Amherst mission: "We have all had reason to concur with Mr. Barrow." There may have been less acrimony in Ellis' *Journal*, but the author's opinion of Chinese society was equally low. He added little that was new to the charges of earlier sinophobes. The alleged pretentions and arrogance of Chinese officials; Chinese propensity for filth, lying, cheating, and cruelty; the primitive state of Chinese science and medicine; and the slavish adherence to customs—all were present. One mildly original criticism by Ellis was his assertion that the bows and arrows with which Chinese soldiers were equipped were inferior even to those of medieval Europe. The bow had a shorter range, the arrow was over-feathered and the Chinese had not yet learned to barb their arrowheads! [53]

In the fashion of Barrow and M'Leod, Ellis was scathingly critical of China's despotic form of government. This was one issue that really split diplomat-authors into two camps. With the shock of the French Revolution still lingering in every memory, men like Macartney, Staunton, Anderson, Van Braam, and Abel admired the efficiency with which Peking controlled the great Chinese masses. But Ellis could not swallow this. Chinese absolutism went too far, and the degree to which one was "placed at the mercy of the caprice of a despot" and even a petty official would not be acceptable "to any civilized person," he concluded.[54]

Frequently, Ellis made it clear that he considered the Chinese a half civilized or semibarbarous nation. Sardonically he accepted the sinophile argument that Canton did not present a true picture of China, adding that his trip to the interior had convinced him that the Cantonese were *more* advanced than Chinese elsewhere due to their contact with civilized Europeans! However, in every part of China, the people and their culture were "inferior by many degrees to civilized Europe in all that constitutes the real greatness of a nation." [55]

Nor did Ellis permit class distinctions to soften his criticisms. For example, in discussing the personal cleanliness of the Chinese, he insisted that "the horrid effluvia proceeding from their persons," emanated from mandarin as well as coolie. "The stench is *sui generis,*" he explained, adding one of his frequent gibes at the sinophiles: "If excess in this quality be a source of the sublime, the Chinese have every claim to that quality." [56]

In his final analysis, Ellis pronounced China destitute of both "the refinement and comforts of civilized life" and the "wild interest of most semi-barbarous countries." He concluded with obvious contempt, "Were it not . . . for the trifling gratification arising from being one of the few Europeans who have visited the interior of China, I should consider the time that has elapsed as wholly without return." [57]

A Russian mission to China in 1821 called forth a travel book by George Timkowski in 1827. Actually this was not a mission in the full sense, as the Russians had been permitted since 1728 a permanent detachment of six priests and four "lay members" for the purpose of maintaining a Russian church in Peking and for learning the Chinese language. The Russians were permitted to trade only by land, and the detachment of Russians in Peking was not a permanent embassy in the normal sense so much as a rough equivalent of the foreign factories in Canton. Nevertheless, the Timkowski book was handled by American editors as a diplomatic rather than a trader account, and the author was considered an important inside dopester since he had spent a full year in Peking and showed additional knowledge of Mongolia and Chinese areas bordering on Siberia. In essence, Timkowski repeated the same criticisms as the other diplomat-authors. Since several American traders had argued that China and Russia were equally despotic, one ruled by the bamboo, the other by the cudgel, it is interesting to note that this Russian diplomat sharply condemned the rigid laws, harsh discipline, and use of inhuman tortures in China.[58] Timkowski's account was less critical of China than several American reviewers seemed to think, however; one accused him of maligning the Chinese, and another of attempting to "confirm Barrow's opinion of the moral inferiority of that country." [59]

The reflections of John F. Davis in 1836, though late in arrival, cannot be omitted from any survey of important influences on American opinion of China. This volume was as ubiquitous as the accounts of Staunton and Barrow in American magazine discussions of China during much of the nineteenth century and went through almost a dozen printings on both sides of the Atlantic. Davis came to China as part of the Amherst mission, remained as an official of the East India Company, and was appointed to the ill-fated Napier mission in 1834. At that time China still refused to accept professional diplomats except as part of special embassies. In between missions there were only spokesmen for the traders, organized along national lines. Indeed, it was Napier's uncertain status that caused the failure of his mission in 1834. With the ending of the East India Company's tea monopoly, the British had attempted to employ Napier as a formal ambassador; but the Chinese were willing to accept him only as a trader primarily and a group spokesman or diplomatic clerk secondarily.[60]

Davis' description of China was decidedly eclectic and compendious. In his introduction the author acknowledged indebtedness to Staunton, Barrow, Ellis, and Abel, which covers quite well the spectrum of British diplomatic opinion concerning China. In part, Davis' volume was a summing up of these diverse views. But his final conclusion was that the Chinese did not fully deserve the severe criticism directed at them by Europeans, that they had been "underestimated, or rather unfairly despised on the score of their moral attributes." Davis did agree, however, that force alone was effective in dealing with the Chinese. He cited the earlier experiences of Commodore Anson and captains Weddell and Maxwell to illustrate that a cannon ball or mailed fist quickly deflated Chinese vanity and made it possible to deal with them. Admiral Drury and Lord Napier had recently ignored this lesson, thereby increasing "Chinese arrogance." He listed the many authorities who had endorsed this precept earlier. "Mr. Barrow, who has really studied China, and understands it well," wrote Davis, "observes that a 'tame and passive obedience to the degrading demands of this haughty court serve only to feed its pride, and add to the absurd notions of its own vast importance.' " [61]

The two final diplomatic accounts were American, products of an embassy sent in 1832 by President Jackson to several Asian kingdoms, exclusive of China, under Edmund Roberts, a New Hampshire sea captain and trader. In Macao, Roberts secured the services of J. R. Morrison, son of the English missionary with whom he had been corresponding for advice. Rebuffed at Hué because he refused to perform the kowtow, Roberts met with great success at Bangkok. He not only succeeded in lowering the duties negotiated there by the British seven years earlier, but almost secured the legalization of opium. [62] An equally successful treaty with Muscat followed; but Roberts, severely ill, postponed his planned trip to Japan and returned to Macao, where he died in 1836. His chronicle was published posthumously in New York. A large portion of it dealt with China, and its harsh criticism was instrumental in shaking the confidence of the pro-Chinese editors of the influential *North American Review.*[63]

Roberts impugned the assertions of other diplomats that despotism in China resulted in order and tranquility. On the contrary, he wrote, "Almost daily, placards are posted in the principal places about Canton and its suburbs, giving accounts of murders and insurrections, robberies, shocking and unnatural crimes of kidnapping, infanticides, suicides, and all the beastly and unnatural crimes of which the world ever heard or read." [64]

Much in the manner of Protestant missionaries, Roberts not

only expressed shock but real indignation over the idolatry and vice he found in China. He was incensed at suggestions that Chinese religious beliefs in any way approached those of Christianity. "They are without God in the world, and estranged from the divine life, worshipping the works of their hands, to the disgrace of human reason," he retorted angrily. Indeed, the vehemence of Roberts' tirades against the Chinese resembled that of Denis Kearney in San Francisco's sandlots four decades later. He characterized the Chinese as "depraved and vicious," inhumanely cruel, and addicted to "pernicious drugs." [65]

The final piece of writing, by W. S. W. Ruschenberger, is a diplomatic account only in a borderline sense. The author was a surgeon aboard the U.S.S. *Peacock* which carried Roberts on his mission. Like Dr. John M'Leod, therefore, Ruschenberger was not a professional diplomat but one who took part in a diplomatic mission. Because of the reputation of the author and his membership in many intellectual societies in America during the 1840s, this book had special importance. Moreover, Ruschenberger was the one American in China with sufficient cosmopolitanism to view the Celestial Empire from a broader perspective. For example, he observed that there were no medical restrictions against eating cats and dogs. "Indeed, if the state of the art of the cookery in a nation were to be received as a criterion of its civilization, I should vote the Chinese the most civilized people on earth." [66] Ruschenberger was almost unique among Americans of his era in thus expressing an awareness of the real worth of Chinese cuisine.

Ruschenberger further corroborated the close cooperation between British and Americans in China, expressing gratitude for the "active sympathies of the British residents" and their "untiring hospitality." Nevertheless, he felt that, "however close their connexions in social intercourse and individual friendship," the Americans had to steer a separate course based on their own commercial and national interests. He was, in fact, mildly critical of the late Lord Napier and of what he considered psychological preparations for war by the British against China.[67]

In spite of Ruschenberger's education and worldliness, his conclusions were scarcely distinguishable from those of Roberts and, in most respects, from those of Barrow, Ellis, and M'Leod. He wrote of the Chinese:

They are a people who destroy their own tender offspring; a nation wherein the most infamous crimes are common; . . . where the merchant cozens his fellow-citizen and the stranger; where a knowledge of the language is the remotest boundary of science; where a language and a literature, scarcely adequate to the common purposes of life, have remained for ages unimproved; where the guardians of morals are people without honor or probity; where justice is venal to an extent unexampled on the face of the earth; where the great legislator Confucius, so much revered, is unworthy perusal, unless we excuse the poverty of his writings in consideration of the ignorance of the times in which he lived; where a chain of beings, from the emperor to the lowest vassal, live by preying upon one another. . . .[68]

In the main the views of these diplomats paralleled the critical themes and division of opinion that emerge from the trader sample. Only Anderson and Abel attempted to totally deny any validity to the major critical themes in the Western indictment of the Chinese. Others—Staunton, Van Braam, and Davis—accepted such charges regretfully and tempered them either with nostalgic reflections on the fancied Cathay of their youthful imaginations or with relativistic arguments on the universality of vice, corruption, and oppression. Barrow, Ellis, M'Leod, Roberts, and Ruschenberger viewed the alleged social and moral depravity of the Chinese with a degree of highly charged moral indignation that was rarely found in the comments of the traders. Timkowski alone resembled the latter in that he repeated the critical themes with no trace of emotion or nostalgic regret. Although resembling the Protestant missionaries in their critically indignant tone, the diplomats were different in one major respect: Even the most critical diplomat, with the single exception of Roberts, expressed great respect for China's religious toleration and general religious indifference.[69]

"Benighted an' haythen Dooley,"
says he, "ye have no God," he says.
"I have," says I. "I have a lot iv
them," says I. "Ye ar-re an oncult-
ivated an' foul crather," he says. "I
have come six thousan' miles f'r to
hist ye fr'm th' mire iv ignorance
an' irrelijon. . . ."

"Hop Lung Dooley" as "a Chiny-
man" and the "baldheaded" mis-
sionary from "Baraboo, Wisconsin."
Peter Finley Dunne, *Mr. Dooley:
Now and Forever*, ed. L. Filler
(Palo Alto, 1954), p. 135.

4

The Protestant Missionary Image, 1807-1870

The Reverend Robert Morrison's arrival in China in 1807 opened
a new channel of direct information about that nation. The Protestant missionary was the third "gate keeper" and one who commanded the widest audience in America. Not only did the missionaries publish a great many books and journals on China and
their experiences, but they had their own missionary periodicals,
the influence of which was multiplied by a much wider religious
press and numerous pulpits from which to propagate their views
of China.

Before 1840, there were only twenty Protestant missionaries in
China, including two printers and one teacher, according to Professor Latourette, whose encyclopedic work offers us an excellent
guide to their activities.[1] But the myriad reports, journals, and
books produced by this group are not of equal importance in shaping the American image of the Chinese. Kenneth Latourette rec-

ognized this in his history of the missionary movement and labeled some of these works "popular and semi-popular." [2] In this chapter, major stress has been placed on those works that were widely reviewed and frequently cited in both the religious and lay press.

An adequate coverage of the religious press during the period under examination presents a more formidable task in view of the sheer number of newspapers involved. New York City alone supported fifty-two religious publications in 1850 and a federal census of that year revealed 191 throughout the United States.[3] Since only nine American organizations established missions in China before 1877, three of which were southern,[4] the primary publications for each organization and for the denomination it represented were used to sample the treatment of China in this medium. Of these, the *Panoplist,* which became the *Missionary Herald* after 1812, was by far the most important. It was the official publication of the American Board of Commissioners for Foreign Missions, the first American organization to field missionaries in China. Although ostensibly Congregationalist, the American Board acted as an interdenominational agency until other Protestant sects formed their own organizations after the Opium War. Its publication was frequently cited as being a leading authority on China by the lay press, and its value was formally acknowledged by the esteemed *North American Review* in 1848: "There is not a number of the Missionary Herald, an inobtrusive monthly published in this city, which does not send abroad through the American churches materials of knowledge which would be issued from the secular press with the longest and loudest flourishes of trumpets." [5]

Another outstanding missionary publication was the *Chinese Repository* published in Canton by the American missionaries Elijah Bridgman and Samuel Wells Williams from 1832 to 1851. Originally intended for Westerners residing in China, this magazine soon reached a much wider audience in the United States where its articles were frequently reprinted in the religious press.

It is perhaps significant that the first Protestant missionary, Robert Morrison of the London Missionary Society, took his departure for Canton in 1807 via New York, rather than directly from London. The efforts to convert China seem to have aroused greater enthusiasm in the United States than they did in England.[6] In fact, Morrison's detour was due to the East India Company's opposition to his adventure. In the United States, however, he was warmly greeted by elements of both the business and reli-

gious communities. William Patterson, director of the Mint, secured for him a letter of introduction to Edward Carrington, the
American consul in Canton, from Secretary of State James
Madison asking that everything possible be done for the English
missionary consistent with the interests of the United States.[7] Un-
beknown to the clergyman, Madison had showed little interest
until informed that it was Morrison's intention to translate the
Bible into Chinese; he then complied with Patterson's request in
order "to benefit general literature." This prevailing skepticism
was reflected in the casualness with which the secular press reported Morrison's visit. One New Yorker gave utterance to the
American mood of the day when he asked the missionary, "And so
Mr. Morrison, you really expect that you will make an impression
on the idolatry of the great Chinese empire?" Morrison's reply was
equally characteristic of the determination and optimism of the religious renascence when he answered, "No sir, I expect God
will." [8]

While the *Missionary Herald* followed closely every accomplish-
ment of Morrison during his first two decades in China, secular
newspapers ignored them. Indeed, *Niles' Weekly Register* in 1822
virtually endorsed official Chinese action against Christian missionaries and their converts. Christianity was a disruptive influence in the Celestial Empire, Hezekiah Niles asserted, tending to
upset arrangements that had "endured so many ages and contributed . . . to peace and happiness." The record of Christianity
was one of endless warfare, Niles argued: "If the emperor of China
acts from the known conduct of European nations, professing
Christianity, he does perfectly right in opposing everything that
may introduce such discordant elements into his empire." [9]

After 1830, the indifference to missionary efforts began to disappear. Not only were missionaries more newsworthy, but sympathy
and enthusiasm for their work began to be expressed by many
American editors. Niles, in contrast to his earlier sentiment, now
reprinted missionary appeals that the "abominable idolatry" in
China not be excused; that Americans not sit back and idly ignore
"that which God abhors." [10] American traders offered free passage
to missionaries and, in 1834, formed with them in Canton the Society for Diffusing Useful Knowledge Among the Chinese. The
trader D. W. C. Olyphant underwrote the expense of publishing
the *Chinese Repository*, until his death in 1851.[11] This enthusiastic support was not simply a response to the arrival of American
missionaries in China in 1829. English missionaries such as Mor-

rison and William Medhurst and the Prussian Charles Gutzlaff were as much American heroes by 1840 as were native-born individuals like Elijah Bridgman, David Abeel, Ira Tracy, Peter Parker, J. Lewis Shuck, and Samuel Wells Williams. The reversal in American attitudes toward the missionary can best be explained in terms of the general religious revival that had caught fire in eastern rural areas early in the nineteenth century and spread to the seaboard cities by 1830. This "second great awakening" manifested itself in several ways, one of which was a heightened evangelical fervor to bring the gospel to the heathen.[12]

It is in the light of the "Protestant crusade," as Professor Billington labeled it, that the style and content of missionary reports on China can best be appreciated. In part, this religious revival "represented a swing away from the liberalism and Deism which had followed the Revolution toward a rigid fundamentalism which rivaled the stern religion of the Puritans of colonial New England," according to Billington.[13] This would account for the missionaries' obsession with idolatry, gambling, and sexual immorality in China, as well as their indifferent or frequently hostile view of Confucius. The tendency of the Protestant missionary to relate Chinese superstition to "Romanish rites," and his continual warning that the "Man of Sin" in Rome possessed a "560 year head start in converting China," may also have been manifestations of the anti-Catholic aspect of this religious revival.[14] In a letter to his mother, the Reverend Samuel Bonney listed the "four great evils of paganism" as "Confucianism, Boodhist and Taou sects, Popery, and opium smoking."[15]

An examination of the comments of European Protestant missionaries in China, however, reveals a style and content that is virtually indistinguishable from that of their American counterparts. Therefore, one is led to conclude that the Protestant missionaries in China were the product of a religious culture and social movement that transcended national boundaries in the West. They represent that part of the transatlantic mood in the nineteenth century which gave birth to the Salvation Army, the Young Man's Christian Association, and the antislavery, women's rights, and temperance movements, in addition to the propagation of the gospel in heathen lands.[16]

George Danton believed that the great majority of the Protestant missionaries were as primitive as the Chinese they converted, utilizing "a type of propaganda which was little more than the attempt to substitute one superstition for another." For this reason,

Danton continued, they were successful in converting only Chinese with severe psychological problems, at least during the early phase of Protestant proselytism.[17] Danton's assertion was not restricted to the lay missionaries who simply left their work benches to preach the gospel in foreign lands without benefit of any theological training, the number of such missionaries in China before 1870 not being very great in any case.[18]

Evidence can be found to indicate that Danton's charge is a serious one. The Reverend John L. Nevius did experiment with conversion to Christianity as a means of exorcising demons in Shantung, and the tactic was officially supported by F. F. Ellinwood, director of all Presbyterian missions. When Nevius finally published a book on his experience with Chinese demons, Ellinwood wrote the introduction and concluded, "it seems a well established fact that in nearly or quite every instance, the person afflicted, speaking apparently in a different personality . . . has confessed the power of Jesus and it [the demon] has departed." [19] Is it so strange "that demons, recognizing Christ's presence with his people should instinctively escape from a Christian atmosphere?" Nevius asked. Does not the Lord's prayer beseech "deliver us from the evil one"? [20] A column for young people in the *Missionary Herald* discussed Chinese demonology in great detail and reminded its youthful readers that the best way to resist demons was to rely on the "Divine Savior." [21]

But Danton has overstated his case. Rather than superstition, it would seem that provincialism better describes the missionary's conception of China and the Chinese. "The civilization which the Gospel has conferred upon our New England is the highest and best the world has yet seen," one set of missionary instructions stated.[22] The admiration for China expressed by Jesuit missionaries more than a century earlier was totally absent in the commentaries of the later Protestant missionaries. The warmest feeling the latter could generate was a kind of paternalism for the Chinese as "children of darkness," condemned souls who could not muster sufficient determination to save themselves. This provincialism was best expressed in the American missionary's initial shock in facing a society in which "the very name of our saviour is disapproved, if not hated by millions." [23] He seemed ill-prepared to come to grips with heathenism on such a grand scale. "Whole cities are given to idolatry!" Elijah Bridgman exclaimed with a tone of disbelief.[24] "I have been here a week," Samuel Wells Williams wrote back to his father in Utica, New York, "and in that

short time have seen enough of idolatries to call forth all the ener-
gies I have. To . . . see the abominations practiced against the
honor of Him . . . and not be affected with a deep sense of the
depth to which this intellectual people has sunk, is impossible to a
warm Christian man." The ubiquitous incense stick literally covered Canton in a cloud of smoke and blinded his eyes, Williams
claimed.[25]

This initial shock for missionaries arriving in China did not
diminish as the century wore on. Evidently their provincialism did
not permit all the reports fed back by Protestant pioneers to adequately prepare them to face "Satan's empire." Their first reports
to friends and religious newspapers continued to reflect a kind of
breathless shock, horror, helplessness, and incredulity. "Our residence in this far off land has brought us into direct contact with
heathenism," one husband-wife missionary team reported back in
1850. "The monster stares us in the face and defies our power.
Never before have we so ardently desired that eloquence that
moves—the ability to utter those words that burn. It has startled
our whole being to find ourselves fresh as we were from the land of
Bibles and Sabbaths, and Christians, placed in the midst of these
teeming multitudes who neither fear nor know the God whom we
love and adore." [26]

The provincial qualities of the missionary were also revealed in
his rather naive expectations to quickly put Satan to rout in China
with his simple evangelical messages—"those words that burn."
When easy victory was not forthcoming, he concluded that the
Chinese were far more than the innocent victims of Satan to be
found in most pagan countries, but were his conscious agents, who
received personal gratification from deliberately dishonoring God
with acts of idolatry and licentiousness. The myriad descriptions
of "orgies of idolatry" in which the missionary perceived a "diabolical ecstasy" seemed to hint at a kind of sexual sublimation in
such pagan rites.[27] At the same time lewd public debauches
were reported in religious metaphors that revealed its motivation
in devil worship. "Girls scarcely twelve years old were given up to
the beastly passions of men. Parents prostituted their daughters;
husbands their wives; brothers their sisters—and this they did with
a diabolical joy," Gutzlaff reported.[28] Lechery preoccupied the
Chinese who were "vile and polluted in a shocking degree," Williams asserted in his classical textbook, *The Middle Kingdom.*
Young girls were never safe abroad alone where they could be
"lured" by "pictures, songs and aphrodisiacs" into "gates of hell"

to perform "abominable acts," he declared.[29] The Reverend Maclay saw licentiousness as universal and unconcealed in China. "Its
corrupting and debasing influences pervade all classes of society
. . . Forms of this vice which in other lands sulk in dark places, or
appear only in the midnight orgies of the bacchanalian revelers, in
China blanch not at the light of noonday; . . . this lust finds
ready access to the precincts of the family, the forum, and the
temple." [30]

More objective and more systematic Western observers have
generally described the Chinese as exceptionally modest, almost
prudish in their dislike for any public display of affection between
the sexes. That the missionary witnessed public sexual orgies illustrates the theory that one does not see and then define but rather
defines and then sees his definition. What the missionary saw can
only be explained in terms of his preconceived notions about all
pagan societies and the need to illustrate his indictment of the
Chinese as conscious agents of Satan. Hence, he did not echo the
trader's laughter at Chinese idols, for such monsters were not to be
explained by superstition alone but had to look to Satan for inspiration. Indeed, the *raison d'être* of Chinese life, to some missionaries, was the desecration of their God.[31] This unholy alliance
with Beelzebub was formalized in the imperial use of the dragon
as its symbol, the very form in which the devil was depicted in the
Apocalypse, it was reasoned. "Surely this great heathen monarch
could not have adopted a more expressive device to indicate his allegiance to the 'Prince of the Power of the air' that worketh in the
children of disobedience," declared a text on China published by
the American Sunday School Union.[32] Indeed, even when directly
accused of "serving the prince of demons," the Chinese "do not
startle, but glory in their shame," Gutzlaff reported.[33]

In contrast to both the trader group and the diplomat-authors,
the Protestant missionaries were disdainful of Confucius and his
philosophy. This may have been part of the antiliberal quality of
the religious revival in the nineteenth century which frequently
resulted in a general attack on "free thinkers," deists, and transcendentalists. The Reverend David Abeel explained "all the admiration heaped upon Confucius and his system" as a function of
"ignorance" among the Chinese and "infidelity" among "more enlightened" peoples.[34] Ironically, there is little evidence that
deists, transcendentalists, or Unitarians ever looked to the Chinese
sage for inspiration. At least such men as Jefferson, Franklin, Joseph Priestly, Henry Ware, William Channing, and Theodore

Parker left no trace of any interest in Confucius. In his study of oriental influences on transcendentalism, Professor Arthur Christy relied totally on Indian and Persian philosophies and failed to document his contention that Emerson utilized Confucius for his ideas about social relationships.[35] Credible as this might seem, Emerson's few recorded statements on China or the sage do not reveal any admiration. On the contrary, Emerson expressed wonder in 1824 that "our forefathers" could have ever been taken in by anything Chinese. All Emerson could find in Chinese civilization, he confessed, was "a besotted perversity" and the peak of Chinese wisdom was making tea. Moreover, the sage of Concord was specifically critical of Confucius for having condoned and rationalized all of China's social inequities. "But I hate China! 'Tis a tawdry vase," he exclaimed. He did hold out some hope, however, that "the huge and sluggard wave of oriental population" would soon "be stirred & purified by the conflict of counter currents," and "cast off the nightmare incubus that has so long ridden its torpid mind." [36]

True, the Confucian cult in eighteenth-century Europe had been closely associated with the *philosophes,* and it is surprising how the mention of Voltaire could still transform an American editor's ink into pure bile a century later. One Philadelphia editor who favorably reviewed Barrow's hostile report on China wrote, "It is not therefore astonishing to find the cavilling spirit of Voltaire, who has entailed ignominy on the *name* of philosophy . . . acquiescing with readiness and approbation, in all the chimeras of Chinese imagination." [37]

Whatever the reasons, Protestant missionaries, the clergy, and religious editors were clearly not enamored of Confucius in the nineteenth century. Even the few missionaries who thought better of him were angered by earlier attempts to extol the similarities between the teachings of their Saviour and the Chinese sage. "Confucius was a wise and good man," Robert Morrison conceded, but "merely a man"; whereas Christ was "God manifest in the flesh." [38] After all, M. Simpson Culbertson cautioned, "the mind is utterly unable, without a revelation, to solve the mysteries of our existence or to find the true foundations of genuine morality." [39] In much the same vein, Ira Tracy expressed dismay that Sir John Davis dared to attribute the "golden rule" to this idolatrous philosopher.[40] "That these doctrines are superior, or even equal, to those of the inspired volume, could never be assented to, by any but those whose hearts are encased in the adamant of infidelity," Mrs. Shuck charged. Even "the little good" to be found in the works of Confucius was "enveloped in ignorance, superstition and idolatry." [41]

Many missionaries simply dismissed Confucian philosophy as dull and banal, but certainly innocuous enough. "To us, Confucius seems no inspired teacher—only a petty pattern of a Benjamin Franklin," who "at least had some knowledge of God," one religious editor explained. "What touch of Nazarene grace and spirit do we find in these words, 'if perchance I catch an old bird, it is because he follows the young ones' ? Which is a fair size of his [Confucius'] use of external facts," he demanded.[42] Indeed, the Reverend Nevius reasoned that the pedestrian quality of Confucian thought demonstrated that "a want of originality, and a servile following of old forms and usages, was a characteristic of this race more than two thousand years ago." [43] Beyond its antiquity and influence in China, this "vain philosophy" had no intrinsic value.[44] It was a "lifeless and coldhearted system," which was "powerless in the present and hopeless for the future world." [45] The only possible danger Confucianism offered, in the opinions of these missionaries, was that the complacency and contentment with which it was accepted in China deterred the Celestials from seeking out the true God.

But others, or even these same missionaries on different occasions, were less indifferent about Confucian philosophy which they thought was insidiously harmful and capable of deluding the Chinese for many centuries. Their complaints, however, were rarely spelled out. They generally remained vague and unstructured. "The false sentiments and pernicious principles . . . outnumber and outweigh all the others" was a typical grievance of this sort, voiced by the *Missionary Herald*.[46] Given the benign quality of Confucian thought, it is understandable that these critics found it difficult to demonstrate or illustrate its alleged dangers. Some critics resorted to *ad hominem* arguments pointing out that Confucius unjustly divorced his wife, and one editor accused him of having been a "despot" who had his critics executed in his lifetime.[47] Williams did cite the case of one young American whose ideas about God and religion were corrupted by reading Confucius.[48] The Reverend Maclay was something of an exception when he specifically singled out secularism and materialism as the evil twin effects of this philosophy. "Man is enthroned," he explained, "all recognized influences, celestial, terrestial, are held to subserve his purposes, and are valuable and worthy of respect only as they contribute to this end." [49]

More generally the sage's severest critics resorted to the argument that Chinese society with all its egregious flaws was directly attributable to Confucian influences. A philosophy must be "judged by its fruits," these missionaries insisted.[50] "Pride, self-righteousness, blind inconsistency, shameful dissoluteness, lurking atheism, and a hungering and thirsting after unrighteous gain, are the prominent characteristics of the present followers of Confucius," Mrs. Shuck observed.[51] Indeed, what more proof was needed than the fact that the last surviving descendant of Confucius was a degraded opium smoker.[52] The Reverend Ellinwood declared angrily that "the apologies which are made for heathen systems" would soon disappear if the apologists could only witness the "orgies of idolatry," and the "ignorant and debased masses" to which such philosophies have given birth in China.[53]

There is little doubt that the reputation of Confucius suffered considerably during the nineteenth century and that the Protestant missionary played a crucial role in effecting this change. Medhurst acknowledged that the missionary's harsh criticism of the sage was an important source of friction between him and the Chinese, but one that he felt could not be avoided.[54] In 1863, the Reverend James Legge, a missionary to China and respected sinologue at Oxford, asserted in his widely acclaimed translation of the Chinese classics that Confucianism was best "adapted to a primitive, unsophisticated state of society." Legge, however, carefully disassociated himself from those missionaries who attributed all of the social evils in China to this philosophy: "I do not charge the contemptuous arrogance of the Chinese government and people upon Confucius. What I deplore is that he left no principles or record to check the development of such a spirit." Legge's conclusion rang with a devastating finality: "But I must now leave the sage. I hope that I have not done him injustice; but after long study of his character and opinion, I am unable to regard him as a great man." [55]

Later in the nineteenth century the reputation of Confucius appears to have recovered considerable lost ground. Very late in his life, Emerson reversed his opinion, praising Confucius as "the singular genius the Asiatics seem to have had for moral revelation," and some admirers were picked up among the American Humanists.[56] But nowhere is this shift more dramatically revealed than in the revised judgment of Legge in the second edition of his translations, published in 1893, which must be compared with the earlier one to fully appreciate how far opinion had traveled in thirty-two years: "But I must now leave the sage. I hope that I have not done him injustice; but the more I have studied his character and opinions, the more highly I have come to regard him. He was a very great man, and his influence has been on the whole a great benefit to China, while his teachings suggest important lessons to ourselves who profess to belong to the school of Christ." [57]

In addition to idolatry, licentiousness, and criticism of Confucius, the practice of infanticide and the barbaric treatment of women appeared consistently in the Protestant missionary accounts of China. While these latter two themes were certainly not new, they were neglected until these missionaries arrived on the scene, and the Reverend Medhurst's boast that they were the first to bring these dreadful practices to the full attention of the West seems amply justified.[58] Actually, many missionaries cited the English diplomat, Sir John Barrow, as their authority on infanticide in China, even making him an eyewitness to the practice, which he never claimed to be. "Some of the scenes he witnessed while at Pekin were almost incredible," Abeel wrote of Barrow. "Before the carts go around in the mornings to pick up the bodies of infants thrown in the streets, . . . dogs and swine are let loose upon them. The bodies of those found are carried to a common pit without the city walls, in which the living and the dead are thrown together." [59] The Reverend James Nevius reported, however, that "benevolent persons" in China had erected "baby houses" into which the infants could be discarded so that their last moments were not made frightful by hungry dogs.[60] Articles on infanticide in the missionary and religious publications often carried illustrations of windowless towers with small apertures into which "heathen mothers without natural affection" could stuff their unwanted children.[61] Protestant missionary estimates of the extent of this practice exceeded those made by diplomats, even Barrow, and any earlier reporter on the Chinese scene. Williams suggested that up to 40 percent of all female infants born in China were "murdered" by their parents, and Abeel calculated that it ran as high as 70 percent.[62] But there was an even more important qualitative difference between the missionary view of infanticide in China and that of diplomats or traders. Most Western travelers to China who reported on the subject explained it as a function of

poverty and therefore restricted to the lowest classes in China. The
missionaries, however, related it to paganism and hence reported
infanticide as a universal practice in the Celestal Empire.[63]

Williams observed that "the two best general criteria of civilization among any people are superior skill in destroying our fellow
men, and the degree of respect paid to women." [64] Very few missionaries criticized the Chinese for their lack of military powers.
On the contrary, Morrison thought that the absence of an "heroic
spirit" made the Chinese temperamentally better suited for Christianity than were Europeans.[65] But the missionaries were less than
philosophical about the Celestial treatment of women. If not murdered at birth, they were shabbily treated until sold to the highest
bidder as wives, concubines, or prostitutes. They were permitted
to live only in order to realize a profit from the smallest possible
investment, the missionary protested. Even as a legal wife, the Celestial female lived in "perpetual humiliation and wretchedness,"
according to most missionaries.[66]

Missionaries on home leave were welcome speakers before
women's rights organizations in the United States, some of which
were eager to exploit China as an example of the immorality and
social decay that must follow in the wake of any unjust treatment
of the female.[67] China had obviously been deprived of women's
refining influences, and the Society for Promoting Female Education in the East and the Female Agency among the Heathen were
formed to tackle the problem in cooperation with the missionaries.
But Mrs. Shuck warned that such groups must keep in mind that
"the sad condition of our sex in China can never be alleviated
until Christianity triumphs in this cruel land." [68]

Although the missionary was preoccupied with the social evils
and character deficiencies he perceived in China, he did not always
dwell on them in his reports back to the United States. To some
extent the substance of his report and the manner with which he
treated specific Chinese institutions depended on his mood at the
time of writing. He tended to fluctuate between states of unrealistic optimism over his prospects for converting the Chinese and bitter despair over his obvious lack of success.[69] Given his singleness
of purpose and apocalyptic belief that God would intervene on his
behalf in China, one would expect the missionary to be somewhat
short on patience and give vent to angry tirades against the Chinese and their social system. But he rarely remained bitter or
despondent, and as his confidence picked up the content of his reports changed accordingly.

During his more sanguine moments, the missionary would stress those aspects of Chinese life that would assure him of quick success. China's reputation for universal literacy and rational values, for example, pointed to a rapid conversion, the missionary reasoned optimistically. Elijah Bridgman ecstatically announced that "no where else on earth" were "so many human beings able to read the word of God." [70] Even more important, the Chinese were "inquisitive,—patient in research,—fond of literature," Abeel declaimed, full of confidence that such habits could only lead the Celestials to Christian truths once exposed to them.[71] They were more approachable for proselytizing than most peoples, Morrison reasoned; they had "no sullen sense of honor," and in contrast to Europeans, "a Chinaman would stand and reason with a man, when an Englishman would knock him down, or an Italian stab him." [72] Armed with these convictions, some missionaries took illegal trips up the coast from Canton fully confident that villagers would be able not only to read their religious tracts but would be willing, if not eager, to discuss the contents with them.[73]

As mounting frustrations shifted the missionary's mood to uncertainty and discouragement, he revised his estimates of Chinese literacy, intelligence, and rationality. Morrison became exasperated at the obstinacy of his servants who refused to discuss religious matters with him at all. "My country not the custom to talk of God's business," one curtly informed him.[74] These missionaries began to argue that far from clear thinking, the Chinese mind was so "filled with sin and darkness" that it was unable to function at all. In his famous text on China, Williams discussed at some length the "debasing effects of heathenism on the intellect," which permitted Celestial thought only on the level of "imitation" but not "invention"—hence the "slavish dependence" on "old customs" which so frustrated the missionary.[75] "The torpor of minds in heathen countries is inconceivable to one who has lived all his life in a Christian land," Williams wrote to his father in the aftermath of his first frustrating attempts to reach the Chinese with God's message.[76] "We have given the Chinese credit for more individual intelligence and courage than is usually granted to that ignorant and timid people," the editors of the *Chinese Repository* concluded in a moment of discouragement.[77]

If it were simply a matter of mental sluggishness, the missionary might have faced this with greater optimism and effort; but as he slid further into despair, he sensed a diabolical perversity in the Chinese cognitive processes. "Their minds appear to have been cast in a different mould; and their thoughts arranged in a manner peculiar to themselves," Medhurst complained.[78] To illustrate this perversity one missionary recounted how a Chinese burned a broadsheet upon which was printed in Chinese: "He that believeth in me shall never die; but he that believeth not in me shall die." Having survived this flagrant act of defiance, the Celestial announced to the missionary and his Chinese audience, "Truly this have fool pigeon." [79] Other missionaries reported that many of their potential converts seized upon Christ's crucifixion as proof that he was not a real god. One Chinese even suggested that Jesus deserved his ignoble death for having denied his natural father, Joseph! [80] Such was the twisted logic and perverted nature of Chinese thinking with which the missionaries had to contend in their efforts to save the Celestial Empire.

Since the missionary was generally fluent in one or more of the Chinese languages, he frequently used them to illustrate the peculiar and perverse Chinese mentality which continued to frustrate his best efforts. There was no generic term for religion in Cantonese, Medhurst asserted, and the concept of sin was absent.[81] Sin was equated with crime, the *Missionary Herald* reported with some astonishment, and while "murder, arson and adultery" were considered crimes, "lying, deceit, fornication, gambling, drunkenness, pride and opium smoking" were not. What can one think of a people who reserve their strongest condemnation for leaving one's country while his parents are still alive but condone fornication "so long as both parties agree"? the article demanded.[82] The Chinese language was so perverse, contended the Reverend Doolittle, that it was almost impossible to conduct "evangelical truths" through its medium. Indeed, Doolittle declared in exasperation, *"The invention of the Chinese language has been ascribed to the devil,* who endeavored by it to prevent the prevalence of Christianity in a country where he has so many zealous and able subjects." [83]

Many aspects of Chinese society were subjected to conflicting interpretations in the writings of missionaries. In one moment the religious indifference of the Chinese might be hailed as a gift of Providence. Thus there were "no absurd dogmas" or serious religious commitments to be rooted out as in other heathen countries, the *Methodist Quarterly Review* happily explained to its readers.[84] At other times the same characteristic was *prima facie* evidence that the Chinese were devoid of any feeling. Not only were Chinese minds "apathetic," but their hearts were so "untouched" and "barren" that "even the tale of the cross finds no response in their mercenary breasts." [85] In moments of utter dejection, the missionary could even argue that the insensitivity of the Chinese was almost subhuman: "Their inmost soul, their very conscience, seems to be seared dead—so insensible that they are as regards a future life, like beasts that perish." [86]

Discussions of Chinese despotism and xenophobia in missionary sources also followed similar vicissitudes in harmony with the cycle of hope and despair in the moods of the authors. Despotism was discounted in hopeful moments as either being exaggerated in the West or simply as being too inefficient to offer any serious obstacle to the missionary. Public opinion was more powerful than Westerners believed and could effectively countervail any governmental arrogance, some missionaries optimistically prognosticated.[87] The Reverend William Speer's buoyant optimism even carried him to the conclusion that China was in fact a democracy: "There are few nations of the world among whom the freedom of the people is more large, more squarely founded on their intelligence, or more carefully guarded against despotism than in China." [88]

But even in their most sanguine moods, no other missionaries went quite this far and were content simply to insist that direct appeals to the people would permit them to bypass China's ineffective despotism. But this optimistic line of reasoning also necessitated the denial that the Chinese people were as hostile to strangers as they were reputed to be in the West. Xenophobia was merely an official policy that did not reflect the true feelings of the people in China, the missionaries concluded in such moments. The Reverend Charles Gutzlaff in 1833 electrified the missionary world with his reports of an illegal trip to villages outside of the Canton region that successfully tested this optimistic thesis. He reported that everywhere he was warmly received by friendly people who eagerly accepted his missionary propaganda. Official attempts to impede his progress or in any way to harass him were frustrated by popular demonstrations in his support, Gutzlaff recounted.[89] His achievements were hailed by missionaries as proof of their most optimistic evaluations of political conditions in China. "The people are not misanthropic but would rejoice in more social intercourse," the *Missionary Herald* declared.[90] "The Chinese people cherish a fondness and hospitality to strangers," announced the Reverend Lewis Shuck.[91] Expressions of renewed confidence in the prognostications for a rapid conversion of the Chinese, once official Chinese restrictions were removed or bypassed, spread like fire through the missionary press in response to the Prussian missionary's reports.

The American missionary Edward Stevens and his English colleague William Medhurst followed in Gutzlaff's footsteps along the Chinese coast. Unlike their Prussian colleague, however, they wisely refused free passage from opium traders, who frequently made such illegal voyages, and at great expense hired their own vessel and crew. The confidence engendered by Gutzlaff, plus the belief in the righteousness of their cause, led Stevens and Medhurst to behave in an incredibly lawless manner. By their own testimony, they disrupted a local court and school, ignored the pleas and orders of Chinese officials, and even resorted to physically pushing Celestial officers aside on a number of occasions.[92]

In spite of their aggressiveness, however, Stevens and Medhurst did not claim the spectacular success promised by Gutzlaff's reports. Moreover, the continued failure to find friendly, receptive audiences, or a substantial number of converts anywhere in China, led to less optimistic appraisals of the efficiency of China's despotism and the friendly nature of her people toward strangers. To some missionaries and editors, the country was "groaning under an absolute despotism," and Christianity could not succeed until the twin yoke of the Manchus and Satan, which had literally enslaved the people, was removed.[93] Far from friendly, the people were "venal, tricky, extortionate and cruel," Maclay blurted out as he reviewed the excruciatingly slow progress of the missionary in China.[94] Williams warned that the "ostentatious kindness" of the Chinese was but a facade: "The politeness which they exhibit seldom has its motive in good will, and consequently when the varnish is off, the rudeness, brutality, and coarseness of the material is seen. . . ."[95] Even Morrison, who appeared to be personally fonder of the Chinese people than most missionaries, could be provoked into lashing out from the depths of despair to characterize the people as "specious, insincere, atheistic in spirit, selfish, cold blooded and inhumane."[96]

In their most jaundiced moods, the missionaries frequently resorted to an apocalyptic phraseology to paint the Chinese as "sitting in darkness and dwelling in the land of the shadow of death."[97] Indeed, "Kingdom of Darkness" was used to refer to China in missionary sources almost as much as were "Celestial Empire" or "Middle Kingdom," and one very popular missionary account of China bore the unlikely title *Darkness in the Flowery Land*.[98] Such terms were rarely clarified but remained vague expressions of despair for most missionaries. "Alas!—this is a dreary land to the spiritual eye, there is no cheering prospect—all is gloomy darkness," lamented Morrison.[99] To Williams, this gloom was "the most fearful immoralities and desolating horrors of paganism" which had resulted in "a full unchecked torrent of human depravity."[100] The "shadow of death" cast by such behavior, as well as the Celestial's stubborn refusal to accept salvation from Christ's messengers, was presumably God's anticipated revenge, although this was never specifically spelled out. Indeed, the missionary in discussing this darkness and death often lapsed into a barely intelligible vocabulary. Maclay, for example, raved that "the foul relentless malady" into which the Chinese were "rapidly sinking" was "indescribable, unutterable and inconceivable."[101] This despair and apocalyptic vision were by no means restricted to Protestant missionaries in China. Facing a similar recalcitrance in Hawaii, one American missionary wrote to his wife: "The people of Hilo are as hard as nether millstone. My heart aches for them. My bowels are troubled. The Lord help . . . or they all die."[102]

The nadir of the missionary's despondence was reached when he began to sense total futility in all his efforts and even faltered in his conviction that God wanted China converted to Christianity. "Without me ye can do nothing," the readers of the *Missionary Herald* were reminded.[103] "How far Satan may be allowed to assist in these delusions none can determine," Abeel confessed in utter dejection.[104] But this extreme loss of hope was rare, and ephemeral in any case. As the missionary wallowed in the trough of his despair, he generally concluded that God could not long tolerate such bleak social conditions in China and would have to respond to them dramatically and soon, a conclusion that started the missionary back on the cycle of hope.

Still more damaging to China's sagging reputation in nineteenth-century America was the intermittent debate among missionaries over whether any pagan nation could be classified accurately as civilized. Few missionaries echoed the pluralistic argument of the editors of the *Biblical Repertory* that China represented "a high degree of civilization," however "opposite to our own ideas of good taste."[105] But they were at the same time reluctant to follow the simple dictum of Rufus Anderson of the American Board who flatly refused to consider any heathen nation civilized.[106] For one thing, Anderson's pronouncement raised the awkward necessity of considering the classical civilizations in Greece and Rome as barbaric.[107] Also, there were obvious differences between China and primitive heathen societies. After all, China did have a government, as "bad" as it was, a system of writing, albeit "primitive," and some science, however "absurd," it was reasoned on the pages of the *Chinese Repository*.[108] Such characteristics, however marginal, clearly placed China "entirely above all other heathen nations," Maclay conceded.[109]

But very few missionaries were willing to consider China as fully civilized, and most settled for a semicivilized classification or agreed with Williams that it was a "defective civilization." [110] There were just too many features of Chinese life, in their eyes, that stemmed from "ignorance and barbarity," some of which "would place China on a level with the rudest tribes of mankind." [111] Underneath "a very polished civilization," warned one editor, the Chinese were "morally a most wretched people. Sin had spread its deadly venom throughout the whole body politic." [112] China's civilization had only "the element of stability but not of improvement," explained Williams, which prevented the Chinese from achieving the perfect civilization associated with Christianity.[113] While reaching a similar conclusion in 1833, the editors of the *Missionary Herald* were careful to stipulate that China was "capable of rising and vieing [sic] with the most enlightened nations." [114]

As the nineteenth century wore on, the Chinese seemed to lose even this distinction. Missionary publications expressed fewer reservations about labeling them "barbarous," and in 1870 the Reverend J. G. Wood apparently suffered no quandary about including the Chinese in his book, *The Uncivilized Races*. The elegantly costumed mandarin seemed strangely out of place in the frontispiece where he was depicted among a fur-clad Tartar and Eskimo, a tatooed Maori chief, and a half-dressed Australian bushman, African hunter, and American Indian who represented Wood's "uncivilized races." [115] The descriptions of Chinese culture commonly given in missionary publications often made explicit conclusions on the nature of Chinese civilization somewhat unnecessary.[116]

In 1864 the editor of the *London Times* taunted the missionaries by suggesting that they were putting the cart before the horse. Using the Taiping rebels for illustration, he contended that people must first be civilized before one could expect them to understand and accept Christianity without distorting it. Infuriated by this reasoning, Samual Morse turned his editorial page over to the missionary Samuel Wells Williams to expose its specious logic. In reply to the London editorial, Williams insisted that Christianity was not only a civilizing agent but without it there could be no civilization.[117] By 1883, however, Williams wrote to the American Board that, in view of a great increase in the number of conversions to Christianity in China, "the time was speedily passing when the people of the Flowery Land can fairly be classed among the uncivilized nations." [118]

A further influence on the American image of China was the Protestant missionary's stress upon China's huge population. Although hardly a new theme, the missionary press and Protestant clergy in general consciously campaigned to make Americans aware of the vast number of pagan souls at stake in the effort to convert the Celestial Empire to Christianity. Missionary appeals often sought to make this number less abstract by comparing it to other national populations or by devices such as asking the reader to imagine a single file of Chinese at six foot intervals girding the earth eighteen times. It would take forty-two years for such a file to march past a single point on earth—that is, forty-two years if the Celestials rested every Sabbath, Maclay explained, in a sublime piece of wishful thinking.[119] "The mind cannot grasp the real import of so vast a number," Culbertson declared. "400 millions! What does it mean? Count it. Night and day without rest, or food or sleep, you continue the weary task; yet eleven days have passed before you have counted the first million, and more than as many years before the end of the tedious task is reached." [120] Furthermore, this gigantic population was "increasing with frightening rapidity," Americans were warned.[121] The *Missionary Herald* exhorted ministers to employ graphs, blocks, posters, or any other means that would awaken their congregations to the significance of China's huge population. Its editors commended the work of one pastor in South Weymouth, Massachusetts, who maintained giant posters in his church demographically illustrating China's population and growth in relationship to that of other nations.[122]

Unquestionably the motivation behind such a campaign was the elicitation of greater support for the missionary cause in China. Yet the effort was bound to have important side effects, particularly in conjunction with the worst of the missionary castigations of Chinese irrationality, cruelty, lack of moral precepts, and sexual perversion. It was just this combination that played into the hands of the sinophobes in the United States and a national concern over China's ability to inundate the country with almost inhuman hordes which was expressed even by those who opposed exclusion as a solution to the problem.

Henry Danton is not alone among scholars in attributing the highly unfavorable image of the Chinese in the West to the Protestant missionary. Professors Chao-kwang Wu and S. Y. Teng made similar assessments, accusing the missionary of "race pride" and even racism.[123] Most recently Oxford's Raymond Dawson has again taken the Protestant missionary to task for having conceived of the Chinese "at best as a people whose greatest minds were necessarily inferior and whose masses were as lost children hungering for the gift of the Holy Spirit, and at worst as subject to what Wells Williams describes as 'a kind and degree of moral degradation of which an excessive statement can scarcely be made, or an adequate conception be found.' And it is to this view," Dawson imputes, "that the darker features of the modern popular image of the villainous Chinese depicted in cinema and comic may doubtless ultimately be ascribed." [124]

The evidence in support of such allegations is indeed impressive. Nothing Chinese escaped the critical pen of the missionary. Even China's esteemed examination system was reduced to trite penmanship exercises in the rote memorization of Confucian banalities.[125] Often the stinging indictments of Chinese behavior to be found in missionary sources could easily have been written by a Denis Kearney in the heyday of sandlot sinophobia in San Francisco or uttered in the halls of Congress during the exclusion disputes. For example, one passage in an American Board pamphlet declared, "Underneath a calm and courteous exterior, foreigners have found them cunning and corrupt, treacherous and vindictive. Gambling and drunkenness, though abundantly prevalent, are far outstripped by their licentiousness, which taints the language with its leprosy, often decorates the walls of their inns with the foulest of scenes by them called 'flowers' and lurks beneath a thin Chinese lacker as a deep dead rot in society." [126] Essentially this is the style and vocabulary of the demagogic sinophobe on the West Coast in the 1870s.

Ironically the Protestant missionary, who favored Chinese immigration to the United States as a further means of converting them to Christianity, had to defend the Celestials against almost identical charges, particularly those dealing with sexual promiscuity and perversion. Oscar Handlin writes that on the West Coast it was charged that "Orientals beguiled little girls to their laundries to commit crimes *too horrible to imagine.*" [127] But it would be a serious mistake to assume that such fears were confined to the Pacific slope, as Professor Handlin implies, or to attribute them to

Count Gobineau and other nineteenth-century racists, as he suggests. These sexual fears were expressed nationally and the responsibility for this particular misconception about Chinese behavior rests firmly on the shoulders of the Protestant missionary.

Undoubtedly the motivation behind these distortions and the missionary emphasis on the worst aspects of Chinese life was to exploit China as a didactic model. The lechery, dishonesty, xenophobia, cruelty, despotism, filth, and intellectual inferiority he perceived in China were all what Williams called "concomitants of heathenism." [128] Thus China served the missionary and minister as a useful illustration of the evils of paganism and the benefits of Christianity. The worst pictures of Chinese society also helped to enlist greater support for the missionary cause. Typically a plea for money and more missionaries in 1833 began, "Alas! How generally is the cry of the exposed and dying infant disregarded in China! Beneath a parade of manners reduced to the most regular form . . . is the nation groaning under oppression and violence, their courts filled with bribery and injustice; their markets with cozening and deceit, their houses with concubines and even worse abominations." [129] But such vignettes of Chinese society were bound to remain in the reader's mind and continue to affect his image of the Chinese long after they reaffirmed his smug conviction that a Christian civilization was the best of all possible worlds or elicited from him some coins to save Chinese babies from their horrible fate.

Nevertheless, it is still highly problematic to ascribe to the Protestant missionary alone the unflattering image of the Chinese that evolved in the West during the nineteenth century. An immediate difficulty is that the one important Catholic missionary account of China during this period, that of Abbé Huc, differs very little from those of his Protestant counterparts. True, Abbé Huc also indicted the Protestant missionary for displaying an ethnocentric contempt for the Chinese. "We must not wholly despise the Chinese," he pleaded, "there may be even much that is admirable and instructive in their ancient and curious institutions." But all the critical themes to be found in Protestant sources are in evidence in Huc's work. He dismissed Confucian philosophy as "true Spinozism," and dwelled on the cruelty, infanticide, and licentiousness he perceived in China, adding a few novel twists of his own. For example, Abbé Huc reported that parents literally butchered their sick children in order to protect the healthier siblings from an evil spirit. Female infants were not simply discarded, according to this French Lazarist, but they were beheaded by the father in order to prognosticate his chances for a male offspring from the manner in which the girl's blood flowed along the cutting edge of his cleaver. The abbé's descriptions of wanton lewdness and public sexual orgies are no more distinguishable from the ubiquitous ones in Protestant sources than is his final exhortation to the Chinese people: "Oh pagans! True children of the demon who delights in blood . . . when will your hearts be moved by the charity of Jesus Christ?" [130]

Those Protestant editors who reviewed Abbé Huc's report valued it as corroboration for their own negative impressions. "We should be glad if it were possible to lay hold upon one lofty principle in this demoralized people to wind up our brief summary of their habits, but . . . we can only hope that this gross darkness is an indication of the dawn of a brighter day," confessed the editor of the *Methodist Quarterly Review* in concluding his review of it.[131]

A more serious challenge to the interpretation that the Protestant missionary was totally responsible for vitiating China's reputation in the West, however, is the influence of the trader and diplomat-author in this process. One trader, W. W. Wood of Philadelphia, anticipated Danton's charge by a full century; but Wood's own book was almost a continuous diatribe against the Chinese and their institutions.[132] Ironically, the missionary Maclay credited the trader with this responsibility, apparently as oblivious as Wood of the important contribution his own book was making to the development of an unfavorable image of the Chinese in nineteenth-century America.[133] Williams laughed off as ridiculous the assertion in a popular geography textbook that it was "so obviously in the interest of the missionary to deprecate the mind and religious character of the Chinese." [134] Not long before, Williams reminded his readers, Sir John Barrow had accused the missionaries of "setting the Chinese in the fairest point of view." [135] But Barrow made this charge in 1803, four years before the first Protestant missionary arrived in China, and obviously had the Jesuit missionaries in mind, as Williams must have known. Only in 1905 did a Protestant missionary concede that his colleagues had played a substantial role in destroying China's esteem in the West.[136] Such introspective sensitivity was a rare quality among nineteenth-century missionaries.

If the missionary is to be assigned even a lion's share of the responsibility for creating a highly unfavorable image, it must be on the grounds of greater efficiency in the dissemination of his views as well as the totality and emotional quality of his criticism. The moral indignation expressed in missionary commentaries is not evident in those of the trader and is certainly less pronounced among the diplomats. The missionary's focus on paganism impugned all aspects of Chinese society and led to a more pronounced assault on the moral and intellectual characteristics of the people and their character development. All of this was amplified by the religious press and in Protestant pulpits, a highly specialized and personalized type of medium upon which modern communication theory places great value in terms of its effect on public opinion. This theory also hypothesizes an interrelationship between a climate of opinion and the substance of communication, so that messages not only affect opinion but the latter also influences the content of the message.[137] In other words a certain degree of inertia is involved in the creation of images and opinion. It is this interrelationship that helps to explain how the missionary, trader, and diplomat reenforced each other's view of the Chinese. The decisive advantages that the missionary possessed in the quality of his messages and the type of communication system he utilized may have been balanced by the head start enjoyed by both the trader and diplomat in whittling away at whatever esteem the Chinese still possessed in the West at the turn of the eighteenth century, decades before the Protestant missionary movement in China really got underway. Obviously the responsibility for China's deteriorating reputation in the United States must be diffused among all three categories of inside dopesters.

Before leaving the inside dopesters, an evaluation of the relative importance of the books on China produced by them is in order. Editorials on China as well as bibliographies, recommended reading lists, and textbooks on the subject continually cited particular authors as authorities on China more than they did others. For example, the works of Du Halde, Barrow, Staunton, and Williams had tremendous staying power throughout the nineteenth century as far as such citations are concerned. Rarely were these authors omitted from a reading list on China. On this basis it is possible to construct a hypothetical American bookshelf on China for the year 1855 in much the same manner that Lawrence Wroth constructed a general colonial bookshelf for the year 1755.[138]

Such a hypothetical collection would include the writings of few traders, whose books were not plentiful to begin with and whose appeal as authorities was not as great to editors as were the missionaries and diplomats. Probably the works of Wood and Dobell would be present along with one less popular book possibly by Delano, Fanning, Shaw, or Holbrook. The diplomat accounts of Barrow, Staunton, Ellis, and Davis would most certainly be on hand, alongside one or two of the lesser works by Van Braam, Timkowski, Roberts, Abel, or M'Leod. Protestant missionary works would dominate the shelf with those of Morrison, Milne, Medhurst, Lowrie, Gutzlaff, Abeel, Bridgman, Shuck, and Williams. But Catholic missionary reports would not be absent. Alongside the Jesuit "classics" by Le Comte and Du Halde would be added Abbé Huc's volumes just published in 1855.

But too much cannot be inferred safely from book lists or even frequent references to a particular author. A further indication of the influence of these reports on the American image of the Chinese would be their reflection in the contents of the mass media and school textbooks. At any rate, after 1840 the events that occurred in China were more important in further defining the American image of the Chinese.

PART TWO

*Events in China
and
the Chinese Image*

A Chinaman is cold, cunning and distrustful; always ready to take advantage of those he has to deal with; extremely covetous and deceitful; quarrelsome, vindictive, but timid and dastardly. A Chinaman in office is a strange compound of insolence and meanness. All ranks and conditions have a total disregard for truth.

"China," *Encyclopaedia Britannica*, 7th ed. vol. VI, (1842).

The character of the Chinese is by no means an agreeable one. The men are servile, deceitful and utterly regardless of the truth. From the emperor to the beggar through every rank of society, through every grade of office, there is a system of cheating, and hypocrisy, practiced without re-morse. . . . No faith whatever, can in general, be reposed in the Chinese.

Samuel Goodrich, *The Tales of Peter Parley About Asia for Children* (Phila., 1859), pp. 57–58.

5

The Opium War Popularizes the Unfavorable Image, 1839-1850

Beyond any question the first Anglo-Chinese war, 1839-1842, served as a catalyst in the crystallization of the American image of China on a popular level. This was due as much to cultural changes within the United States as it was to the sensational appeal of the war itself. The two decades between 1840 and 1860 represent a pivotal period in the evolution of American culture, during which the people shed much of their provincialism. As the cultural historian Carl Bode describes it, "the United States was a simple nation when the forties began and a complex one when the fifties ended. The people and the printed word came together." [1] One crucial factor in this change was the development of the nation's first real mass medium which played a vital role in bringing

83

the Opium War to the full attention of the American people. The penny press, that ancestor of the modern popular newspaper, was instituted in the 1830s and its struggle with the older, more "respectable" Wall Street press reached a climax in 1840. In a manner reminiscent of the Spanish-American War at the end of the century, the Anglo-Chinese conflict in 1840 furnished a convenient battleground in the larger struggle for domination between this new genre and the more established newspapers. The penny press thrived on war and scandal and used such aggressive tactics as boarding inbound ships from China off Sandy Hook, New Jersey, in order to scoop their older competitors who furiously protested that they alone were "authorized" to get the news on board. James Gordon Bennett obviously enjoyed the competition, crowing ecstatically over every "beat" scored in a rash of extras on the Opium War. Not only was the Celestial Empire being vanquished but that "lazy, rotten, corrupt, unprincipled, ignorant, barbarian, selfish, bankrupt, dying Wall Street press" was suffering a similar fate in the process.[2]

The descriptions of China in these newspapers, which had largely ignored that nation up to the Opium War, reflected a highly unfavorable conception of the Celestial Empire. The front page sketch in a Boston newspaper in 1840 is a good example of the contempt for China expressed in the penny press at the very outset of the conflict: "There is a pompous and pedantic land, which boasts supremacy in wisdom and in science from an epoch anterior to all human record save its own—China, the land of many letters, many lanterns, and few ideas. Peopled by the long eared, elliptic-eyed, flat-nosed, olive colored, Mongolian race, it offers a population singularly deficient in intellectual physiognomy; though to its absurd ugliness, the women of the higher classes occasionally offer striking exceptions." [3] This image of the Chinese was not plucked out of thin air but is related to the kind of treatment China had been receiving in American magazines and textbooks for at least a decade before the Opium War.

An examination of fifty-nine magazines and fifty-five newspapers published between 1785 and 1840 reveals certain trends in the treatment China received in this media before the Opium War. First of all, one can exaggerate the interest in China sustained by the first half century of America's trade with that nation, particularly in the newspapers. Captain John Green's first successful voyage to Canton in 1785 did send editors on a hasty search for information on the Celestial Empire. Parts of a popular geography text,

Du Halde's work, and Cook's journal were serialized in a number of newspapers. The emphasis was largely on Chinese trivia. "Much hath been said lately about *China,* a few anecdotes respecting it, we doubt not will be acceptable," a Providence editor prefaced his tidbits of information in 1785, such as the weight of the bell in Nanking, the number of troops stationed in Canton, and the streets of Peking which he described as "long and narrow but exceedingly clean." [4] The return of the *Pallas* to Baltimore three months in Green's wake failed to provoke any more sketches of Chinese life outside of the local press in that city, and little interest in Captain John O'Donnell's polyglot crew of Chinese, Malays, and Lascars. [5] Salem's first ship to Canton in 1787 stimulated no more curiosity about China, even in the local press. [6] Until the Opium War, newspapers pretty much restricted their comments to economic intelligence and inflated hopes for the wealth that the China trade would engender.

Serious commentary on the Chinese was left up to the magazines before 1840, and even here it was limited until a decade before the Anglo-Chinese war when articles on the Celestial Empire increased sharply. For the first three decades of the trade American editors demonstrated a marked preference for the older, more favorable conceptions of the Chinese. They quickly discovered the European controversy in progress over the merits of Chinese civilization. "The accounts given of this place by Pères Le Comte and Du Halde are in everyone's hand," a Philadelphia editor wrote in 1785. "These authors have been lately accused of great exaggeration by M. Sonnerat . . . who is as desirous of tearing everything Chinese down as the Jesuits were of exaggerating them," he explained. [7] Because of their relative ignorance of China, and their disadvantage in not having been there to see for themselves, these editors felt somewhat helpless in the face of the growing criticism of the Chinese on the part of traders returning or writing from Canton. The complaint of the editor of the *Boston Magazine* typifies this situation: "Much hath been said for and against the Chinese. Some travellers have extolled them in the highest terms whilst others have run to the contrary extreme; these last have of late been more numerous than the former. When we hear . . . a report [on China] loaded with reproach, founded on real or pretended facts, we have no means of contradicting; though unknown to us, it is natural for the sake of human nature, to wish that they may not be true." [8]

But this clearly articulated editorial preference for a more flattering image of the Chinese does not mean that the sharp criticism that was becoming more prevalent in European intellectual circles at the end of the eighteenth century was ignored by American editors. Adam Smith's caustic comments on the subject as well as those of Cornelius De Pauw, whose lengthy diatribe was published in an American edition in Bath, Maine, in 1792, were reproduced in American magazines.[9] Moreover, many of the exotic descriptions reproduced from the works of Jesuit missionaries were not always so flattering. Chinese soldiers were typically depicted as dressed in petticoats, armed with fans, and riding gelded horses "as timid as their riders." [10] But strong hostility was even less characteristic of federal era American public views of the Chinese than was Matthew Carey's unabashed adulation of the Celestials. Few of his colleagues in 1792 parroted his contention that "nothing is more remarkable, nor better calculated for good government than the means used in China." [11] Most American editors at this time assumed a position of cautious and reserved respect or ignored the subject of China altogether.

Port Folio magazine of Philadelphia was considerably ahead of its time when in 1811 its editors picked up Sir John Barrow's book on China and used it as the basis for a series of sinophobic articles over the next decade. Significantly, one of its editors was Dr. Charles Caldwell, professor of Natural History at the University of Pennsylvania and a key figure in the early evolution of modern racist theory, who used the magazine as a forum from which he could attack the accepted monogenesis explanation of the origins of mankind.[12] The disparaging descriptions of the Chinese may well have served as further illustration of the polygenesis thesis that such vastly different peoples as Mongolians, Negroes, and Europeans could not belong to the same species. However, it was artificial to separate the Tartars and Chinese, it was reasoned on the pages of *Port Folio,* since the two peoples not only resembled each other in appearance, but also in their mental "idiocy." [13]

Port Folio remained virtually a minority of one among American periodicals until the works that emerged from Lord Amherst's embassy provoked a few more magazines into joining the overtly sinophobic camp.[14] The conclusion of one of these editors in 1818 reflects the disillusionment being created by the works of professional diplomats, American traders, and the two English missionaries, Morrison and Milne: "The truth is, that we are now tolerably well disabused of those notions respecting Chinese wisdom and perfection which the interested representations of the Jesuits had succeeded in creating. . . . [Of late] every book on China repeats the same report of the semibarbarous state of a country which was once regarded as the abode of virtue and refinement." This same editor, who once admired the Chinese, now not only denied them a civilized status, but went so far as to rank China well below other Asian nations. He was at a loss to account for the almost inhuman behavior in China and wondered if the answer was to be found in the climate, peculiar social institutions, and adherence to custom or "in the character and genius of the Chinese themselves?"[15] Caldwell's journal never experienced any trouble in answering such a query: "The Chinese never can become a great and independent people because they do not possess that energy of soul and physical conformation, which are necessary to produce such a result. They are constitutionally a feeble race of men. . . ."[16] But such a purely racist explanation had to wait several more decades for any degree of popular endorsement. Until then, interpretations of Chinese behavior generally relied on religious or political determinants rather than genetic ones.

Actually the diplomatic accounts of China produced by both the Macartney and Amherst missions did not receive any widespread acknowledgment in American magazines until after 1825. One editor declared in 1828 that "the names of Macartney, Barrow and Sir George Staunton are now familiar to every reader." From this he concluded erroneously that the Macartney mission in 1793 was immensely popular in the United States.[17] In fact that mission and the books resulting from it were largely ignored and only discovered three decades later when American magazines became more interested in China.

By 1830 many features of Chinese life, such as the exotic ingredients in the cuisine and pharmacology, which had earlier elicited wonder or amusement, began to provoke disgust and suspicion in American magazines. Cats, dogs, and rats displaced such culinary delicacies as lizard eggs, peacock combs, and bird's-nest soup in descriptions of the Chinese cuisine. As early as 1818 one editor imputed sinister qualities to "the filthy feeding of the beastly inhabitants of China . . . in preference to wholesome meat."[18] But such attitudes were expressed more commonly after 1830. One Albany, New York, editor reported with horror that the Chinese murdered young girls in order "to drink certain fluids from their bodies" for medicinal purposes. It was believed that "grains of rice steeped in a freshly cut gall bladder" was a powerful antidote for many diseases, he disclosed.[19] Such grotesque beliefs gained in currency as the century advanced. They were enhanced by the fascination that many magazines displayed after 1830 for Chinese tortures and public executions which were described in grisly detail. Even Hezekiah Niles, who heretofore was concerned mainly with economic intelligence on the China trade, ran descriptions of such Celestial activity and reported that public executions were so numerous that the mandarins refused to attend "unless five criminals and upwards are put to death." [20] The lurid description of one execution reminded the editor of the *New York Mirror* of Robert Morrison's warning: "People in this part of the globe know very little about their fellow beings in the east." [21]

Reports on the cruel treatment of women had already received wide circulation in ladies' magazines before 1830. It was charged that "a mere animalism" had enslaved the Chinese female "for the indulgence of a groveling sensuality." [22] The influence of the Protestant missionary was reflected by the wider circulation of this theme during the decade preceding the Opium War. "We burn with indignation" that the women of China "are considered by the laws of that country as the born and appointed slaves of men," protested the editors of *Atkinson's Casket* in 1835. This editorial carried the usual maudlin appeal to American sentiments on the female: "The fairest and weakest of the human race: mothers, sisters, daughters, names which thrill to the sensorium of Europeans . . . is in the case of Chinese females a sorrowful task; pity in its extreme feeling is awakened. . . . In childhood slighted—in maidenhood sold—in mature womenhood shackled. . . ." [23]

By 1835 the criticism had reached enough of a crescendo to evoke a protest from the editor of the *New England Magazine* that the pendulum of opinion had swung too far in a hostile direction:

The Chinese are neither so good nor so bad as they have been represented. The early travellers and missionaries . . . were prone to over value it. . . . Two opposite parties in France vied in extolling the Chinese—the Jesuits to show the importance of a country they were converting—and the philosophers, that they might prefer the doctrines of Confucius to Revelation. Subsequent travellers finding much of this praise undeserved, were, perhaps disposed to deny credit to the Chinese for their actual virtues and described them, in general terms, as dishonest, inhospitable, cowardly, false, ungrateful.[24]

Nowhere is this shift in opinion about China more dramatically revealed than on the pages of the *North American Review*. From its inception in 1815 until 1835 this prestigious publication was China's champion in America, and many of its articles approached the adulation that is usually associated with the seventeenth-century Jesuit missionaries. The Middle Kingdom was, in the eyes of the editors, "a second civilized world, much more ancient and populous, in some respects happier and wiser . . . than the one with which we are acquainted." They recommended that the Chinese language be put on a par with Greek and Latin in American schools "as one of the branches of liberal knowledge." [25] The wave of critical accounts of China was simply ignored by these editors until 1828, when they conceded to review Timkowski's report. In dismissing it as "calumnious," they acknowledged the works of Barrow and Ellis for the first time, but only to cite examples of prejudiced slander against the Chinese that surpassed even the subject of the review.[26]

By 1828, however, the tone of the *Review*'s articles on China began to take on a faintly defensive quality. The translation of a Chinese novel into French was hailed as a refutation of the growing criticism of the Celestial Empire: "It gives us a much more favorable idea of the Chinese government, than would naturally be derived from the accounts of the persons attached to the recent British embassies of Lords Macartney and Amherst." The reader was reminded how hypercritical English travelers and self-appointed philosophers had been in the United States. There was more than one way to "reconcile the liberty of the people with a tranquil, wise and vigorous administration of their common concerns," the editor-reviewer expounded. China's examination system really accomplished the same thing as popular elections did in the United States, he asserted. In fact the editor confessed that he was unable to choose between these two systems. In his opinion China's means of selecting leaders more closely approached Plato's ideal and it had stood the test of millennia, a test which a system that had just elevated the Jacksonians to power might not survive, the reviewer hinted. At any rate the Chinese novel demonstrated that "the constitution of the Chinese empire, instead of being, as is commonly supposed, an absolute and unmitigated despotism, is evidently one of the most popular forms of government that ever existed. . . ."

In this same review, any social weaknesses, measured by Western standards, that appeared in this novel were glossed over or treated humorously. Was polygamy, or the treatment of the Celestial female in general, so evil when it produced the familial "warmth and tenderness" described in this novel? Of course, polygamy could be "injurious to polite literature" since no suspense could be built up over the necessity of a hero choosing between two eligible heroines, he suggested lightly. The reviewer conceded that a backwardness in science existed, but this was a function both of the empire's great antiquity and the emphasis placed upon "civil polity" as "the great science." [27]

Other editors seized upon this same novel as important evidence of what life in China was really like. "The Chinese novel may be the best source of information on China, and her laws, the works connected with the Western embassies not excepted," the editor of the *Southern Review* asserted in order to undermine the growing criticism of the Celestial Empire in American magazines. Contrary to popular beliefs, "everything in the novel indicates a polished state of society, enjoying the comforts and elegancies attendant on the highest civilization." [28]

Interestingly enough, Robert Dale Owen ran long excerpts from this novel in his *Free Inquirer* for quite different reasons. He saw in the novel a useful didactic model through which one could more easily recognize the foibles in his own society. "Not perhaps, that the prejudices are stronger, the caprices greater, or the follies more glaring in China than in the Western Hemisphere," he explained, "but they are Chinese prejudices and caprices and follies; of a form and complexion and dress so different to our own, that we hold up our hands in wonder at the taste that tolerates and the blindness that approves them." [29]

By 1834 the respect and adulation for China associated with the *North American Review* began to evaporate. A review of Vico in that publication used China to illustrate the philosopher's cyclical theory of civilization, concluding that the Middle Kingdom was destined "at no very distant day to share the fate of Rome, Memphis and Babylon." In criticizing British demands for extraterritoriality, the editor conceded that Chinese laws were indeed inflexible and primitively vindictive but he insisted that foreigners still had to obey them or stay at home, a line of reasoning followed by several American publications which once euologized China's "perfect" legal system.[30] In sharp contrast to its earlier praise for the "mutual respect and harmony" between the sexes that was depicted in the Chinese novel, the *North American Review* took China to task in 1836 for her shabby treatment of women. Still more shocking was the contemptuous dismissal of Chinese literature by this publication that eight years earlier had hailed a

Chinese poem as "Pindaresque" and expressed the hope that the translation of literary efforts would be accelerated by Western scholars. In 1836, the editor saw in Celestial literary efforts "proof . . . of the amazing weakness of the Chinese intellect. The tone of thought . . . never rises above a contemptible mediocrity."[31]

The *coup de grace* to any lingering respect on the part of the editors of the *North American Review* was supplied by the reports of Roberts and Ruschenberger. In a joint review, the editors excoriated Chinese behavior and China's "curtain of overwrought ceremony" which they explained as "a true *cordon sanitaire* against a real trial of strength between a more manly energy, and the scanty resources of a worn-out barbaric despotism." These editors who once viewed the examination system as a means of producing philosopher kings now found it worthless. "Hence it seems, after all, that a professor of penmanship would stand the highest chance of being secretary of state," they observed. "Alas! how few of our great men would stand the smallest chance of political elevation in China." A decade earlier the last comment could only have been directed at the quality of American political leadership, but in 1838 the deterioration of China's reputation had gone so far that the plaint had to be literal and damning. The editors commended Jackson for wisely instructing Roberts not even to attempt to negotiate with the Chinese during his mission to Asia. They recommended that Americans simply flout China's laws by trading in other ports if they wished, reminding them that the missionary Gutzlaff had cowed a Chinese fleet with no weapons at all—this from the same editors who were so critical of Britain's demands for extraterritoriality only a few years earlier. In conclusion, they pontificated,

For ourselves, we think it is time we should cease to denominate the Chinese the glory of the Asiatic race, merely because they boast to have produced a sort of barbarian Plato some hundreds of years before the Christian era, shave their heads to ape the baldness of wisdom, print by means of embossed blocks of wood, in no better artistical style than that of the ancient Peruvians, and have a fashion of instructing their youth in crude, unnatural monstrosities, and in poems which, to hear, would have made Hafiz and Sadi break their lyres, in a fit of epilepsy.[32]

Blow after blow continued to fall on China's sagging reputation in America. Peter Stephen Du Ponceau, a naturalized American and amateur philologist and ethnologist of international reputation, pronounced the Chinese language to be more primitive than those of the most savage tribes of American Indians, which seemed to lend further scientific support to the unfavorable trend of opinion.[33] Several editors consciously and regretfully acknowledged the rapid passing of the older image of China based on "the idealess abstractions on porcelain and tea-chests." [34] Only a few after 1835 still clung tenaciously to the friendly, idealized view of China. The *Southern Literary Messenger* of Richmond, Virginia, became the new journalistic champion of China and continued to sing her praises even after the Opium War.[35] Nathan Dunn's Chinese exhibit in Philadelphia in 1839 reflected the older image of the Middle Kingdom, and one editor expressed the hope that it might counteract the damaging commentaries of more recent travelers to that nation.[36] By 1839, however, inertia was clearly on the side of China's critics in America.

Few of these editors could have been very surprised at the outcome of the Opium War. Too much had been said about China's military backwardness. The Amherst mission and the action of Captain Maxwell in Canton provoked one editor in 1818 to declare that the country "slumbers, like a drowsy and emasculate Mammoth . . . til invasion, from the East or West shall enter her realms, and with fire and sword, purge away the gross and stagnant humors that clog her distempered frame." [37] An article in *Port Folio* even declared that it "would be an act of real humanity if the powers of Europe were to combine against this . . . ferocious despotism." In a fashion less humanitarian than adventurist, however, the author went on to describe the Chinese soldiers as "food for cannon; and I might add, amusement for the bayonet." [38] But once again *Port Folio* was ahead of its time and such sentiment was not widely expressed until after the Opium War. The more general reaction among American editors was a recognition that China was coming apart at the seams and offered easy prey to a European nation. "We cannot deny the evidence of our senses," Samuel Morse wrote. "And oh, should the bands of government be once broken asunder, and this immense mass of population—an ocean of human beings—be thrown into confusion, the scene would be awful." [39]

The depiction of the Chinese in American textbooks up to 1840 parallels the treatment they received in American magazines. Geography was one of the first disciplines to develop textbooks in the United States and the only one to have a special concern with China. A sample of forty-nine such texts reveals a highly unflattering picture of the Chinese by 1820, one that dominated this genre over the next two decades, if the sample is at all representative. Of the thirty-six geographers who wrote these texts, twenty-one were severely critical of the Chinese, while eight admired them and seven were ambivalent or defied classification. Significantly, five of the eight authors who treated the Chinese favorably published before 1820, whereas seventeen of the twenty-three critics did so after that date.

Professor John Nietz attributed the unfavorable conception in geography texts to a single English author, William Guthrie, who had, in his opinion, imposed upon "all Asiatics a more or less unfavorable characterization" as "a legacy to generations of geographers." [40] There is no question that Guthrie's geography was popular in America. Much of it was serialized in the *United States Chronicle* of Providence, Rhode Island, in 1786, and one historian tells us that few traders left for China in the first two decades of the trade without their copies of "Guthrie's Grammar." [41] Jedidiah Morse, America's first geographer, acknowledged the importance and popularity of Guthrie's book, and paid it an even higher tribute by plagiarizing portions of it. Indeed, the same description of the Chinese as "the most dishonest, low, thieving set in the world, employing their natural quickness to improve the arts of cheating" was cited by Nietz to illustrate Guthrie's contempt for the Chinese and by Professor Ruth Miller Elson as evidence of a similar disparagement in the works of Morse.[42]

But both Guthrie and Morse balanced this slur with a good deal of praise for China's great antiquity and orderly social system. Morse appears to have personally revised his estimate in 1796 when he delivered a blistering attack from a pulpit in Charleston on the "depraved people" of China and their tyrannical government.[43] Yet the older, more balanced evaluation of Chinese society to be found in Morse's first geography text in 1784 continued to reappear in his subsequent works until 1812.[44] Apparently these early geographers did very little rewriting but rather put new texts together with scissors and paste, transferring whole sections either from earlier works of their own or from those of other geographers. In any case, the sections on China in the works of Guthrie and Morse were closer to the more favorable treatment of the Chinese in geographies published before 1820 than they were to the caustically critical descriptions that prevailed in such textbooks after that date.

The work of the world-famous Danish geographer, Conrad

Malte-Brun, published in Boston in 1828 and extremely popular
in the United States, was more typical of the kind of treatment
afforded the Chinese after 1820. He excoriated their social institutions before dismissing the Chinese as "a set of subjugated and dis-
ciplined barbarians." [45] But Samuel Goodrich, "the McGuffey of
the East Coast," was probably more instrumental than any other
geographer in creating a popular disdain for the Chinese in the
United States. Goodrich wrote scores of geographies, histories, and
gazetteers for adults and children. Some of these appearing under
the *nom de plume* Peter Parley were written in the first person
and present tense as though the author were reporting directly
from the land about which he was writing. Such a highly personalized form of communication, together with the number and popularity of his works, makes Goodrich an important figure in the
evolution of the unfavorable image of the Chinese in the eastern
United States. His conclusion about China in 1833 remained basically unaltered throughout his writing career: "Few nations, it is
now agreed, have so little honor, or feeling, or so much duplicity
and mendacity. Their affected gravity is as far from wisdom, as
their ceremonies are from politeness." This condition Goodrich
attributed to both natural and institutional causes, which hinted
at a racist explanation of Chinese behavior that was more common
later in the century.[46]

Not all of the works in the sample were hypercritical of the
Chinese after 1820. A popular atlas by T. G. Bradford in 1835 presented a flattering description of China.[47] The work of a Scot,
Hugh Murray, was inclined favorably enough toward China for
Celestial officials to select it for translation into Chinese.[48] But
such works were exceptional in the decade before the Opium War.
The unflattering description to be found in geography textbooks
published between 1785 and 1840 elicited the wonder of the author of a doctoral study of these books, that in spite of America's
economic interest in China "few pains were taken to better relations by developing better attitudes in American schoolrooms." [49]

In the absence of more precise means of measurement, it would
seem safe to conclude that as far as opinion makers are concerned
the favorable image of China in the American mind before 1840
conjectured by some historians did not exist. On the contrary, it
seems more probable that these opinion makers entertained a
highly unfavorable conception. One need not be surprised that
the popular lecturer Edward Everett should have included the
Chinese among the two-thirds of mankind who were "pagan savages, or the slaves of the most odious and oppressive despotisms" in

an oration at Yale University in 1833.[50] Such a conclusion would naturally follow the kind of treatment the Chinese were receiving in American magazines and geography textbooks.

If the hypothesis suggested by this evidence has any validity, there must have been some reflection of a limited American sympathy for the British attack on Canton in 1840. Professor Thomas A. Bailey flatly rejects such a possibility. The Opium War was fought in "an era of British-hating," he reminded his readers. The Treaty of Nanking ending the war and the Ashburton Treaty settling the Maine boundary dispute were signed in the same year.[51] That Americans almost unanimously supported their esteemed Chinese friends against another blatantly imperialistic venture of a mutual enemy was the conclusion left as a legacy to generations of American historians by the famous diplomat-historian John W. Foster in 1904.[52]

A lecture on the Opium War by no less a figure than John Quincy Adams raises questions about such an assumption, or at least makes one pause before accepting the logic of Foster's assertion. In support of England, Adams argued that "law and right" were not "convertible terms." Citing Vattell and anticipating the classical rationale of the Victorian era, this distinguished elder statesman insisted that the cultivation of commerce was "among the natural rights and duties of men." This natural right was "emphatically enjoined by the Christian precept to love your neighbor as yourself," he explained, since "there is no other way by which men can so much contribute to the comfort and well-being of one another as by commerce." But "the fundamental principle of the Chinese empire is anti-commercial," Adams pointed out. Unlike the more altruistic Christian nations, the basic motivation behind the "churlish and unsocial" Chinese behavior and "the foundation of their system of morals is selfish enjoyment," he declaimed. Far from condemning England's attack on China, Adams applauded her for rectifying "this enormous outrage upon the rights of nature" which had been "too long connived at and truckled to by the mightiest Christian nations of the civilized world." Indeed, Adams argued, that "after taking the lead in the abolition of slavery" and the "degrading tribute to Barbary African Mohammedans," England was simply extending "her liberating arm to the farthest bound of Asia." Britain had "the righteous cause" in the war, which had been brought about not by opium, but by "the kotow!—the arrogant and insupportable pretentions of China," he concluded.[53]

Historians have either ignored this lecture of Adams, or treated it as a singular and almost inexplicable aberration in the American view of the war. The refusal of the *North American Review* to print his lecture seems to confirm the belief that the sinophobia expressed in it flew in the face of an overwhelming American sympathy for the Chinese.[54] Adams himself recorded a strong reaction to the speech: "The excitement of public opinion and feeling by the delivery of this lecture far exceeds any expectation that I had formed." [55] The exact meaning of this remark is somewhat Delphic, but it has been commonly assumed that his sinophobia was offensive to America's sentimental ties to China. The simpler explanation that the "strong current of popular opinion" to which Adams referred was anglophobia rather than sinophilia has not been suggested. Yet in view of the caustically critical comments on China in the *North American Review* before the war, it would seem safer to conclude that the editors objected not to Adams' contempt for the Chinese, but to his justification of England's imperialistic adventure in China.

Adams was not the only American who was able to compartmentalize his traditional mistrust of England so that he could attack her actions along the Canadian border or on the high seas and still view her invasion of China as a defense of basic human rights. The anglophobic *New York Herald* excoriated England in 1841 for "aggressions and aggrandizements," citing Canadian border incidents, claims to the Northwest Territory, the seizure of an American merchantman off Africa, and the burning of the *Caroline* four years earlier.[56] The omission of the Opium War from this list was no oversight as only two months earlier James Gordon Bennett had hailed Britain's attack on China, comparing it to the defeat of the Mexicans and establishment of the Texas republic. "It is another movement of the Anglo-Saxon spirit in the remotest east, against the barriers of semi-barbarians and a half-civilized race, who have been stationary for twenty centuries or more," Bennett opined.[57] William Cullen Bryant's *Evening Post* was also able to declare that "for once England's motto, *Dieu et mon droit*," could be "most justly made the cry of her sons on the shores of the Celestial empire." [58] Adams' fellow Bay Stater and idol of the lecture circuit, Edward Everett, also strongly supported the English in the Opium War.[59]

This is not to imply that a majority of Americans supported England in the Opium War. Clearly this was not the case. But a small and important minority did champion England's cause in China, and it was probably influenced by American traders and missionaries in making such a decision. Professor Dennett acknowledged that Adams was "intimately acquainted" with merchants in the China trade, and Professor Bemis noted that the ex-president was an avid reader of travelers to the Celestial Empire, presumably traders, missionaries, and diplomats.[60] The documents that Adams had amassed in support of his position included evaluations of the Chinese by these groups as well as reports of the famous Terranova trial in 1821 which occurred while Adams was secretary of state.[61] Yet these historians never considered any possible influence on Adams from merchants or missionaries. On the contrary, Dennett stated flatly that Americans in China, as well as "religious and philanthropic circles" in the United States, strongly disapproved of the war being waged by England, an assertion that he supported with a single article from *Hunt's Merchants' Magazine*. Nor did Dennett find it strange that the American medical missionary Peter Parker should have recommended that Adams be appointed commissioner to China after his "infamous" lecture on the Opium War. Parker himself was "actively engaged in arousing and educating public opinion on the Chinese question," Dennett wrote, leaving the reader to infer that Parker was sympathetic to the Celestials.[62] In fact, Parker's position on the war was almost identical to that of Adams.[63]

John W. Foster also quoted two American missionaries to China who favored England's cause in order to demonstrate that Adams was not totally isolated in his view of the war. But Foster made it clear that these two missionaries were as much mavericks among the Americans in Canton as Adams was at home.[64] Again, no one has systematically tested the assumption that the Americans in China opposed English actions there, an assumption that rests more on logic than any real evidence. Yet if the conclusions drawn in the earlier chapters of this study are at all viable, Americans in China must have supported their English friends against the Chinese, of whom they were contemptuous.

The recorded sentiments of traders in Canton indicate that the overwhelming majority of this group did support the English in the Opium War. In view of the close cooperation between the two English-speaking groups in Canton, this is hardly surprising. When the English merchants quit the city after Commissioner Lin seized their supply of opium, Americans continued to fill the orders for Chinese goods of their Anglo-Saxon cousins who had retreated to Macao.[65] Back in Providence, the trader and former consul to China, E. C. Carrington, received letters from six traders

in China during the hostilities, five of whom warmly supported
English actions there. One of these, Isaac Bull, was no anglophile
and suffered some mental anguish in reaching this position. "I
want protection for my property against Englishmen, not Chinese" he indignantly complained in 1839.[66] Within a few months,
however, he began to conceive of the struggle as one between the
Chinese and all "foreigners" in Canton, expressing the hope that
it would be brought to a head and settled permanently. "Affairs
between the Chinese and foreigners have been going on gradually
toward the desired end, viz. a final rupture between China and
England," he reported to Carrington.[67] A few weeks later he was
delighted that the Chinese ordered the English out of Canton, as
England would be left with no alternative but to fight.[68] Bull
even favored the English blockade, reasoning that if it were raised
before a final settlement, no concessions would be made by China.
"The English may talk reason with the Chinese until the day of
judgment, the latter will not give them what they want without
force," he wrote.[69] This was an almost unanimous belief among
the American community in Canton and one that several American newspapers took up during the war. A trader or missionary
was no doubt behind the statement in the *Providence Journal:*
"From the Chinese government we must expect nothing but false-
hood, deception, breaking of promises and treaties, treachery in all
its most revolting forms, flattery, cringing, suppleness, . . . pride,
haughtiness, contempt and unrelenting cruelty if successful.
. . ." [70] Meanwhile, it was an old China trader, J. M. Forbes, who
was instrumental in convincing Daniel Webster that the Chinese
only understood and respected force.[71]

It was initially difficult for Augustine Heard, Jr., to support
British demands in China in spite of his close and friendly relations with English traders. His diary described the slow evolution
of his endorsement; at first condemning "despicable" actions on
the part of Chinese officials, Heard finally expressed regret after
the war that England had not completed the job.[72] For William
Henry Low there never was such a problem, and he not only supported the English from the beginning of the difficulties but actively served Captain Elliot as a courier once the fighting broke
out.[73]

A number of traders commented on the virtual unanimity of
American sympathy in Canton for the British at the outbreak of
hostilities. Perhaps this was to be expected from such traders as
Whitman, Ritchie, Augustine Heard, and R. B. Forbes who were

sympathetic to British actions in China.[74] But it is more interesting to discover that two traders whose hostility to the British put
them in a position to challenge any such consensus readily acknowledged that their own views were not in tune with the majority of their compatriots. Thus Captain Martin, who was satisfied
that "the English are now suffering the judgment of their evil
deeds," chastised his compatriots in Canton for supporting them.
He was "sorry" that they too had been "transgressing China's
laws" and complained to Carrington that he had "no idea of becoming an outlaw" when he left Providence.[75] William Hunter
who characterized the Opium War as "one of the most unjust ever
waged by one nation against another" also conceded that this view
of the war made him practically a minority of one in the foreign
community in Canton.[76] Actually Hunter published his account
forty years after the event and seems to have conveniently forgot-
ten the anger with which he described Lin's "act of piracy" in
1839, and his own expressed hope that "the Chinese gov't will
have to pay for all this . . . violent imprisonment of all foreigners in Canton . . . till opium, *not their own,* is given up to this
Scoundrel of a Commissioner. . . . He has caught us in a trap,
but please God, he may be well thrashed for it yet." [77]

Americans also had lost their share of the British held opium
when Commissioner Lin seized it. This illegal trade had already
badly strained the relationship between Chinese officials and
Western merchants, which was never too cordial to begin with.
The missionary Samuel Wells Williams testified that the years following Lord Napier's expulsion in 1834 were "gloomy" ones, during which foreigners were confined to factories, native servants
were ordered to leave the compound, and restrictions on missionaries were increased.[78] An official Chinese attempt to strangle a
Chinese opium dealer in front of the foreign factories was beaten
off by English and American merchants, only to provoke a coun-
terinvasion by hundreds of Chinese ruffians. Such incidents embit-
tered most members of the foreign community.[79] Hunter testified
to the rapid deterioration of respect for Chinese officials and
people in general during the years preceding the first Anglo-
Chinese war, a trend that he thoroughly deplored.[80]

In 1840, the successful execution of a Chinese opium dealer
under the American flag caused the consul, Peter Snow, to haul
down his colors in protest against this "direct and positive insult"
to the United States. In his report to Secretary of State Forsyth,
Snow made it clear that he sympathized with the English and

found Commissioner Lin's demands totally uncivilized. "That the blood of the innocent shall flow for the crime of the guilty is too monstrous for a civilized government to submit to . . . ," Snow complained, with reference to Lin's demand that all foreign traders put up bonds which would be forfeited if they dealt in opium. The somewhat innocent tone of Snow's report did not jibe with his own claim to Lin that 1,540 chests of opium seized from the British belonged to Americans.[81] Indeed, Professor Chang estimates that "the relative significance of the American share in the trade" was "considerable," and after the hostilities much of the British opium traffic was "continued with American help and protection." [82]

Consul Snow concluded his report with an acknowledgment of his "obligations" to Captain Elliot for providing Americans with "protection," and expressed the hope that "this friendly and honorable conduct" of the British would "be duly appreciated by our government at home." [83] If this was not quite a plea for official support of the English cause, R. B. Forbes and other American traders in Canton supplied the lack. They petitioned Congress to denounce the "robbery" of British merchants by Lin's "high handed measures," and justified the English blockade and military action to "reduce the Chinese government to a willingness to listen to all the just and reasonable demands of the foreign powers." In conclusion they urged that the United States government "take immediate measures; and if deemed advisable act in concert with the governments of Great Britain, France and Holland, or either of them, in their endeavors to establish commercial relations . . . upon a safe and honorable footing. . . ." [84]

While Abbot Lawrence was presenting this petition to Congress in January 1840, a group of Boston and Salem merchants countered with a second petition which urged Congress not to take any rash actions in China. They agreed that a naval force in Chinese waters was necessary, but they cautioned that it should remain strictly neutral. A significant difference between these two groups of petitioners was in age: the second group of signers represented the older "China hands." [85] But the second petition merely expressed the need for caution and not any sympathy for the Chinese.

The support by American missionaries for the English in their conflict with China was no less overwhelming than that of American traders in Canton. Williams explained to the readers of the *Missionary Herald* that China needed "a hard knock to rouse her from her fancied goodness and security." [86] Sam Brown, the missionary-teacher, was anxious lest Britain refrain, as it had done in 1834 following Lord Napier's expulsion: "How long will England continue to wear the lion as her crest, and yet play the part of the hare?" [87] The Reverend Boone of the Episcopal Board hailed the blockade as a guarantee that the English were going to fight this time: "There is but one single barrier to the establishment of hundreds of missions among these literally perishing heathen idolators, and that barrier is of a political nature, which might be removed in a day. . . ." Boone predicted that the English would "throw open to our residence before the current year is past, cities whose inhabitants . . . outnumber all the inhabitants of our Atlantic cities put together." [88] Mrs. Shuck confessed: "How these difficulties do rejoice my heart; because I think the English government may be enraged, and God, in His power, may break down the barriers which prevent the gospel of Christ from entering China." [89] Bridgman and the editors of the *Missionary Herald* joined a score of American missionaries in calling the Anglo-Chinese rupture "the great design of Providence to open China to Christianity." [90]

Unlike the traders, however, the missionaries were more concerned about the role played by opium smuggling in bringing about the war. As a group they strongly condemned this illicit trade and found it necessary to wrestle occasionally with their consciences and work out elaborate rationalizations to justify the war. In publishing the text of Adams' lecture, the editors of the *Chinese Repository* expressed gratitude for the "lucid manner" in which Adams demonstrated that "the Chinese government has not the right to shut themselves out from the rest of mankind" and that the war largely sprung from "Chinese assumption, conceit and ignorance." Yet they could not accept easily the argument of Adams that opium was no more a cause of the war than the throwing of tea in Boston Harbor was a cause of the American Revolution. The editors finally took solace in the rationalization that the ways of God could be strange but that all would agree that "the almighty Governor of the nations would in his own chosen way educe lasting good to both parties" as a result of the war.[91]

Peter Parker insisted that the war was necessary to terminate the opium trade: "It is the occasion of great joy that the opium traffic is to close. But it has to be done in a manner that is peculiar to a nation that regards itself as the principal part of the world and all other nations as mere handfuls of men who come to share in its boundless compassion." How the war would end the opium trade Parker never explained. Such details he left to God: "May the will of the Lord be done; and may every change hasten the coming of his kingdom here!"[92] Parker personally took his case to the United States where he lectured throughout the country, in Congress, and to the President's cabinet on "the true nature of the war." There were two common errors in American thinking on the war, he complained. Every American in China knew that England was not embroiled in the struggle "to perpetuate the Opium Trade, and there was no concealed object of conquest." The real purpose of the war was "indemnity for the past and security for the future." [93] Bridgman, Abeel, and Williams joined Parker's attempt to educate the American people on these points through a steady flow of letters to editors in the United States.[94] Even a letter from the Prussian missionary Gutzlaff to a friend in Scotland managed to find its way into the *New York Herald*. England's victory was "fraught with the highest benefit to commerce and civilization, and indeed the truest and best interests of the human race, and China especially," Gutzlaff declared.[95] One Sunday school textbook explained that the Celestials would benefit from the British invasion through the destruction of "the despotic web of paganism, and superstition" under which they were suffering.[96]

However much Williams insisted later that "everyone in China" knew British actions involved "far higher principles than the mere recovery of opium," [97] he still had found it necessary to justify his endorsement of them continually on the pages of missionary magazines:

Should England not feel herself called upon to demand explanations for past grievances, we [missionaries] fear that the authorities will become still more overbearing and exclusive. . . . Alas! Our hearts sink at the bare possibility of such a result. We deprecate war. . . . While we pray, therefore, that if consistent with God's holy purposes, it may not be inflicted, ought we not to plead with even still greater importunity that if Great Britain pursues a peaceful policy, the pride and prejudice of this people may not swell into still higher barriers, than they already oppose to our influence.[98]

The editor of the *Southern Literary Messenger* was not far from the truth when he accused American missionaries of listening "if not impatiently, at least anxiously, for the sound of the first gun. Well may the statesman of China look suspiciously upon the efforts of religious missionaries, and regard them as covert designs to subvert the Chinese government. . . . There they stand before the gates of the Chinese empire . . . with matches lighted and weapons bared, and cry as they knock: 'Peaceably if we may; but forcibly if we must.' " [99]

This aggressive stance of the missionary existed throughout most of the nineteenth century. Long before the Opium War the *Chinese Repository* expressed disappointment that the British did not retaliate over the Lord Napier incident. "It is certain that the more forbearance and indulgence are shown to them [the Chinese] the more proud and overbearing they become," the editors advised the English. The rationale developed by this American missionary publication anticipated that of John Quincy Adams by seven years. Only force would "compel China to a course more consistent with their rights and obligations," and to give up her isolationism which was in "open violation of the law—thou shalt love thy neighbor as thyself." [100] Apparently few Protestant missionaries at this time questioned the wisdom of using grape shot in order to enforce the law of love.

During the discussion over extraterritoriality which followed Napier's expulsion, Williams and Bridgman expressed disgust over the consensus among American editors that China did have a right to make her own laws and foreigners an obligation to obey them however absurd such laws might be. Bridgman asked scornfully, "And why not ask: 'Have the banditti and pirates on high seas a right to make their own laws?' " [101] Their publication, the *Chinese Repository*, predicted in 1836 that Americans would soon come to realize that force was the only means of dealing with the Celestials.

When the Opium War failed to produce the dramatic changes anticipated, American missionaries continued to clamor for the use of additional force in China. In a letter to a group of Boston merchants in 1855 the Reverend Peter Parker, who was at the time moonlighting in the position of United States commissioner to China, explained that diplomacy had no effect on the Chinese. "It is from influences more potent than those of the ablest diplomatist, that any important changes are to be looked for in the relations subsisting between China and the Western nations . . . ," our chief diplomat and leading missionary advised.[102] Williams continued to hammer away at the same theme. The Chinese "would grant nothing unless fear stimulated their sense of justice for they are among the most craven of people, cruel and selfish as heathenism can make men, so we must be backed by force, if we wish them to listen," Williams pleaded.[103]

Only a few American religious publications questioned the wisdom of such arguments and were scornful of any conception of God's will coming to man in the guise of the Royal Navy. The editor of *The Friend* expressed shock over "the many Christians who are delighted with British military preparations in China. Strange! That reflecting minds can ever believe that the wrath of man will be able to work the righteousness of God: and still as strange that they can be brought to hope or desire that the gospel of Jesus Christ may be, or can be, brought to the minds of unbelievers by the sword, or that through the slaughter of thousands of our fellow mortals, the kingdom of the Prince of Peace is to be established." [104] The editors of the *Christian Examiner* joined the protest accusing John Quincy Adams and his clerical supporters of national and race prejudice. It was unreasonable "to try the Chinese by the standards of Anglo-Saxons" and fatuous to ascribe the British invasion of China to God's will. "While God may turn evil to good, the character of evil and the evil-doer remains unchanged," they advised.[105]

The trader and missionary views on the war, together with the generally unfavorable treatment of the Chinese in magazines and textbooks, were influential enough to make the most anglophobic newspaper editors pause before condemning British action in China and to put some in the uncomfortable position of supporting England for the first time in their lives. Out of thirty newspapers—representing New York, Boston, Philadelphia, Washington D.C., Baltimore, Providence, Salem, and Albany—six editors gave England consistent support while seven vociferously denounced Albion's latest venture in imperialism. Fifteen newspapers wavered back and forth between praise for Britain's chastisement of the vile Celestials and criticism for her brutal attack on Canton. Two publications simply ignored the war altogether, although one of these, curiously enough, did not blank out news of China but featured a series of articles on the *curiosa* and *admiranda* of the Celestial Empire in a manner reminiscent of the eighteenth century.[106]

Only one of England's critics in this journalistic sample could be said to have been motivated by any real sympathy for the Chinese. The others actually expressed as much contempt for the Celestials as they did hatred for the British. A popular refrain among these critics was that "neither China's conceit, ignorance, nor ludicrous institutions" justified an armed attack.[107] Horace Greeley demanded to know just how the sight of a Christian nation "deliberately setting aside all the restraints of law and justice, and entering upon a contest with a semi-civilized country" would set an example for other "idolatrous savages" in the rest of Asia.[108] "This quarrel seems to us to reflect upon the Christianity and Civilization of Great Britain," the editor of the *New York American* declared, because the Chinese, in his opinion, were "semi-barbarous" and racially inferior—a nation of "children or idiots." [109] In adding the Opium War to Britain's "sad catalogue of outrages upon humanity," *Niles' National Register* listed "China and her imbecile world of mortals" as England's latest victim.[110] Clearly the admiration and sentimental ties to the Chinese conceptualized by several American historians were absent in the editorial commentary on the Opium War.

Critics of the war were largely motivated by traditional anglophobia and by fear of an English monopoly in China. Little concern was expressed over the opium trade. These editors simply could not conceive of the "conquerors of India"—those "insatiate monopolizers of the trade of the world"—sharing the fruits of a victory in China with any other nation.[111] This fear was by no means absent among those editors who endorsed England's attack on China. On those occasions when editors such as Bennett and Bryant saw the struggle as a racial one "between the Caucasian and Tungusian races," they supported their fellow Anglo-Saxons; but on other occasions they expressed anxiety over the "growth of the grasping British oligarchy." [112]

No editor expressed support for the English in China with complete equanimity, and the editorial pages of the *Providence Journal* provide us with a good example of the mental anguish that was involved for an anglophobic editor to concede that for once England had acted correctly in warring upon another nation. Hailing on one occasion a British victory in China as the only means of opening up that "selfish" nation to commerce, this editor would a month later remind himself that "John Bull is not in the habit of opening oysters for other people to eat." [113] But continued reports of alleged "insults and injuries" heaped upon all foreigners in China by "this most absolute and oppressive despotism" shored up his confidence that the English attack was the proper action in this case. His main concern turned to the possibility that there would be an insufficient number of British troops on hand to complete the job, or that treacherous mandarins might with false promises trick the English into withdrawing prematurely.[114] Once the British were victorious, however, this editor felt compelled to express the wish that the necessary job had been carried out "with purer hands than those that conquered India." [115] Nevertheless, a few weeks later he was insisting that it was a great victory for America as well as for England.[116]

Other editors reached this conclusion much earlier. The editor of the *Boston Atlas* found it difficult to understand how anyone could think that the United States would not benefit from an English victory in China.[117] As the *Columbian Centinel* expressed it, John Bull was holding the horns of the cow while America milked her.[118] The *New-York Journal of Commerce* was convinced early in the war that "the humbling of such a power as that of China, will be considered one of the greatest blessings that could be conferred upon the commercial community of every trading empire." [119] The outcome of the war could only be "the complete success of civilized man," the *Morning Courier and New-York Enquirer* declared.[120] "As for the permanent acquisition of the country or any portion of it, that is out of the question," the *New York Commercial Advertiser* assured its readers. "The indignation of the whole world forbids it even if it were physically possible. Great Britain, mighty as she is, and unscrupulous, would not dare to practice upon China such a course of aggression, injustice, inhumanity and fraud, as resulted in the conquest of India." [121] An editorial in the *New York Sun* claimed that the war would actually liberate the Chinese from an unpopular, tyrannical, Tartar government, abolish the opium trade (!), establish free trade, and open up the country to "the Anglo Saxon race" with all its benefits—"The introduction of civilization among these benighted nations," a "better form of government," and above all, "enlightened and liberal Christianity." [122] This editor pointed out that since Americans experienced no difficulties trading with a "British India," there was no reason to expect that they would in a "British China." [123]

Armed with such convictions, some American editors even counseled the British to be more aggressive in China and not to stop short of a total victory. "If Elliot permits himself to be trapped into negotiations with China, he should be sacked," one New York editor advised. "Nelson would have been just the right sort of man for such an occasion; he had a particular genius for cutting Gordian knots and sweeping away all the diplomatic rubbish." [124] But this same editor by 1841 could write of the same war: "In its origin and its progress, we conceive that justice, human rights and the rights of nations and humanity are outraged." [125] The role of the British in China was like that of "buccaneers in the old times who slaughtered without mercy." [126] Half of the editors fluctuated between warm support for and strong condemnation of Britain. While this could be explained in terms of the inertial effect of our traditional anglophobia or the fear of a British monopoly countered by a hope for the opening up of China as a result of the war, there was a pattern to this editorial vacillation that can be related to American relations with the British and Chinese. Many of these editors sided with the English early in the conflict when Americans in China were also experiencing difficulties with the Celestial government: a Chinese opium dealer was executed in front of the American factory, mobs attacked all foreigners, several American ships were temporarily seized on suspicion of smuggling opium, and some Americans were arrested and then expelled in 1839 and 1840.[127] At the same time, some of these editors expressed surprise that England was being "remarkably conciliatory" on the Maine boundary dispute in 1839. President Van Buren "frankly admits that both parties have been in the wrong," an Albany editor informed his readers.[128] The Royal Navy's annoying habit of stopping American vessels off the coast of Africa for examination was renewed, however, which revived the bitterness of the *Caroline* affair and helped to sour much of the editorial endorsement of the Opium War in 1841.[129]

But the letters of Peter Parker and the famous speech of John Quincy Adams, together with China's expulsion of all Western merchants from Canton—or more precisely, Whampoa—won some of these editors back to the British cause before the war ended. The *Daily National Intelligencer* published a letter of Parker's that convinced the editor of the righteousness of the British cause in China.[130] Parker had less luck with the editor of the *Northern Light,* who was impressed by his "persuasive arguments" but feared that such "diplomatic subleties" could be "a cover for opium." At any rate, he could never buy the famous missionary's conclusion that "the British government, so far from meriting censure, should receive the congratulations and thanks of Western nations." It simply flew in the face of everything this Albany editor knew of the English.[131]

John Quincy Adams was far more successful in convincing American editors that China had violated international law and that England's attack was more than justified. But Adams' speech came at the end of 1841 when the anger over the Royal Navy's arrogance seems to have cooled a bit, and when more publicity was being given to the difficulties between Americans in China and xenophobic Celestial officials. Twelve editors in the sample agreed with the ex-president, although four of them qualified their endorsements by accepting his severe judgment of the Chinese but diluting his view of the British as liberators of the Chinese and champions of the West. It is not surprising that the *Sun, Herald,* and *Morning Courier* in New York; Boston's *Advertiser, Morning Post, Atlas,* and *Columbian Centinel;* and the *Philadelphia Gazette* and *National Intelligencer* concurred to some extent with Adams. These newspapers had expressed sympathy for England's policy in China on other occasions during the preceding two years. The *New York American,* however, had been consistently critical of the English, particularly on the opium issue. But Adams finally convinced this editor that "the opium question was but a trifling incident in the cause of the war." [132] Equally unexpected was the adamant refusal of the *Evening Post* and the *Commercial Advertiser* in New York to accept either the logic or the conclusions of America's senior statesman.[133] Not only had these publications generally supported the war, but the editor of the latter newspaper had continually praised John Quincy Adams, "honored and revered by all who have a reverence for lofty intellect, profound learning and lofty patriotism." [134] The editor of the *Boston Evening Transcript,* which had been essentially neutral, was won over by "the matured thoughts" of Adams on the war in China. "The opium question" had been "such a bugbear in the public mind," he admitted and thanked Adams for having "set the record straight." [135]

It would seem, however, that the opium issue was for these editors little more than a moralistic peg on which to hang their opposition to the war. The real "bugbears" in their minds were anglophobia and the fear of a British monopoly in China. In an editorial on the "intrinsic merits of the question," the editor of the *Boston Atlas* argued that Americans should ignore opium and international law and judge Britains's action solely on whether or not America has anything to gain from the war: "Whether the Chinese committed an outrage in seizing so much British property or whether the 'outer barbarians' are right in persisting in carrying on the opium trade against the will of the Emperor—for the Chinese people, it is presumed, are hardly consulted in the matter; this we leave . . . to debating societies who are fond of discussing abstract questions of right." Commissioner Lin and Lord Palmerston would ignore the results of such a debate in any case, the editor added, and the real issue was that the Chinese had to be taught that they could no longer abuse foreigners with impunity.[136]

The actual reporting of the conduct of the war did not help China's image in the United States. While some anglophobic editors enjoyed Peking's bombastic edicts addressed to the "Royal Barbarian Victoria, Queen of an Obscure Island," they also found the Chinese conception of the English as "rebels," with its implication that the whole world was subject to the dragon throne, baffling and irritating. The emperor's threat to unleash the "vengeance of heaven" and sweep the English from the seas was either foolish or blasphemous.[137] Ironically, an English writer who attempted to excuse these bits of braggadocio as mere rhetoric designed for domestic consumption in China was taken to task by a New York editor who pointed to the long history of arrogant ethnocentricity, xenophobia, and delusions of omnipotence on the part of the Chinese.[138]

The utter rout of the Chinese in the war was also damaging to their image in America. In spite of a general awareness of China's military weakness, American editors were not adequately prepared for the debacle that took place. "The universal opinion is that the force of the British is inadequate to make any important impression . . . ," one editor wrote as English warships and transports were joining up off Macao.[139] This view was widely expressed and Bennett appears to have been one of the few editors who predicted the extent of China's defeat on the grounds that her tyrannical government would be unable to muster fully her large population in order to slow down the British. Yet even Bennett found the statistics of battle in China difficult to believe.[140] Whole cities were reported taken with less than a handful of British casualties; Chinese flotillas were destroyed without the loss of a single seaman. Estimates of the rates of fatalities ran up to four hundred to one in favor of the British.[141] H.M.S. *Nemesis,* probably the first steam warship to engage in combat, sank forty junks in one afternoon; and the crew amused themselves with the Chinese costumes found floating in the wreckage. Some sailors rigged "a Chinaman's tail" at the back of their necks and donned mandarin hats to produce "a comical sight" it was reported with amazement.[142]

A few editors saw China's weakness as final proof that the nation was uncivilized, although others thought the number of casualties questioned the popular belief that the Chinese were abject cowards.[143] Considering their superstitious nature, obsolete equipment, and ludicrous leadership, one correspondent reported, "you will hardly believe that the Chinese stood to their guns to the last." [144] Continued slurs on Chinese manliness irked the editors of one magazine who angrily retorted, "We do not understand how prejudice can be strong enough to question their courage." [145] But the pro-Chinese *Niles' National Register* more closely approached the average editorial reaction to China's utter impotence when it expressed disgust that the Chinese had not at least extracted a higher price for the British victory and lamented: "With every successful collision between the Chinese and their invaders, the imbecility of the former appears more and more manifest." [146] For the pro-British editor of the *Boston Atlas,* Chinese conduct in the war was best explained by the fact that "the insolent and the treacherous are invariably as prone to fear as they are ready to injure; and their submission is usually as servile as their presumption was arrogant." [147]

One fascinating side effect of the Opium War was a very faint stirring of what could be considered yellow perilist fear, probably its first public expression in American history, although certainly not the first in the West. No doubt the yellow peril concept goes back at least to the thirteenth-century European reaction to Genghiz Kahn. A series of articles in *Gentleman's Magazine* in the eighteenth century had argued that China was the fourth beast of Daniel that "shall devour the whole earth, and shall trample it down, and tear it in pieces." [148] In 1840 rumors circulated in America that Napoleon had warned the members of the Amherst mission who visited Saint Helena on their way home from Peking that, should the English invade China, they would teach the Chinese how to fight and imperil the world.[149] This rumor provoked one editorial in the *Providence Evening Herald* that was full of foreboding over the possibility that China would be "awakening from the lethargy of centuries." [150]

Bennett dismissed these rumors and fears in his customary ethnocentric fashion. Why hadn't British conquest taught the Indians how to fight? he asked rhetorically. British ascendency was "derived not from her physical power merely, but from that moral force which superior intelligence and a high degree of civilization confer on nations," Bennett explained. Such attributes have only been conferred on Western nations, however, so that the Chinese or Indians could never dominate the West. Like ancient Rome, England was simply exercising her "moral supremacy" over "Barbarian hordes" in the East, Bennett concluded.[151]

The debate over England's moral culpability in attacking China did not terminate with the end of the war, but continued sporadically in the mass media for more than a decade as new Anglo-Chinese tensions built up over opium smuggling. A number of editors who had been vehemently anti-English in the war reversed their opinions and belatedly justified Britain's attack on China in 1840. For one thing the feared British monopoly never materialized. Instead, "the thunder of British batteries" had induced the Chinese "to enroll themselves in the list of governments who meet upon an amicable footing of mutual trade and commerce, and are bound by . . . international law," the editor of *Hunt's Merchants' Magazine* admitted in 1845.[152] Moreover Americans fully expected to capture a larger share of the China trade which was expanded to several Celestial seaports as a result of the war. "It would appear that the major part of the British victory is to fall into American hands," one editor rejoiced. "Our clipper fleet outstrips the wind and leaves their competitors . . . quite in the background." [153]

The belated reversal of opinion on the Opium War may also have had something to do with the bitter American disappointment with the Taiping rebels by 1854, as well as with the expulsion of some American businessmen from Japan in 1855. All of this seemed to point to the wisdom of England's decision in 1840 to use force in China. The *North American Review,* which had refused to print Adams' lecture in 1841, granted full indulgence to the English in 1854 attributing the Opium War to "Lin's obstinacy and stupidity." [154] Another of England's earlier critics, *Graham's Magazine,* expressed disgust in 1853 with those Americans who were still criticizing Britain's role in China, comparing them to the "shallow philanthropists" of Rabelais "who live in their little barrels and survey mankind through the bung-holes." [155] But Bennett observed in 1855 that Americans were beginning to understand that "the use of force on Asiatics" was "in the long run more humane" than were peaceful negotiations.[156] No moralist, Bennett conceded that the war he had applauded fifteen years earlier was "in all probability . . . recklessly unjust and unjustifiable"; but, he quickly added, "the benefits of that war to the British, to the Chinese, to commerce and to the world at large, cannot possibly be exaggerated." [157] In the end the British were bringing "progress" to "savage people" in India and China, Bennett insisted, whatever the means.[158] Interestingly enough, Bennett's anglophobia on other issues was by no means diminished, but it was in the spirit of a noisy family quarrel. Against the "savages" he demanded a united Anglo-Saxon front.

Perhaps the most significant about-face after the war was made by Caleb Cushing, if the account of John Quincy Adams is correct. Had he seen the evidence on which Adams had built his case, Cushing confessed, he would have been persuaded earlier.[159] Yet the English bluebooks on the affair amassed by Adams were not that impressive; and most of the evaluations of the Chinese by traders, diplomats, and missionaries had been available to the public in magazines or books. Indeed, some of these books were in Cushing's own private library.[160] It would seem that Cushing's alleged change of heart would have been more influenced by his own experience in China, where he had to threaten force to overcome Chinese recalcitrance in his negotiations with them on behalf of the United States government. Moreover, his interpreters in Canton were the missionaries Parker, Williams, and Bridgman, all of whom were partisan to the British cause and hypercritical of the Chinese.[161]

In conclusion, the Opium War served as an important catalyst in popularizing the anti-Chinese themes developed and polished by diplomats, traders, and missionaries over several decades. Such themes had already received ample reflection in American magazines and geography textbooks long before the war. Indeed, they were strong enough to influence a substantial minority of American newspaper editors and important opinion leaders to suspend their anglophobic predilections and support England in her war on China. Moreover, the majority of Britain's journalistic critics in the United States were not sympathetic to the Chinese by any means. The inertia of anglophobia, plus a fear of an English monopoly, appears to have been the real motivation behind such criticism, however much of it was cloaked in moralistic considerations concerning the opium trade.

The development of an unfavorable American image of the Chinese was an evolutionary process that accelerated noticeably between 1835 and 1850. No single event, person, or group can be isolated as being primarily responsible for this development. The important point to keep in mind is that the unfavorable image of the Chinese is discernible among American opinion makers long before the first Celestial gold seeker set foot upon California soil. Subsequent developments after 1850, both in China and the United States, provided the capstone to a process that began with the China trade in 1785.

In spite of the Burlingame Treaty, and all the advances which American and European civilization has made toward establishing a friendly feeling with the Chinese, it is evident, from recent events that these people remain as barbarous as ever. Their pagan savageness appears to be impregnable to the mild influences of Christian civilization.

New York Herald editorial, Oct. 30, 1870.

Th' time has come f'r the subjick races in the wurrld to rejooce us fair wans to their own complexion be batin' us black and blue. T'was "Wow Chow, while ye'er idly stewin' me cuffs I'll set fire to me unpaid bills." "I wud feel repaid be a kick," says Wow Chow. . . . But now its all changed . . . th' wurrud has passed around an ivry naygur fr'm lemon color to coal is bracin' up.

Peter Finley Dunne, Mr. Dooley at His Best (New York, 1938), p. 131.

6

The Mass Media Era, 1850-1870

The Opium War initiated a widespread American interest in China, in much the same manner that Commodore Perry's visit to Tokyo Bay performed that function for Japan. But subsequent events in China maintained a high level of interest in that nation over the next few decades. The Taiping Rebellion from 1850 to 1864, the *Arrow* incident in 1856 and ensuing Anglo-Chinese conflict until 1860, the Burlingame mission in 1868, and the Tientsin Massacre in 1870 all served to keep China in the public eye. Because these events coincided with the first two decades of Chinese immigration to the United States, they provided an important background to the national debate over Chinese exclusion.

A sample of twenty-seven newspapers representing ten cities and four towns in northeastern United States was examined for reports on these events in China and editorial reactions to them. There is

no expectation that a meticulously accurate account of these occurrences from the perspective of an expert in Chinese history will
follow. For example, every newspaper examined for its reaction to
the Tientsin Massacre accepted at face value the French charge
that Chinese officials had deliberately goaded the populace into attacking the missionaries with accusations that they had kidnapped
Chinese children in order to mutilate their bodies. Yet Professor
Paul Cohen insists that imprudent behavior on the part of the
French nuns helped to engender such grotesque beliefs without any
official encouragement.[1] However, more important to this study
than the reality of the event itself is the perception of it by American editors. These perceptions not only affected the image of the
Chinese, but in turn clearly indicate the viability of the image
shaped by missionaries, traders, and diplomats. This interrelationship between perception and image forms a crucial part of the the-
oretical framework of this study.

More than any single occurrence in China during the nineteenth century, the Taiping Rebellion aroused widespread excitement in the United States. In many respects this revolution
was a harbinger of later revolutions in Asia. Led by Hung Hsui-
ch'üan, it was a peasant uprising against the Manchu rulers in the
name of Christianity that featured a communistic economy. But
like the Chinese use of Marxism a century later, the Taipings
adapted a Western religious doctrine to their own needs and freely
mixed in with it some Chinese traditions. The initial success of
these rebels and its promise of a Protestant Christian China
alerted editors of the most obscure rural American weeklies.[2] In
1854 the Taiping struggle competed successfully with the Crimean
War for space in the American press. The long stalemate between
rebel and imperial forces that continued for another decade, and
the role of colorful Western adventurers in the war, such as Major
Charles ("Chinese") Gordon and the Americans Frederick Townsend Ward and Henry Burgevine, helped to keep China in the
news, and probably conditioned the press to give greater attention
to the *Arrow* incident and the second Anglo-Chinese war.[3]

During 1852 the insurrection went almost unnoticed in the
press, and the few scattered references to it failed to mention any
religious significance. The *New York Times* first reported the
rumor that the Taiping rebels were Christians, but the editor
quickly dismissed it as too fantastic to be true. A few days of
cogitation, however, led this editor to entertain the possibility
more carefully. After all, he reasoned, the humanistic elements in

Confucian philosophy could have prepared the Chinese for such a sudden conversion.[4] Bennett in the *New York Herald* scoffed at these rumors and cavalierly dismissed the Taipings as "Chinese Spirit Rappers." Yet Bennett was at a loss to explain why the missionary and acting U.S. Commissioner Peter Parker should support the rebels. Perhaps, he suggested, the missionaries saw in the insurrection another opportunity to wring more concessions from a weakened Celestial Empire.[5]

By the summer of 1853, however, the American press was brimming with talk of the "Protestant" Taipings whose leader had been converted by an American Baptist missionary, Issacher Roberts. Moreover another American missionary, Charles Taylor, managed to get to the rebel camp, and his report appeared in newspapers throughout the northeast. Taylor testified that the rebels addressed him as "brother," and that the first thing they did following a victory was to passionately destroy the hated idols in China: "So gratifying a scene of devastation I certainly never before held. Here were gilded and painted fragments of images strewn about in every direction. The altars and tables, incense vases and candlesticks, Buddhist books and all the paraphernalia of idolatrous worship, were broken, torn, and scattered here and there in irrevocable ruin; and this too, by the very ones who, not three years ago, were willing votaries at just such shrines." [6]

More reports from inside dopesters in China began to fill the mailbags of American editors. In some cases these were simply letters to friends or relatives in the United States who turned them over to local editors whence they were picked up and reprinted in a succession of newspapers.[7] Anything from China during the summer and fall of 1853 was hot news. Most of the letters published were from missionaries, ecstatic over this totally unexpected victory in China. It confirmed their expectations for divine intervention at the right moment. Their colleagues who had visited the rebel camp reported omnipresent signs of Christianity. Protestant services were held three times a day and the Ten Commandments were strictly observed. Perhaps the Taipings were a bit zealous in executing individuals for "lewd glances of the eye, lewd movements of the heart, smoking opium, and singing lewd songs," some missionaries conceded, but such Draconian measures were rationalized away with a reminder of Chinese propensities for lechery and other vices.[8] The Reverend W. A. P. Martin in a letter to Caleb Cushing likened Hung to Oliver Cromwell: "On the one side . . . dissolute and atheistic or idolatrous Imperialists; on the other abstemious, devout and image-breaking followers of Tai-Ping." [9]

The traders were more reserved about the religious nature of the Taiping Rebellion but no less enthusiastic about the golden opportunity it presented to replace the Manchu government with one more friendly to commerce.[10] One trader called for American and British arms to accelerate the change and the editor of the *Evening Traveller* in Boston agreed: "By the side of England, the customer to the extent of sixty million pounds of tea, should stand the United States the taker of forty million pounds." [11] Another trader suggested that Americans simply "advance more boldly" with their wares in the wake of the rebel victories. The Taipings were rooting out the afflictions suffered by China for millennia—"a kind of dropsy: a surfeit of population and conceit; of conservatism and vanity; of prejudice and superstition." Whether the Taipings were Christians or not was irrelevant from his point of view since commerce could only benefit from such extirpation.[12]

Because the traders harbored fewer illusions about the Christianity of the Taipings, they continued to support them as a welcome change even in the wake of disclosures that Hung considered himself to be the brother of Christ and another rebel leader to be the "Holy Ghost." One trader pleaded that Hung's use of the Bible was no different than Mohammet's use of the "Jewish Bible," and that Americans would be foolish to get too excited over such shadows and lose the substance of commercial opportunity.[13] Only with the discovery that the rebels were just as xenophobic and anticommercial as the imperialists did the traders bitterly denounce them.[14]

In spite of the enthusiastic endorsement of the Taipings in 1853 by both missionaries and traders, American editors were surprisingly cautious about fully committing themselves to the rebel cause. Bennett's response to the eyewitness accounts of missionaries was fairly typical of the initial editorial reaction in the sample during the summer of 1853: "When Dr. Medhurst first suggested that the Chinese insurgents were mainly Christians, . . . we, in common with the bulk of the British and American press, treated the idea as a delusion of an over sanguine missionary. Events, however, have since contributed to strengthen the strange theory . . . not only of Christianity, but of Protestantism." But Bennett nevertheless remained wary of accepting these reports at face value. After all, it was possible that these "former thieves" were simply putting on "a show of Christianity" in order to win Western support. Of course, such "a cunning scheme" would make the Chinese "far more able rogues than anyone suspects," Bennett mused as he struggled with the problem without coming to any conclusion.[15]

By the end of 1853, however, all of the editors in the sample gave the Taipings some measure of support. Horace Greeley explained in his endorsement that the rebels had simply been too influenced by the Old Testament rather than "the forgiving temper of the new," which accounted for the excessive slaughter of the enemy.[16] An Albany editor insisted that "the slaughter of infidels is praiseworthy," but he admitted to some concern over their un-Christianlike, wanton destruction of property.[17] The editor of a small town weekly expressed amazement that any American should be concerned over the fate of Buddhist priests or their property. For him it was enough that "any change can hardly be for the worse: any kind of agitation is better than the dead stagnation of Chinese life."[18] A Boston editor argued in his endorsement that the Taipings "either sincerely or for political reasons have renounced idolatry and embraced something which bears resemblance to Christianity," a substantial gain in his eyes.[19] But few editors could agree on how the Taiping movement resembled Christianity. Some asserted that it was a kind of Calvinism, while one editor in Rochester, New York, called it "a sort of Jewish description of Christianity," and another in Washington likened it to Mormonism.[20] Probably the most important single influence on American editors was Bayard Taylor, the Philadelphia journalist who reported from China in 1853 as a kind of freelance foreign correspondent. His conclusion, that the heathenism, despotism, and vice in China called for change and that any change could only improve the situation, closely resembled the position taken by many editors in the sample.[21]

A few editors were less equivocal in their praises for the Taiping rebels. An editorial in Boston's *Evening Traveller* argued that "this wonderful revolutionary movement" could only be ascribed to the hand of God, and not to the missionaries in China. "A good translation of the Bible is certainly the last thing the Jesuits would have put in the hands of converts"; on the other hand, "Protestant missionaries could never have originated a movement of this kind, it being utterly inconsistent with their principles . . . not to meddle in this way with the civil affairs of a country."[22] Now that the Chinese were being converted to Christianity by the sword of Taiping-Wang, Americans would have to make adjustments in their image of the Celestials, another Boston editor warned: ". . . . it is time for those who have derived their sterotype cut in geographies, in which an oblique eyed, mild looking individual, with shaven poll, lengthy queue and voluminous breeches, is presented hawking about 'rats and puppies for pies' to turn to more reliable sources for information. . . ." As a substitute for these maligning texts, the editor suggested the works of William de Rubruquis and Marco Polo.[23] But this editor was himself unable to make a clear break from that unfavorable image of the recent past, so that references to "the usual habits of the Chinese" or to "this new morality" of the Taipings continued to slip into his editorials.[24]

On the whole, the letters to newspapers from readers displayed much more enthusiasm over the news of the Taiping insurrection than did the editorials. Indeed a great number of the former were complaints against the editor's "tepid response" to this "great historic event" which was only the "beginning of a world-wide conversion to Christianity." [25] Of course, a disproportionate number of these letters were written by members of the Protestant clergy who pleaded for greater patience and understanding of the rebels. "One cannot expect a barbarian, a heathen to pass instanter from his idolatry to the service of the True God, without a spot or blemish," one cleric implored in a letter to the *New York Herald*.[26] Another letter reminded an editor that revolutions were always taking place in remote parts of China and suggested that the Taipings were being assigned the faults and excesses of other groups.[27] The "doubting Thomases" were angrily denounced by a minister who demanded that such critics explain how it was possible for the rebels to have encountered such spectacular success in the field "without the aid of Divine Providence." [28] A returned missionary in a letter to the *National Intelligencer* called for an end to such senseless bickering. It was enough, he argued, that the rebels had "raised the standard of Christianity" without subjecting the substance of their beliefs to petty scrutiny.[29]

Ironically, it was often in the admissions of missionary apologists that American editors first learned of some of the worst Taiping excesses. An English missionary writing to the *London Times* conceded that Hung claimed divine status for himself, but by way of mitigation added that such terms as "holy" and "supreme" were reserved for God. But the American editor who reprinted the letter expressed some shock over Hung's outrageous pretentions.[30] A lengthy defense of the rebels in the *Biblical*

Repertory disclosed that Hung "fancies himself to have been on one or two occasions taken up to heaven," where he conversed with his brothers, the other sons of God: Confucius, Moses, and Christ.[31] Editors of the secular press were dumbfounded by such revelations, and were unable to share the conclusions of religious editors that the Taiping movement necessarily represented something better than the paganism it was replacing.

Late in 1854 newspapers in the United States featured a dramatic reaction against the Chinese rebels. A headline screamed "Blasphemous Pretentions of Tai-ping Wang" in the *New York Herald,* and an editorial in the *New York Times* bore the title "The Blackguard 'Heavenly King' of China." [32] "In their religion, the rebels are blasphemous, fanatic and superstitious," declared the editor of Boston's *Evening Traveller* who once hailed the Taipings as the candle that would light up China's "heathen darkness." [33] Hung was rather commonly referred to as a "knave" in editorials, and one editor wondered if the rebel leader had ever recovered from his earlier insanity.[34] In a blistering editorial attack on the Taipings in 1854, Bennett expressed great annoyance over "our profound ignorance of the true nature and business" of the rebels, who "mingled the doctrines of the Bible with the absurd fables of their own mythology. . . . The barbarity and folly of their actions equaled the absurdity and blasphemy of their words. Their whole progress has been a series of savage cruelties, and ruthless acts of destruction leaving whole villages . . . steeped in blood." [35]

The bitterness expressed in these newspapers calls for special explanation in view of the reluctant and skeptical endorsement journalists had given the rebellion in the first place. In June of 1854, the new American commissioner to China, Robert McLane, visited Nanking to arrange a commercial treaty and suffered humiliating rebuffs from the rebel leaders. McLane returned "thoroughly convinced that the success of the Taipings would in no way benefit the foreign powers." [36] Angrily, one editor reported that the rebel leaders demanded the kowtow of foreigners whom they addressed as "hairy devils" or "barbarian slaves," and "taunt us with imbecility" in much the same manner as have the Manchus.[37] Visitors to Nanking were informed, according to new reports, that the world was under Taiping jurisdiction and that all ambassadors were tribute bearers to Hung.[38] Many of these complaints boiled down to the effect that the rebels were just as anticommercial and xenophobic as were the imperialists. The Reverend Dr. Dyer Ball reported that even missionaries were addressed rudely as "foreign white devils" by the rebels,[39] and news reached American editors that their consul Benjamin Spooner had been fired on by Taiping batteries.[40] The American government had put up with this Chinese nonsense too long, Bennett declared. He suggested that McLane or Spooner be sent back to the rebel camp "with a suitable force and demand to trade with Nanking. Their refusal would allow us to act, and it is not unlikely that some incident would occur which would afford us as ample grounds for hostilities, as there were for the Opium War." [41]

This disillusionment with the Taipings was a boon to the reputation of Humphrey Marshall, McLane's predecessor, who had been *persona non grata* with American missionaries, traders, and editors for having recommended a year earlier that American aid be given to the emperor in suppressing the rebellion.[42] Marshall had been "very roundly taken to task by our newspapers . . . for favoring the imperial government," Bennett admitted sheepishly, as subsequent evidence seemed to justify that position.[43] Even the missionary Elijah Bridgman who had furiously demanded the former U.S. commissioner's recall asked, "Is it possible, after all, that Humphrey Marshall knew what he was about?" [44]

The American religious community was badly split over the Taiping issue after 1854. Many feared that Hung would merely substitute what Parker called "a theocracy with blasphemous ideas" for the existing paganism.[45] Some insisted that there was "nothing of Christianity in Nanking but its name falsely applied . . . to a system of revolting idolatry," as the Reverend J. L. Holmes asserted in the *Missionary Herald*.[46] But others clung to the illusion that however "mongrel" their Christianity, the Taipings would at least "pave the way for the gospel in China." [47] In 1871, the Reverend Russell Conwell was still lamenting the missed opportunity presented by the Taiping Rebellion, a failure that he attributed to the traders and narrow commercial interest: "All sympathy with justice and Christianity fled at once before the money god's magic wand. . . ." [48] As late as 1896 W. A. P. Martin was still angry over the missed opportunity.[49] But Peter Parker appeared to be closer to the majority of missionaries when he avoided taking a clear stand on the issue in 1854. He described the "frightful cruelty" practiced by both sides in the Chinese civil war and concluded, "Alas for China. It would seem that the declaration, that the nations that will not serve God shall be destroyed, is about to be fulfilled. Our only consolation is—the Lord reign-eth!" [50]

The anger of American editors was not restricted to the Tai-pings for very long. It was soon reported that Commissioner Mc-Lane was also rudely rebuffed at Pei-ho by the imperial govern-ment when he joined Britain's representative, Sir John Bowring, in an attempt to negotiate with Peking. Captain Buchanan of the United States Navy accompanied McLane on these trips, and he made good copy for American reporters. His advice from the first was that the only way to deal with the Chinese, rebel or loyalist, was "to give them a million shot a minute," which he repeated so often that it earned him the nickname "Old Million." [51] He bore striking resemblance to "Captain Blast 'em all," a character in a popular New York play entitled "China, or Tricks upon Travel-lers." [52] McLane returned to the United States shortly afterward and was replaced by Peter Parker who was officially appointed the United States commissioner in China after having served tempo-rarily in that capacity on a number of other occasions. Decades later, McLane was able personally to avenge himself when, as a Maryland representative to Congress, he was able during the ex-clusion debates to exploit his experience in China to document his deprecation of Chinese character. [53]

As a result of the alleged insults committed by both sides in the Chinese civil war, Bennett changed his position and counseled neutrality in the opinion that a victory for either the imperialists or rebels would be a Pyrrhic one, and the West could then step in and shape the future China to its own needs. [54] But American edi-tors seemed to be getting bored with China when a new incident in 1856 catapulted the Chinese back onto the front page and into editorial columns of American newspapers. Imperial government officials had seized the lorcha *Arrow,* an opium runner manned by a Chinese crew but commanded by an Englishman who flew the Union Jack. When the English protested this insult to their flag the mandarins quickly released the ship and crew with apologies, although they had already executed a few of the hands who had notorious records as opium smugglers. The British were not satis-fied with mere apologies, however, and wanted it stipulated that such seizures would not take place in the future. When the Chi-nese officials refused to give this assurance, Admiral Seymour of the Royal Navy stormed Canton.

Interest in the *Arrow* war was greatly enhanced by the report that the American consul in Hong Kong had not only joined the British assault but carried "Old Glory" with him over the battered walls of Canton.[55] Six weeks later the USS *Portsmouth* exchanged fire with a Chinese battery, and Commander Foote successfully assaulted two forts with marines. When Commodore Armstrong dispatched a boat to take soundings preparatory to moving his fleet up in support of Foote, the Chinese fired on it, killing the man heaving the lead. At the same time an American merchantman was taken under fire by Chinese guns until an English man-of-war came to her rescue and demolished the redoubt.[56]

The bellicosity exhibited by American editors and their pro-British sentiment in discussing these incidents is in sharp contrast to the journalistic reaction to the Opium War seventeen years earlier. Virtually no newspaper in the sample discussed the opium question, although the *Arrow* was engaged in this illegal traffic and one of the results of the ensuing Anglo-Chinese war was the legalization of opium in China.[57] Instead, these editors almost unanimously accepted the British version of the *Arrow* seizure which was invariably reported as "another Chinese outrage." The stress was on China's flagrant violation of treaty rights and insolent defiance of international law.[58] The editor of the *New York Times* reacted to the firing upon Commodore Armstrong's boat as though it were entirely unprovoked, although his own news pages made clear the aggressive purposes of taking the soundings.[59] The Chinese simply could not win a point in the American press. When they quickly apologized for firing on Foote, the press interpreted this as proof that force was the only effective way to deal with the Celestials, immediately assuming that no apologies would have been forthcoming without the navy's strong retaliation. On the other hand, when the mandarins refused to apologize for firing on the merchantman with the excuse that it was too difficult to differentiate between the British and American flags, it was taken as further illustration of Chinese idiocy, perfidy, and trickery. "The stupidity and obstinate superstition of the Chinese should not be permitted to stand in the way of the only protection we can give to our fellow citizens in a distant land," the editor of the *New York Times* declared.[60]

Only three American editors in the sample were initially critical of the aggressive reaction to these incidents and two of them soon swung into the majority position of support for British policy in China. Uncertain at first, Boston's *Evening Traveller* instinctively interpreted the British actions as a continuation of the grasping imperialism begun by Sir Francis Drake and featured an article that was highly critical of Foote's "impudent conduct." [61] Within days, however, this editor decided that Britain had acted with "deliberation" whereas the Chinese were "unreasonable," and the attack on that "stationary nation" was "totally justified." [62] When the Chinese sued for peace he cheered the British victory: "China has at last been bombarded into the family of nations, the emperor having ordered peace to be made at any price." [63] The *Albany Evening Journal* was mainly concerned over the effect the war would have on the cost of tea. The editor reasoned that the American vessel was probably too close to the Celestial fort in the first place; and since the Chinese were such poor gunners, the alleged British rescue could only have been a grandstand play to win American allegiance.[64] But a few weeks later he, too, began to justify British policy in China and decided that "the enfeebled Mohammedan and Mongol races are destined" to fall under the advance of the Anglo-Saxons, just as the Mexicans and Indians "melt away before the advance of American settlers." [65]

Only Horace Greeley remained adamantly critical of the British in China, and in contrast to 1840 it was the pro-Chinese editor who bore the brunt of his colleagues' disapproval. The editor of the *National Era* noted that Greeley also defended Russia in the Crimean War implying that he was soft on despotism. The Chinese were hardly the innocent victims of the "rascally English," this editor asserted in answer to Greeley. "We know something of the Chinese from personal observation and experience. They are mean, treacherous, grossly immoral, irreligious, practically atheistic, intolerant, self-conceited and insolent—always indisposed to treat foreigners with justice or civility. . . . There is nothing in their history to give them any claims to the special sympathy of the civilized world." [66]

Nor were English dissenters safe from correction by the *New York Times,* whose editor took to task one journalist who argued that his nation's bombardment of Canton was disproportionate to "an apparent insult to a strip of British calico." Obviously Admiral Seymour's action was in response to more than this, the *Times* reasoned. "When a nation so grossly violates its treaty stipulations" and "acknowledges none of the responsibilities which public law imposes—the only course left for the outraged party to pursue is to inflict upon the offenders severe and summary punishment." [67]

Although the newspapers in the sample almost unanimously

supported England's view of the war, they rejected the plea of the *New York Times* for a "united action" on the part of the United States, England, and France to subdue China quickly and bring her "within the compass of nations." [68] Most of the editors sampled believed that the Chinese "insults" had been sufficiently avenged by Seymour and Foote and that it was time to negotiate new treaties. The editor of the *New York Times*, however, agreed with Foote that with the Chinese there could be "no correspondence except the correspondence of guns." [69]

Only the *New York Herald* agreed that more "decisive measures" against China were still necessary, but Bennett opposed any formal alliance to accomplish this. The Western nations should simply continue to bombard China independently without any "premeditated plan" :

In a word, the four leading nations of the world appear to be forced by circumstances to make an end of China. For our part we see this consummation with unmingled pleasure. For years the intercourse of the civilized and commercial nations with Asiatics has been degrading, senseless and absurd. . . . We submit that the world is too small, and life too short for us all to wait till blockheads of this denseness learn common sense by experience. . . . Bombardment is the only argument that should be brought to bear on them. While we regret to counsel bloodshed, it is a consoling circumstance, however, that there are in China nearly four hundred millions of people, and that lusty boys are not worth over four dollars at the sea ports, and good looking girls three. When the material is so plentiful and so cheap, a little of it may be wasted without much injury. . . . If the great rivers are opened by such a war, it is a worthy investment.[70]

Over the next two months Bennett sporadically ran jingoistic headlines asking "Shall the United States Go to War?" and answering yes, "on every ground—policy, expediency, justice and humanity." [71] Of course, consistency was not Bennett's forte, and in between such headlines he would sober up and quietly muse that it was perhaps more prudent simply to let England do America's fighting in China.[72]

But Henry Raymond in the *New York Times* apparently had a more developed sense of national honor than did Bennett and pleaded that America's reputation was being "sullied" by avoiding war in China only to reap the harvest of a British victory.[73] When Lord Napier left Washington with nothing more than President Buchanan's pledge for "moral cooperation" in China, Bennett was furious that no concessions had been guaranteed in return for such a pledge.[74] Raymond, on the other hand, expressed disgust that "the bugbear of entangling alliances" had prevented the president from fully meeting his obligations in China. If Americans believed that neutrality would be rewarded by the Chinese, it was "pure nonsense," he insisted; the only distinction between foreigners made by the Celestials was one between "two kinds of 'foreign devils,' " and "whatever privileges Americans enjoy in China are the product of British arms." [75] "Those persons in this country who have persisted in regarding the war now waging in China as a war of conquest, provoked by England, in which we as Americans, have no possible interest . . . should read the correspondence between American merchants in China and Commodore Armstrong," another editorial in the *New York Times* recommended.[76] To Raymond, American policy in China had to be predicated on "two truths" : that the Chinese do not distinguish between foreigners and that Americans in China have "virtually been under the protection of the British flag." [77]

Officers in the United States Naval Academy apparently took the jingoism of a few newspapers and magazines seriously. At least, the class of 1857 was prepared for a war in China, and middies were told during a howitzer drill that the weapon could "destroy a host of Chinamen." The seniors were warned that they were bound for ships fitting out for China where they "may soon have the opportunity of repeating the shell and grape practice in earnest." [78] The new United States commissioner in China in 1857, the missionary Peter Parker, was also scheming to involve his country in the war and seize Formosa for her in the process.[79]

With the appointment of William B. Reed as Parker's successor at the end of 1857, the United States was represented by an official who was more scrupulously neutral than his predecessor. But Reed, too, was nevertheless rebuffed by Commissioner Yeh at Canton, who told him that he "could not think of admitting any barbarian inside the walls," it was reported.[80] The neutralists should be satisfied, crowed the *New York Times,* now that "we have lost respect on all sides." [81] When Lord Elgin received the same treatment in his attempt at negotiations, he simply called in the Royal Navy, assaulted Canton once more, and carted Yeh off to India as a prisoner of war. The *New York Times* expressed gratitude to England for having "vindicated the honor of Christendom." Will the Americans ever learn from their Anglo-Saxon cousins whose "relations with China have been marked by peculiar foresight and wisdom"? "The American eagle stood perched aloft while the lion pulled down his prey; and now that the danger is over, it does not object to play the part of the vulture," declared Raymond with disdain.[82]

As a result of Lord Elgin's action the Chinese agreed to meet with representatives of Western nations at Tientsin in 1858 to draw up new treaties. Once there, the mandarins did not move fast enough to suit the British representatives, and the Royal Navy kicked over a few more "mud forts," as they were popularly called, in order to speed up Celestial deliberations. Not a single editor chided the English for their impatience or aggression, and many began to agree with the *New York Times* that this was the only way to deal with such "cunning and treacherous" people: ". . . anyone conversant with the history of affairs in China during the past eighteen months can arrive at no other conclusion than that by force, and force alone, can the Chinese government and people be compelled or persuaded to accept and recognize the principles of International Law." [83]

Just as the Chinese question seemed to be settled, another incident recaptured the spotlight for China in the American press in 1859. Arriving at the mouth of the river to Tientsin to present the 1858 treaties fully ratified by their governments, representatives of England, France, and the United States found new barriers erected in the Gulf of Pei-ho replacing the ones destroyed by the Royal Navy a year earlier. Impatient over this, the British began to blow them up once more when they found themselves caught in a murderous crossfire at Taku. To the shock of all present, five English gunboats were sunk and a combined French and British landing force was repulsed with a great many casualties. It was in this battle that the American Commodore Tatnall rushed to aid the English with the now famous remark attributed to him, "Blood is thicker than water." [84]

Professor Tyler Dennett ascribed Tatnall's action to the fact that both he and Ward were Southerners who quickly saw in the battle "a conflict of color." Stephen Decatur's diary records that he heard Tatnall swear that he would "be damned if he'd stand by and see white men butchered before his eyes." [85] Whether or not a sectionally engendered racial conception motivated Tatnall and Ward, it does not account for the fact that most Americans in China and Yankee editors back home shared their sympathies in this case. Samuel Wells Williams, who was present at the battle of the Taku forts, wrote home to his brother, "I never, I think, felt such a disappointment as when I saw the English defeated last June. . . . I am sure that the Chinese need harsh measures to bring them out of their ignorance, conceit and idolatry; why then deplore the means used to accomplish this end so much as to blind our minds to the result which God seems to be advancing by methods whose inherent wrong he can punish at his own time." [86] Another American witness, George Washington Heard, Jr., expressed the same sentiment in a letter to his parents immediately following the battle, and he insisted that his reaction was unanimously shared by all Americans on the scene.[87]

Editorial comments in the United States paralleled the feelings expressed by American witnesses on the scene of the battle. China's successful ambush of the landing force was characterized as "clearcut treachery" and used to strengthen the stereotype of the Chinese as a cunning and deceitful people. England's defeat was "a hidden and calamitous event" for "the civilized world," mourned one editor. "The sinister Chinese showed no guns or soldiers in the forts" (while the Royal Navy was innocently blowing up the river barriers in an unselfish effort intended to bring civilization to the Chinese, one must presume), when suddenly the Manchu garrison opened fire in what this editor called "a premeditated act of treachery." [88]

It took "the perfidy of the Chinese" at Taku to fully convince the editor of the *Springfield Republican* of the wisdom of British policy in China.[89] "The fact is, the Chinese are as treacherous as they are timid. They have a keen sense of fear, but a dull sense of honor. It is one thing to get them to sign a treaty, and quite another to get them to abide by it," wrote another editor to justify his unequivocal support for the use of force in China after the Taku "ambush." [90]

The editor of *Littell's* did question "the haste" with which the press took "for granted, what no doubt is the natural and most obvious interpretation of this calamitous affair—that the Chinese government had treacherously determined to break faith with the English and entrap them into a murderous slaughter." [91] Some correspondents were also critical of the American press reaction to Taku. If the Russians had taken Liverpool in a war and then sent a powerful fleet to London to conclude a peace treaty would the English permit it to enter the Thames? one demanded in the *New York Evening Post*.[92] Another correspondent even suggested, incorrectly, that the allies had blundered into the wrong river, the barricade to which had not been destroyed a year earlier, and that the mandarins were waiting to greet the diplomats at the correct estuary a few miles away.[93]

But few editors sampled responded to these suggestions. Greeley continued to caution his readers that "China is as much sinned against as sinning," [94] and others expressed concern over the usurpation by Tatnall of Congress' prerogative to declare war; but no one accused him of aiding English imperialism, of abetting the opium trade, or of racism for that matter, as would have been the case in 1840.[95] A Boston editor could not refrain from gloating a bit over England's defeat "at the hands of an army that has been the laughing stock of all civilized nations." [96] But the overwhelming majority of American editors expressed indignation over what they proclaimed to be a carefully planned and treacherous Chinese act that violated all bounds of human decency. As the *North American Review* expressed it, the ambush was "a provocation by these Oriental heathens such as has never been given before, and in comparison with which the petty indignities—the burning of opium-chests and the penning up of a plenipotentiary in the Canton factories . . . are as nothing." [97] From its refusal in 1842 to publish John Quincy Adams' justification of the Opium War and the Taku incident in 1859 this journal had indeed come full circle. It had the company of the *Christian Examiner,* one of the few religious publications in the United States that had refused to endorse the first Anglo-Chinese war. Now it too supported the British and described China as "the most illiberal, narrow-minded, cruel, despotism in any of the semi-civilized empires of Asia," whose "weak and besotted monarch" was "a perfect example of Chinese pride, bigotry and tyranny." Under such conditions war between the stagnant Chinese and progressive Europeans was not only necessary but almost inevitable, the editorial concluded.[98]

The treatment of U.S. Ambassador John Ward, who had gone to Peking after the Taku incident as a neutral, was seized upon by several overwrought editors. "Mr. Ward and Legation Boxed Up in a Most Undignified Manner," one headline squalled.[99] Reports that Chinese official notices proclaimed Ward a tribute bearer and that in Peking the American legation was held prisoner were published. Not since Macartney's mission in 1793 had representatives of a Western nation been so humiliated, two editors protested.[100]

The following year, news that the allies had returned to Taku, razed the troublesome forts, and burned the emperor's summer palace was greeted by most journals as well-deserved retribution for the "insolence" of Peking: "However much we may disapprove of the process of making customers by force, we cannot but wish the allies well out of this." [101] There were no such qualifications on the pages of the *North American Review,* which felt that Lord Elgin had avenged a century of Western "humiliation" in China, and only regretted that Sir George Staunton could not have lived to see it.[102] But Bennett also warned that should Peking's authority be destroyed in the process it would play into the hands of the Taipings with whom it would be just as impossible to deal. "Perfidy and deceit are the great elements of Celestial diplomacy" for both the imperialist and rebel, he reminded his readers.[103]

A great deal of journalistic attention was given to "atrocities" committed by the Chinese during the clashes between 1856 and 1860. The first incident to attract notice was the murder of Howard Cunningham, an employee of Heard and Company, by a Chinese mob in 1856.[104] After the fighting over the *Arrow* incident began, a report reached the United States that the Chinese had decapitated several Americans under the impression that they were English and publicly displayed their heads. This was described in the *New York Herald* as a "wanton act of barbarity" that had "incensed" the American people.[105] In general, military actions of the British were treated as legitimate, whereas Chinese attempts to retaliate were reported with horror and repugnance. Thus, the destruction of foreign factories by the Chinese was reported with a loathing that approached disbelief, and the execution of forty Britons and Americans was labeled a "vicious massacre." In contrast Britain's bombardment of Canton seemed a "just retaliation for the violation of treaty rights by Chinese officials." [106] As the editor of the *Evening Transcript* in Boston explained it, "the violation of the treaty in such a treacherous manner, calls forth demands for a terrible vengeance." [107]

Chinese actions were reported with tone words that connoted barbarity. The European factories were reported destroyed "with the savage fury of a pagan people." [108] At the same time, Sir John Bowring charged that mandarins had attempted to poison the entire English population in Hong Kong. His official report was published on the front page of the *New York Times* under the headline, "The Chinese Barbarities." Arsenic had allegedly been put into the bread used by the English community, but in such a large dose that the victims rejected the nauseating pabulum and there were no fatalities. "This mode of warfare is hard to deal with . . . ," Bowring wrote. "Large premiums have been offered

. . . to anyone who shall set fire to our houses, kidnap or murder us." [109]

The Anglo-Chinese conflicts between 1856 and 1860 served to endorse or nationalize some of the charges commonly brought against the Chinese by traders, diplomats, and Protestant missionaries over several decades. It is not possible to measure how many additional Americans became converts to the unflattering image of China that had long been standard belief in these groups. However, by comparing American press reactions in the two Anglo-Chinese conflicts, one can easily see the degree to which the unfavorable stereotype of the Chinese had affected American editors between 1840 and 1857.

So contrary to the natural order of things was the defeat of the British at Taku as to generate a belief that Russian, not Chinese, gunners had been responsible. Young G. W. Heard recorded in his diary that Royal Marines who got close enough to one fort heard the Russian word for powder being used. Whoever manned the guns, Heard reasoned, "understood the science of gunnery too well" to have been Chinese, and he concluded that they had to be "runaway sailors" or Russians.[110] This offered a convenient rationalization of the defeat for the British military and a fascinating bit of intrigue for some American journalists.[111] Sir John Bowring exploited this rumor with warnings that Russian soldiers were pouring into China and that Siberian soldiers serving China were primarily loyal to Russia. "There are growing signs of brotherhood" between "the fur clad Russians" and the Chinese, warned *Littell's*.[112] Bennett used the fear of such an unholy alliance to justify his demand in 1857 that Americans go to war with China if only to make sure that Russia did not gain a foothold there. Reports of a Russian fleet in Chinese waters enhanced his anguish over the American failure to fully appreciate the danger.[113]

This faintly expressed fear of Russian influence is significant only in that the first phase of an articulate yellow peril theory envisioned Russian-led and -tutored Chinese soldiers overrunning the West. By coincidence, General G. J. Wolseley, an important architect of the yellow peril concept, was a veteran of the second Anglo-Chinese war.[114]

Perhaps these latent fears caused some American editors to attribute greater significance to the second Anglo-Chinese war than was warranted. "This Chinese war may yet come to be the leading event of the middle of the century," Bennett suggested.[115] Karl

Marx had predicted that China's weakness would invite a struggle there between the European powers which would accelerate the downfall of the ruling elites back in Europe. As a special correspondent for the *New York Tribune* in 1853, Marx wrote: "It may seem a very strange, and a very paradoxical assertion that the next uprising of the people of Europe, and their next movement for republican freedom and economy of government, may depend . . . on what is now passing in the Celestial Empire. . . ." [116]

The Crimean War distracted Marx for a time; but when it failed to achieve his anticipated destruction of the old order in Europe, he once again turned to China in his reports to the *Tribune* as the scene of the last self-defeating struggle between European powers over Chinese spoils. In 1857, Marx was fond of stressing the irony of China bringing about his predicted disorder in Europe while England and France claimed that they were only interested in restoring order in China. [117] For a number of American editors, the Sepoy Mutiny in India, the Royal Navy's shocking defeat at Taku, and the persistent rumors of Russian machinations in China heightened the sense of a "new era" in Asia, one that was full of significance and potential danger for the West. "We are led to the irresistable conclusion that behind the dissimulation and treachery that have marked the official intercourse of the Asiatics with Europeans, there is something far deeper than a mere wish to deceive," Bennett wrote, in a fantastic attempt to relate Cawnpore, the *Arrow* seizure, and Taku to some sort of Asian conspiracy against Europe that extended from Delhi to Peking. But Bennett's style was so manic that in the same editorial he went from a sort of yellow peril foreboding to jubilation over the economic opportunity that an Asian revolt against Europe might present to Americans. As he shifted moods, he was happy that the United States had remained neutral and, forgetting his own castigations of the Chinese and earlier counsel for war, decided that America had remained China's friend all along. The Celestial immigrant returning to China would also help America's reputation because of "the favorable treatment in California" that he received, Bennett added, impervious to the indignities such immigrants suffered and to some of his own editorials denouncing this immigration. [118]

American interest in China was understandably diminished during the Civil War in the United States, although the final defeat of the Taipings by Charles Gordon's "Ever-Victorious Army" in 1864 made an ephemeral splash on the front pages of American newspapers. Once again the Chinese were depicted as a savagely cruel and treacherous people. The rebels had struck a bargain with Gordon, it was reported, but that pledge was ignored by the mandarins who had the leaders of the insurrection beheaded, while imperial troops plundered, raped, tortured, and slaughtered their followers. With the Americans preoccupied with their own civil war, it was feared by a few editors that "perfidious Albion" would now take over China "as Pizarro did of the Peruvian Inca." [119] This return to the more traditional suspicions of British imperialism in China may have been influenced by English sympathy and aid for the Confederate cause in the war between the states.

Only two years after Appomattox, however, Peking's appointment of the retiring American minister, Anson Burlingame, as a roving ambassador for the Celestial Empire rearoused American public and editorial interest. Overnight, China became "civilized" and on the threshhold of entering "the family of nations." A favorite editorial theme was the romantic conception that the United States as the youngest nation had a special destiny with China, the most ancient one. Fate had decreed this relationship, and within it lay unbounded opportunity for the United States, on which that "shrewd Yankee," Burlingame, would surely capitalize. The cautious restraint displayed by the American press toward the news that the Taipings had turned Christian was totally abandoned in the editorial response to the Burlingame mission.[120] One editor who habitually characterized the Chinese as barbaric and treacherous suddenly declared, "When the forefathers of our best Boston people were digging for roots in swamps and forests . . . , the Chinese were rich, civilized, fertile in poets, philosophers, economists, moralists and statesmen." [121]

In the process of leading the Chinese back to civilization, Burlingame would, of course, Americanize them so that they would become our best customers and allies in Asia, one editor gloated, noting that already one of the New England diplomat's chief Chinese assistants was a Seu-Ki Yu, who had been in disgrace for writing a book on the West twenty years earlier in which he eulogized George Washington.[122] "American supremacy" in China and all of Asia was in the making, this editor maintained.[123] The sample of editors thought this was to be the American century. It seems that neutrality in the Anglo-Chinese wars finally paid some dividends, and "the Chinese really love us Americans better" than Europeans, Dana observed in the *New York Sun*.[124]

While editors were bestowing lavish praise on Burlingame and his mission, Americans in China seemed less happy with the arrangement. The eagle-eyed Bennett pointed out that a good many Americans in China were attacking the Burlingame Treaty.[125] Letters from missionaries and a few traders to domestic newspapers argued that Burlingame was being exploited by the Chinese, who were scheming to get the Westerners to lay down their arms without making any real concessions of their own. As one missionary put it, the West was "being bamboozled by the Yankee Chinaman without a tail," and he urged a quick return to Britain's "old Bulldog policy." [126]

Ironically, a key spokesman for this critical minority was Burlingame's successor and newly appointed American minister to China, J. Ross Browne, who was abruptly dismissed by President Grant for his transparent hostility to China. Browne rejected the prevalent belief that China had adopted a "more enlightened policy." As "a pagan state," he insisted that she would never recognize treaty obligations in terms of international law and urged a vigorous Anglo-American program in China, or what various New York editors described as "gunboat diplomacy" or a "throat policy." [127] It is interesting that the editors of the *New York Times* and *New York Herald* were particularly caustic toward Browne and his followers, conveniently forgetting that a decade earlier their own publications had counseled Anglo-American force as the only way to civilize China. But in 1869, Bennett dismissed the ideas of Browne and his "British party" as "laughable." There they are, "God and Mammon side by side," said Bennett of the American missionary and British trader.[128]

The missionary opposition to the apparent rapprochement symbolized by Burlingame's appointment led to sharp editorial attacks on men of the cloth in China.[129] Bennett suggested that missions be withdrawn from Asia as a "bad business." He lampooned the missionaries as "apostles of Exeter Hall . . . interesting and venturesome ladies, Brahmapootra explorers, writers for the magazines and dabblers in the sale of naval stores." [130] In another editorial Bennett observed how few converts had been made in China and exclaimed, "Can we wonder . . . when we see such ignorance, assumption and narrow minded bigotry in these missionaries? But their role is ended. They belong to the times that are passed. Greater agents of civilization have replaced them." [131]

Such a crudely direct assault can easily be dismissed as a product of Bennett's mercurial temperament. But the growing tendency of other editors to omit Christianity from their conceptions of progress is hard to ignore. Technological innovation and commercial development now seemed more important instruments of civilization than religious proselytism. Bennett was specific on this—"the new Gospel of Peace, progress and civilization, is found in the telegraph and steam power"—whereas in the remarks of others it was more a case of emphasis by omission.[132]

Plainly the long alliance between commercial and religious interests in China was coming under serious strain. The missionary usually attributed this to his conscientious attack on the opium trade. The validity of this assertion is difficult to assess. The missionaries did condemn the opium trade as immoral but they did not focus on their friends and compatriots in Canton who were responsible for it. Gutzlaff accepted free passage on opium traders plying the Chinese coast, and Williams even approved of legalizing the trade in 1858—if only to remove its corrupting influence. "The honorable English merchants and government can now exonerate themselves from the approbrium of smuggling this article. Bad as the triumph is, I am convinced that it was the best disposition that could be made of the perplexing question; legalization is preferable to the evils attending the farce now played, and we shall be the better when the drug is openly landed, and opium hulks and bribed inspectors are no more." [133] But no missionary went so far as to agree with Sir John Bowring that opium was "as harmless as tea." [134]

The Reverend Nevius argued that the first real crack in the edifice built by God and Mammon in China was the growing racism on the part of the merchant, who "would not distinguish between Christian Chinese and pagan Chinese." This was also true in the United States where the racist conception of the Chinese was dominant, Nevius complained. Too many Americans refused to believe that the Chinese could become Christians—not "reliable ones" at least.[135] Whatever the causes, the gulf between the two groups appeared to be widening in 1868 and an editorial in the *New York Observer* complained, "There is a lamentable want of sympathy in China between the commercial and religious interests of the Western nations. Seldom do we meet an Englishman or an American engaged in commerce in that portion of the East who seems to have a favorable regard for the labors of the missionary." [136]

Professor Bailey has called attention to California's quick disillusionment with the Burlingame Treaty because of its immigration provisions. "Interestingly enough, the West—particularly California—applauded the arrangement at the time, although this section was seen to change its views," Bailey summarized.[137] But the pattern of reaction in the less well-studied eastern states closely resembled what took place in California, except that it was not restricted to the immigration issue alone. Sanguine journalistic hopes for a new China which were dominant in 1868 and 1869 had been utterly blighted by 1870. The massacre of missionaries and Chinese Christians, reports of the murder of shipwrecked sailors, and the general harassment of all foreigners in China destroyed the confidence of the nation in Burlingame as a Yankee miracle-worker. The very editors who a few months earlier had welcomed China effusively into the family of "civilized" nations now dismissed the Burlingame Treaty as a "dead letter" and demanded "stronger measures" against the Celestial Empire.[138] Belatedly the *New York Times* apologized to ex-Commissioner Browne and agreed that force alone would change China: "We had as a nation been made the victims of overweening confidence and hopes, and the minister's [Browne's] statements were neither popular nor acceptable." [139]

The "Tientsin Massacre" was the most notorious of a series of popular reactions against Christians, missionaries, and foreigners in China. The first such disturbances in 1869 came at an awkward time with the last of the editorials proclaiming the "New China." Many editors refused to accept the validity of the reports at first. Bennett complained that those "favoring the British view" were "hinting that this new evidence of the barbarism of the Celestials ought to be taken as conclusive against any liberal or fair treatment of such people." The truth of the matter, suggested Bennett, was that the riots were due to the rivalry between several Christian sects and had nothing to do with Chinese officials.[140]

The *New York World* was one of the first publications to break the spell and accept the reports of xenophobic and anti-Christian violence at face value. The editor expressed wonder that Americans were "so credulous and soft hearted as to think that the mass of the Chinese people have become tolerant, benevolent, and merciful" simply by appointing an American minister and signing a treaty. He recommended perusal of a recently published book by Henry Lock, who had been imprisoned by the Chinese in 1859 while under a flag of truce and unmercifully tortured and beaten before his release. Deeply engrained national characteristics cannot be "revolutionized" by a treaty, the editor declared, "but this is the jargon which is talked, and which, we regret to say, passes current amongst us . . . in the very heyday of gushing sympathy with Pagandom." [141]

It was still six months before the murder of French nuns and priests at Tientsin, an event that was impossible to ignore and that finally convinced most editors that the Burlingame Treaty had not altered China's ancient tendency to xenophobia. The reports were "so horrible that they can scarcely be believed," one editor exclaimed.[142] Front pages were given over to lurid details of how nuns were stripped, raped, and horribly mutilated. Huge headlines announced, "The Massacre of Christians," "Another Chinese Outrage," "Chinese Perfidy," "Horrible Barbarities of the Chinese." These stories were accompanied by impassioned editorials denouncing the Chinese, demanding swift and terrible punishments, and expressing dismay that Burlingame had changed nothing.[143]

True to form, Bennett made the most radical shift, and began to give the developments in China a distinct racial twist. His editorials bore such titles as "Mongolian Intolerance," and he made it clear that the "fiendish behavior" was natural to "almond eyed heathens" whose atrocities were incident to "a war of race." [144] He also produced a horror story which accused the Chinese of drugging Christian children in an orphanage run by the Sisters of Mercy so that they could be shipped to Shanghai where their eyes and "private parts" were removed for the preparation of "mysterious drugs." Ironically, this was similar to the grotesque beliefs about the nuns which had goaded the mob into attacking them at Tientsin. Bennett noted this similarity but reminded his readers that it was "absurd" to conceive of such behavior on the part of Christians, whereas anyone familiar with the pagan Chinese knew that they were quite capable of these hideous acts.[145]

Late in the summer of 1870 documents reached the American press that seemed to prove that the violence at Tientsin was no spontaneous action but the result of "insolent Chinese officials" who provoked the "depraved common people" into attacking the missions.[146] In the words of the *New York Times,* the massacre was "a deep laid and carefully prepared conspiracy incited if not actually projected by the mandarins." [147] Unwilling to let the missionary escape with a clean bill of health, however, some editors added that the "injudicious zeal of the missionary" was a "secondary cause." [148] The new evidence was the translation of pamphlets allegedly written and disseminated by mandarins in which the missionaries were accused of kidnapping, torturing, and sexually molesting Chinese children—charges, in fact, which sounded remarkedly similar to tracts published by American nativists about Catholic convents in the United States. But none of the editors sampled saw this parallel, any more than they saw a similarity between the violence at Tientsin and domestic riots directed against the Chinese in Los Angeles that very same year.[149]

These new documents angered American editors more than the details of the massacre itself. Horace Greeley, who only the week before their disclosure was urging caution in assigning the Chinese government responsibility for the atrocities, now conceded that no other explanation was possible. "The full details furnished by our correspondent forbid us longer to indulge in weak excuses for the Chinese," Greeley explained.[150] The *New York Times* declared that the Chinese had torn up the Burlingame Treaty and thrown the pieces in the face of the West. Each "unconscious barbarism truly Chinese" was new proof that the Western nations could not rely upon traditional diplomacy in dealing with such people, and the editor urged his government "to cooperate with other nations in taking any measures . . . which may be found necessary." Decisive action against the Chinese was long overdue: "We can scarcely wonder that our countrymen . . . in China are getting impatient under our do-nothing policy." [151]

Bennett, too, issued a call to arms almost continually during the last few months of 1870. This time, he not only agreed to a formal alliance with other nations in dealing with the "evil cunning" and "vicious treachery" of the Chinese, but also he was angry enough to include the Russians whose influence in China he habitually feared.[152] Bennett even regretted that Napoleon III was not around any more to dash impetuously into action against the "Chinese barbarians," conveniently forgetting how he had ridiculed that hapless French leader when he was in power.[153] The cunning Chinese had in fact focused on French missionaries because the mandarins believed that the Franco-Prussian War would make retribution unlikely, Bennett charged. Hence, it was imperative that a united Western front teach China that treaties cannot be violated with impunity. France and Prussia should "shake hands in Tientsin and then all parties go straight to Pekin," he suggested.[154]

This time, however, the *Times* and *Herald* in New York were not alone in demanding that Americans take an active part in a punitive expedition against the Chinese. Every newspaper in the sample expressed such sentiment at least once during 1870. The "fiendish and demonic atrocities" demanded swift action by all nations in the civilized world, agreed the editor of the *Albany Evening Journal*.[155] Is it possible that Americans would shrink from their duty to help put down this "ill-bred, lawless race of wolves" in China? demanded the *Salem Gazette*.[156] The longer Americans delayed in reacting to the massacre at Tientsin, the more likely that the Chinese will start in on Americans in China, reasoned several editors in New York and Massachusetts.[157] A Boston editor dug up the thirty-year-old lecture on the Opium War by John Quincy Adams to support his argument that if an "exclusive nation" refused to "enjoy friendly intercourse" with other states, "it was the right and duty of progressive humanity to compel them to be neighborly and reciprocal."[158] Even Greeley reluctantly joined his colleagues in calling for joint action, although a week earlier he had counseled restraint in Washington.[159]

Most of these editors were satisfied, however, with the arrival of an American naval squadron in Chinese waters under Admiral Rogers, the swift Celestial apologies to the French, the summary execution of fifteen Chinese in Tientsin, and the dismissal of two mandarins in the area. Indeed, the speed and efficiency with which the culprits were rounded up and beheaded without benefit of costly and time-consuming trials by jury won the admiration of Bennett who declared that "our criminal jurists must take a few lessons from or in Pekin."[160] But disturbing tales soon began to filter back to the press that once again the cunning Chinese had hoodwinked the West and had actually made heroes out of the executed. Their heads had been sewn back on to preserve in death their physical integrity, an honor never afforded a criminal. They were buried in sumptuous coffins befitting great men, and their families were handsomely rewarded by the Celestial government.[161] The dismissed mandarins were in reality elevated to higher posts elsewhere; and the executions, intended to placate the French, were of fifteen common criminals who had nothing to do with the massacre, it was also reported.[162]

On the heels of these disclosures new "outrages" were reported in 1871, this time against American missionaries, Protestant churches, and shipwrecked crews of various Western nationalities.[163] The *New York Times* attributed the new wave of violence to Peking's decision to make "martyrs" out of "murderers," the sacking of Prince Kung, the only Celestial official in whom "there was room for belief in a real desire for progress," and the weakness of the Western response to the Tientsin Massacre.[164] Two weeks later the *Times* ran translations of new antiforeign pamphlets allegedly still being distributed by Chinese officials; and under a headline "A Death Blow to Corrupt Doctrines," it was declared that this latest evidence fully impugned any "lingering hope yet indulged in by some of Chinese good faith and desire for progress."[165] Bennett returned to his demands for action in China, running flamboyant headlines announcing "Another Chinese Outrage" or "Chinese Perfidy—Will There Be War?" A week later Bennett answered that question in another headline: "What China Wants—A Good Sound Thrashing and the Armed Occupation of Pekin by the Outside Barbarians."[166] Bennett was incensed that one xenophobic tract had described Christians and foreigners as "a depraved non-human species," although the *New York Herald* had relegated all Chinese to a similar category on more than one occasion.[167]

Reports of Chinese atrocities against foreigners and Christian churches continued to inflame American editors over the next decade.[168] Perhaps the apogee of indignation was reached when it was learned that Chinese mobs were destroying the railroads and telegraph lines being built by Westerners in China. Nothing more clearly demonstrated the stupidity, superstition, and perversity of the Chinese than this retrogressive policy.[169]

The greatly increased attention afforded by the newly established mass media to events in China between 1850 and 1870 brought the question of Chinese civilization to the notice of millions of Americans who had previously ignored its existence. In the process, the unfavorable stereotype of the Chinese initially shaped by traders, missionaries, and diplomats was marketed more widely. The editorial reactions to these events attest to the viability of the image of the Chinese created by these three "inside dopesters." No new themes about the Chinese were created by these occurrences, but new illustrative material was developed lending credence to those already established.

The distortion and vitiation of the Christian message by the Taipings reenforced the belief in the obliquity and perversity of the Chinese mind that had long been stressed by missionaries. It rendered more plausible the contention of the exclusionist that the Chinese were incapable of being Christianized. The conception of Celestial cunning and treachery was strengthened by the alleged ambush at Taku and the deceitful appointment of Burlingame to mislead the West into believing that Peking was ready to

abide by international law. Reports of the violation and torture of
French nuns supported the axiom of Chinese cruelty and sexual
perversity. Sensational handling of Sir John Bowring's charges further promoted the fear of the Chinaman's diabolical art in mixing
and administering strange and lethal poisons. It provoked a long
article on this alleged Chinese skill in the *American Journal of
Science and Arts.* "It is not our purpose to point out all the viru-
lent agents which unscrupulous Chinamen are likely to employ
against an enemy," the author prefaced his description of various
deadly Chinese concoctions, some of which would be inhaled by
the intended victim. He also asserted that some of Commissioner
Lin's advisers in 1840 had suggested infecting the British invaders
with leprosy, but it was deemed impractical since the effect would
not be quick enough.[170] Stories of strange poisonings in Chinatowns in the United States were legion during the last three decades of the nineteenth century, and it was believed in 1883 that
an entire jury in Philadelphia had been mysteriously poisoned for
acquitting a white "rough" who had murdered a Chinese resident.[171] Undoubtedly these fantasies were triggered in part by
the weird concoctions of Chinese apothecaries, but they were also
confirmed by the sensational treatment of Bowring's accusations.

Even more detrimental to China's reputation was the corroboration perceived in these events to support the conviction that the
Chinese were, in the words of the *New York Times,* "incapable of
civilization." [172] Articulated before, particularly by despondent
missionaries, the Taiping experience, China's alleged failure to
live up to treaties, and finally the destruction of Western technological improvements enhanced the belief at a time when modern
racists were theorizing a biological or genetic basis to civilization.
It was this combination of racist theory and the unfavorable image
of the Chinese that provided the exclusionist with one of his most
persuasive arguments.

American editors did not always consciously relate the happenings in China between 1850 and 1870 to the question of Chinese
immigration into the United States. But this was not always necessary. The Chinese in California—and in New York, New Jersey,
Pennsylvania, and Massachusetts by 1870—were uppermost in the
minds of Americans; and it would not have been easy to separate
reports of barbarity and perversity in China from the Celestial
immigrants. The *New York Times,* wanting to continue Chinese
immigration for its economic benefits, made conscious attempts to
mitigate the effect that the reports from China would have on the

immigration issue. "John Chinaman at home is a somewhat different kind of being from the meek and submissive person who
quietly endures a good many unmerited kicks on this continent
and elsewhere," the editor explained in the middle of his denunci-
ation of the xenophobic mobs in China.[173] But such assurances
failed to assuage the fears of many eastern editors; and one in
Auburn, New York, expressed a common concern when he wrote
in response to the news of the Tientsin Massacre: "This is the
refined nation, and these are the people, which some of our fellow
citizens are very anxious to have emigrate to this country . . . we
prefer that they should stay at home." [174] It was this relationship
that was so frequently exploited by the sinophobes, even the more
sophisticated ones such as Edwin Meade, who, in a lecture before
the Social Science Association of America, described how the nuns
were exposed, violated, and "deliberately cut in pieces" which
were then thrown to the "infuriated mob," before he asked:
"Capable of such deeds, can the injection of such a race into our
body politic be viewed by any thinking American without anxiety
and alarm?" [175]

PART THREE

Developments in the United States and the Chinese Image

As the type of the Negro is foetal, that of the Mongol
is infantile. And in strict accordance with this we
find their government, literature and art are infantile
also. They are beardless children, whose life is a task,
and whose chief virtue consists in unquestioning
obedience. Were Mr. [John Stuart] Mill an anthropologist, we might point out to him . . . the racial
element in humanity.

"On the Mongolian Race of Eastern Asia," *Anthropological Review*, IV (1866), 120.

It is true that ethnologists declare that a brain capacity of less than 85 cubic inches is unfit for free
government, which is considerably above that of the
coolie as it is below the Caucasian.

Edwin R. Meade before the Social Science Association
of America, Annual Meeting in Saratoga, N.Y., Sept.
7, 1877, p. 17.

7

Domestic Adaptations of the Negative Stereotype, 1850-1882

The rise of the penny press, which was the newspaper sector of the
mass media revolution of the 1840s, had brought a vastly increased
emphasis on overseas developments, including those in China. At
the same time, Jacksonian America saw an upsurge of interest in
domestic developments that were likely to be social rather than
primarily political in nature. The magazines, unable to compete
with the daily newspapers for the freshest news from Washington
and overseas, turned naturally to subject matter that involved relatively slow change and detailed description and analysis. As a result, they constitute as important a source for observing the do-

mestication of sinophobic attitudes as the brash and noisy dailies.

One part of the adaptation process was the endorsement of older themes, by repetition and re-rooting in the American environment. A second was the creation of important new themes that owed little or nothing to developments in China, except of course the underlying suspicion and contempt for Chinese people and Chinese civilization. Chief among these newer critical themes were the fear of slavery, the emphasis on racial difference, and the menace of loathsome, contagious disease.

The newer themes owed much to certain key phenomena inside the United States that occurred just as the first Chinese immigrants began to trickle into the country. These phenomena exercised a crucial role in convincing the eastern states that the Chinese should be excluded. For one thing the Chinese arrived in the middle of the slavery controversy and were never able to shake the "coolie" label. They also arrived during the period when the work of Holmes, Lister, and Semmelweis made Americans more conscious of the relationship between dirt and disease. By the time the first exclusion law was enacted, these fears had advanced to the more sophisticated level of "Chinese germs." The period between 1850 and 1882 was also one in which a pseudo-scientific rationale for modern racism developed. Lastly, this period was what economic historians have labeled the "take-off period" in industrial development, when Americans more than ever equated change and technological innovation with progress. All these developments had a direct bearing on the national decision in 1882 to exclude the Chinese from American society and were throughly interwoven with the discussion that preceded it.

The themes about Chinese character that had been developed by traders, missionaries, and diplomats continued to appear in American magazines with increasing frequency after the Opium War. Every aspect of Chinese life was scrutinized, usually with a critical eye, by editors and contributors. Even Chinese underwear was the basis of one short article.[1] By opening up the interior of China, the Anglo-Chinese wars were partially responsible for the increase in reports and, incidentally, for testing the sinophile argument that the most egregious flaws in Chinese society did not extend beyond Canton and its environs. As though systematically contradicting this reasoning, reports poured in of surveys in interior villages where each villager admitted that he personally had disposed of three to six of his own offspring.[2] Such "empirical" reports led one editor to conclude that more than half of all infants born in China were murdered by their mothers.[3] "It appears from the evidence . . . that the practice of infanticide in China . . . really exists," the editor of the *Philadelphia Sun* stated with some surprise.[4]

Post-Opium War reports also included eyewitness accounts of poverty, disease, filth, and cruel executions throughout China. One lurid eyewitness account of the execution of a woman who had murdered her husband described how the breasts, buttocks, and fleshy parts of her legs were removed before final decapitation.[5] Indeed the association of cruelty with the Chinese was so general by 1856 that one American editor, on receiving the news that Chinese officials had erected the first imperial hospital, could not resist the chance afforded for a bit of sarcasm: "Founding hospitals in China! What? In China, whose ditches, canals and rivers are reported to be strewn ever and anon with the bodies of infants that of course have been killed by their horrid mothers. . . . Is it possible that, in the breasts of the Chinese, there can be one drop of the milk of human kindness, at least for children? " [6]

The Anglo-Chinese wars also served to open up China for Western women who heretofore were relegated to Macao while their husbands were in Canton. In the main it was the wives of missionaries who took advantage of this new privilege, and in a sense they constituted a new type of inside dopester. While iterating the same themes about the Chinese generated by their husbands, these wives tended to focus more on the family and role of women in China. Their reports of the filth that permeated the Chinese home and the horrors of opium smoking, polygamy, and infanticide found a ready outlet in the ladies' magazines which were multiplying with such fecundity in the middle of the nineteenth century. Missionaries had mentioned the filth in China before, but it was rarely clear whether they were referring to sexual habits and thoughts or to a lack of physical cleanliness. Their wives stipulated that the Chinese were both physically and morally unclean. Writing in the *Ladies' Repository,* Mrs. Barnaby reported that "the dwellings of even the wealthiest Chinamen are very rude . . . generally dirty with a disagreeable odor about them. . . . The floors are sometimes greasy enough to slide on." [7] So ingrained was the association of the Chinese with a personal and collective filth, that one New York tourist in California found it difficult to believe the immaculate appearance of Chinese immigrants: "They seem to come out of their filth as the eel from his skin, with a personal cleanliness that is marvelous, and to most, incredible." [8] An article in *Scribner's Monthly* in 1876 explained this paradox by asserting that "individually, John Chinaman is a clean human, collectively he is a beast. Follow him home and you will find . . . a herd of animals living in a state of squalor and filth at which even a Digger Indian would shudder."[9] A reputable American encyclopedia edited by George Ripley and Charles Dana in 1863 informed its readers that the Chinese were so filthy that they never changed their underwear until it wore out on their bodies.[10]

Americans became more conscious of the use of opium as a result of the wars in China. Detailed descriptions of the mechanics of smoking the drug and its degenerating effects were much more common in American magazines after 1840. The opium pipe became as much a symbol of Chinese culture as the queue or the tea cup, and the mass media gave the impression that Chinese adults of all classes were universally addicted to this pernicious drug.[11]

But more important in terms of its influence on the decision to exclude the Chinese immigrants was the relationship of these conceptions to particular social and intellectual changes taking place in American society in the nineteenth century. In a discussion of the transformation in his own lifetime of the image of China from "a paragon of nations" to "a most infamous and degraded people," the editor of the *American Quarterly Register* confessed that for him the hostility to progress in China was the strongest influence in this process.[12] Articles and reviews of books on China rarely failed to comment on the stagnation of Chinese life. For some contributors it was simply a question of race: The Chinese were by nature "imbeciles" and incapable of progress. But others related the Chinese resistance to change to their language and examination system which imprisoned the imagination and encouraged a reverence for the past.[13] It is amazing how much ire this alleged deficiency could arouse in some Americans. "You feel a horrible contempt of that beaverish people, that with all their pretention to literature, never cared to improve on the clumsy and contemptible jargon which served their purposes two thousand years ago; and you think all that yelping and chopping . . . were far better abolished," exclaimed one contributor to *Graham's Magazine* in 1853. The whole culture, particularly "the diabolic Chinese alphabet, the grammar, the *belle lettres*—all the tea-chest literature, in fact—ought to be burnt," he recommended, although he conceded to leave the Chinese their "idolatries" if only "to keep up the hearts of the missionaries."[14]

During the debate over exclusion, sinophobic congressmen

thoroughly exploited this theme. Contrasting China's great antiquity with her depraved contemporary state, they charged that the
Chinese were hopelessly devoid of any sense or capability of
progress. "Authors of the compass, they creep from headland to
headland in coasting voyages. . . . Discoverers of gunpowder,
they supply the world with firecrackers, while their soldiers fight
with bows and arrows," California's Johnson quoted from *Harper's* on the floor of Congress to support his argument that the Chinese could not fit into the American scheme of things and would
contaminate the spirit of progress in this country.[15] Ohio's William Mungen, in a plea to outlaw Chinese immigration in 1871,
stated, "Although at a period as early as the date of Thebes, in
Egypt, the Chinese had a settled form of government, what are
they now but a poor, miserable, dwarfish race of inferior
beings. . . ."[16] Fearful that this persuasive argument would
secure passage of an exclusion act, the editor of the *New York
Times* complained that "we shall instantly admit her [China's]
claim to be called civilized when she demonstrates her ability to
kill men in a scientific manner.[17]

The sharply contrasting manner in which Americans viewed the
Japanese at this time underscores the important role that their
perception of progress played in evaluating other societies. When
a few Americans experienced some difficulties in trading with the
Japanese in 1855, there was a briefly expressed tendency in American editorials to conclude that all members of the "Mongolian
race" were not only treacherous but retrogressive.[18] But few
Americans, except for the missionaries, had anything but praise
for the Japanese. As one trader expressed it, they were "a brave
race" and "much cleaner in their personal habits" than were the
Chinese.[19] Although the *New York Times* had objected to making military efficiency the criterion for civilization, it too admired
the Japanese in 1867 for "fielding troops in uniform," armed with
"breech loaders" and "well equipped men of war." It was no wonder that they had so "outstripped" the Chinese.[20] Even as visitors
to the United States, "the Japanese are quick to appreciate the advantages of foreign improvements of all kinds, and readily adopt
our manners and customs when travelling among us," while the
Chinese remains "a law unto himself."[21] The ultimate proof of
Japan's progressive spirit was her readiness to make war on China
in 1872. "They have shown an eagerness to avail themselves of the
advantages of our civilization, while their opponents [the Chinese]
continue to wrap themselves up in a selfish and haughty isola-

tion," Bennett declared. Carried away by his enthusiasm for a Sino-
Japanese war, Bennett announced that "Japan through the
United States" would "regenerate Asia"—in a series of "liberat-
ing" wars presumably.[22]

A recent study of nineteenth-century school books by Professor
Ruth Miller Elson reveals a similar preference for the Japanese as
"the most progressive people of the mongolian race." [23] In reading
the commentaries on the Chinese in geography texts, newspapers,
magazines, and congressional documents, one gets the impression
that this perceived lack of any sense of progress on the part of the
Chinese was as crucial as their alleged vices, paganism, and allegiance to a despotic form of government in rendering them totally
nonassimilable in the eyes of Americans.

But equally as influential in convincing America that it was
necessary to terminate the flow of Chinese workers into the country was the fear that this immigration was instituting a new form
of slavery here. Long before the first Chinese immigrant reached
California, the coolie system had aroused the suspicion of abolitionist circles in England and America. At first the term "hill
coolie" was applied to Asian Indians who were employed as contract laborers on plantations in Asia and Latin America under
conditions that provoked some protest from abolitionists.[24] The
Taiping disturbances in China had created conditions that encouraged Celestials to seek refuge on these plantations, and by
1852 the term "coolie" had become synonymous with the Chinese
immigrant irrespective of his destination.

Because American ships were frequently involved in carrying
Chinese coolies to South America and Caribbean islands, abolitionists in the United States were particularly suspicious that a
new slave trade was in operation. Stories about the "Odius Coolie
Trade," as it was labeled in a Boston headline in 1853, began to
appear in the American press.[25] The loss of the *Sea Witch* off
Cuba with hundreds of "coolies" on board precipitated a congressional investigation and a report by President Pierce on *Slavery
and the Coolie Trade* in 1856.[26] On a return trip to the United
States, the Reverend Peter Parker called on all righteous Americans to oppose both the opium and coolie trades.[27] News that
other famous American clippers such as the *Winged Racer* and
Westward Ho were involved in this "new slave trade" caused
enough of a scandal in Boston to force their owners to abandon
the business hastily.[28]

All of this led to a concern over the possibility that "Chinese slavery" was being instituted on the West Coast, a fear expressed in one Boston newspaper as early as 1853.[29] This provoked constant reassurances that the Chinese in California were not coolies but voluntary immigrants, and in this spirit Congress in 1862 passed a law stipulating that every Chinese immigrant bound for the United States had to be certified by an American official at the port of departure as a voluntary emigrant who fully understood the terms of his contract. Similar to the British Passengers Act passed by Parliament in 1855, Congress also prohibited American vessels from transporting "coolies" anywhere.[30]

With Negro slavery a dead issue after 1865, greater attention was focused on the coolie trade. Descriptions of coolies suffocating in crammed quarters on "slave decks," being burned to death or drowned in nautical catastrophies, and committing suicide or staging desperate and bloody mutinies conjured up all the horrors of the old "middle passage." [31] An extended headline in the *New York Herald* succinctly captured the journalistic reaction to these reports: "Slavers in the Pacific—The Coolie Trade—Dreadful Scenes on Board a Coolie-Trade Ship. Worse than Slavery. Death a relief—Barbarous Treatment of the Coolies—Bound and Beaten —Fortunate Relief—Fearful Tales of Suffering." [32] Horace Greeley demanded an immediate investigation of this "new form of slavery." [33] But Bennett was no abolitionist, and true to form he began to worry about excessive hysteria being created over the coolies after his newspaper had helped to sound the alarm. "Too much ignorance" was confusing the voluntary Chinese immigrants in California with the coolies in the Caribbean, he complained, and reminded his readers of the unwarranted hysterics in 1862 that had produced anti-coolie legislation.[34]

Only a few months after Bennett's sober second thought, however, a coolie revolt occurred on a plantation in Peru; and alarm took command again as he described the "most ferocious instincts on the part of the almond-eyed heathen. About two thousand of them armed with clubs, knives and axes, murdered the families of the plantation owners, and then prepared to sack a small village." [35] This report made Bennett wonder about the wisdom of permitting such "a degraded class of semi-barbarians" to enter the United States freely. But he also noted that the bloodthirsty but cowardly mob was dispersed by a mere two Peruvian officials and concluded that Californians should be able to control their Chinese long enough to exploit their cheap labor.[36]

New reassurances that the Chinese coming to America were not coolies proved necessary. To placate these fears, the secretary of state made public his repeated instructions to the American consul at Amoy to double check to see that each emigrant understood the terms of his contract and was leaving voluntarily.[37] The secretary of the treasury announced publicly that the law of 1862 was still in effect, and Bennett suggested that the government emphasize that the contracts bringing Chinese to this country were the same used to bring Germans and Irish.[38] In 1867 the editor of *De Bow's Review* expressed great surprise over "the dismal howl of the Republican press" at the arrival in New Orleans of twenty-three coolies. It was so "humanitarian" to remove them from Cuba, the editor confessed, that it made him feel "very much like an abolitionist. . . . These Northern cousins of ours are determined that the common and poor men of tawny hue shall not be permitted to come here. . . ."[39] More shipments of Chinese workers to New Orleans in 1870, two months after the arrival of seventy-five in Massachusetts, provoked another statement from the secretary of state to the effect that these were voluntary immigrants eager to return to China once their contracts had expired.[40]

In spite of the many public and private assurances to the contrary, the Chinese immigrant never lost his association with the coolie, an appellation readily bestowed upon him by friend and foe alike. Every newspaper, whether or not it supported the use of Chinese workers under contract, referred to the Chinese as "coolies." For example, a Boston editor who warmly greeted the arrival of Chinese laborers in his state in 1870 entitled his welcoming editorial "The Coolie in Massachusetts."[41] Russell Conwell was unusual in specifying that the term referred only to the lowest elements in the laboring classes which, he contended, made up but one-third of the total immigration of Chinese into California in 1869.[42] Unheeded were the protests of others who argued that "coolieism" implied slavery and should not be applied to the voluntary Chinese immigrants who alone were permitted to enter the United States.[43] Every editor in the sample, whether or not he favored the continuance of this immigration, expressed some fear at one time or another over the dangers of instituting a new form of slavery. For some it was a humanitarian concern, but for the overwhelming majority the fear was that another civil war could result.[44]

Southerners seemed to be unconcerned about reenforcing the impression that the Chinese was being imported to replace the

Negro slave who, now that he was emancipated, would simply die
out like the Indian.[45] "Opinions vary as to the character of the
Coolie; some authorities describing him as a demoralizing blight
to any community . . . ," *De Bow's* reported, "while on the other
hand travellers in *Mauritius, California* and *elsewhere* give him a
very good character." [46] Mauritius was the site of some of the
worst abuses of the "coolie system" reported in the press, and its
association with California in *De Bow's,* together with the use of
the term "imported" for describing the process of immigration,
could only confirm the worst suspicions of northerners.

Conwell added fuel to the fire by explaining that, even if the
Chinese immigrant was not actually a slave, his family back in
China would be sold into a very literal slavery if he defaulted in
paying his debt for passage. An illustration of the Chinese wife of a
delinquent emigrant to America on the block with her three children was included for effect. Conwell alleged that Chinese females
in California continued to be outright slaves, as most of them had
been in China.[47] Even the *New York Times* accepted it as a fact
that Chinese women were publicly auctioned in California and
sometimes even pawned; and the *Newburyport Herald* complained, "In spite of the war . . . proclamations and bills of
rights in constitutions, the heathen among us have slaves—buy
and sell women for the purpose of prostitution." [48]

In the congressional debates over Chinese immigration during
the 1870s, the issue of slavery was preeminent. Eastern congressmen were often more unyielding in their hostility than colleagues
from California who settled for such terms as "quasi-voluntary
servitude" and "quasi-slavery." [49] Henry Wilson of Massachusetts
considered Chinese immigration to the United States and elsewhere as a "modern slave trade system" pure and simple.[50] Congressman Robert McLane of Maryland, who had been commissioner to China between 1853 and 1855, personally testified that
coolies bound for California were held in jails prior to their departure.[51] Senators James Blaine of Maine and Thomas Bayard of
Delaware, Congressmen Peter de Uster of Wisconsin and Roswell
Flower of New York persistently echoed Wilson's charge: The
Chinese immigrants did not come of their own volition, but were
rounded up in China like a herd of animals and sold as slaves to
satisfy human greed.[52] "These coolies are more absolute slaves
than ever the negroes of the South were," declared C. E. De Long,
the former minister to Japan.[53]

The degree to which the fear of slavery affected national leaders on the Chinese question is perhaps best measured by President Grant's plea in his annual address of 1874:

I call the attention of Congress to a generally conceded fact that the great proportion of the Chinese immigrants who come to our shores do not come voluntarily, to make their homes with us and their labor productive of general prosperity, but come under contracts with head-men who own them almost absolutely. In a worse form does this apply to Chinese women. Hardly a perceptible percentage of them perform any honorable labor, but they are brought for shameful purposes, to the great demoralization of the youth of these localities. If this evil practice can be legislated against, it will be my pleasure as well as my duty to enforce any regulation to secure so desirable an end.[54]

The Chinese were also unfortunate in arriving in the middle of another controversy which helped to incubate modern racist theory and render the Chinese nonassimilable on biological grounds. American intellectuals in the 1850s were hotly debating whether the races of mankind had sprung from a single origin (monogenesis) or diverse seeds (polygenesis). Although the latter viewpoint was defeated, the fear of miscegenation and the germ theory of culture appear to have been important by-products of the controversy. They caused a loss of American confidence in the melting pot as far as the Chinese were concerned.

Until 1850, most American intellectuals clung to the concept of monogenesis, for both religious and political reasons. All men were the children of Adam and Eve and in 1776 had been declared equal. Racial differences were seen as a function of environmental variation. Moreover, all the great names in the field of science from Linnaeus and Buffon to Blumenbach and Lamarck supported environmentalism and monogenesis. It was not that Americans underplayed racial differences, of course, but they were confident that by reordering the environment they could alter the specimen both physically and culturally. The melting-pot concept came easily to people who held this theory of racial differences.[55]

Only a few challenges to this view were manifested before 1840. Reports on China stimulated a Boston editor to ask in 1784: "Are all mankind derived from the same common origin? If so, . . . how comes it to pass, that there is such an almost infinite dissimilarity between men of different nations, as to Statue, Form, Colour, Understanding, &c?" Two months later came his response, endorsing the genesis story and dismissing those contemporary mavericks who argued that there were three Adams and Eves of different colors.[56] Early in the following century, Dr. Samuel Latham Mitchell suggested that the differences between the white, black, and tawny races could not be explained by climate alone. He spoke of "an internal physical cause of the greatest moment," though he still regarded the three races as members of the same species.[57] The first direct challenge to the belief in the indivisibility of mankind came from Dr. Charles Caldwell's *Thoughts on the Original Unity of the Human Race* (1830).[58] Caldwell had expressed these ideas earlier on the pages of the journal he helped to edit in Philadelphia, *Port Folio*. This was also the first American magazine, in 1811, to criticize the Chinese severely in terms that approached racism.[59]

But serious consideration of polygenesis had to await a more systematic means of measuring racial differences, which ethnologists such as Retzius in Sweden and Samuel G. Morton in Philadelphia supplied in the form of skull measurements. The earlier "aesthetic" approach, as Stanton labels it,[60] which described physical differences verbally in terms of facial angles, head shape, facial configuration and skin coloring, led to a good deal of confusion. This is perhaps best illustrated by one editor's quandary over the fact that everything about the Chinese pointed to "Mongol," yet "the facial angle would place many Chinese in the Caucasian race."[61] Confusion over inexact indices led some to classify the Chinese as a "Mongolian softened down" and others to relate him to the Hottentot.[62] Dr. Charles Pickering finally concluded that there were two whites races (Caucasian and Abyssinian) and three brown ones (Mongolian, Hottentot, and Malay).[63] By arranging Blumenbach's five races according to the mean internal capacity of their skulls, Morton not only offered a neater system of classification, but a seemingly more scientific means of evaluating racial differences. Surely the race with the largest skull, the Caucasian, was superior and after him the Mongolian, Malay, aboriginal American, and Ethiopian in that order. While the Chinese were second, and in the words of Morton "ingenious, imitative and highly susceptible of cultivation," they were clearly inferior to and separate from the Caucasian race.[64] As a distinct species, their presence in the United States would pose the threat of hybridity, something to be strictly avoided, in the view of the polygenecists.

Men like J. C. Nott, George Glidden, and Louis Agassiz did not rest their case for pluralism on craniology alone, however. Indeed, they made free use of "aesthetics," phrenology, cultural attainments, and even linguistics, which they regarded as a special enemy of the pluralistic position, to attack the concept of the unity of mankind. That is, the "pyramidal" shaped head of the Chinese, and their "primitive" language were merely corroborative indices of racial inferiority.[65] Their cranial deficiency was not simply one of size alone, for the inadequacies of the skulls of "the Mongol, Indian and Negro, and all dark-skinned races," Nott contended, were "especially well marked in those parts of the brain which have been assigned to the moral and intellectual faculties." The low order of social development of these peoples further illustrated their natural inferiority. Indeed, they were biologically incapable of imitating the Caucasian, and introducing them to Western institutions and ideas was "warring against the immutable laws of nature," as far as Nott was concerned. He demanded, "What have been the results of missions to Africa, to China, to India, to the American Indians? . . . it would seem as if these philanthropic efforts, so far from producing good fruits for the dark races, in the main do more harm than good. The dark races borrow the vices, but never the virtues of the white man. . . ." [66]

Louis Agassiz, after Morton, did more than any other individual in America to render the pluralistic thesis more respectable since he was not only an eminent scientist, but deeply religious as well. He contended that polygenesis did not challenge the scriptures since the Old Testament never mentioned American Indians, Mongols, Malays, or Negroes. Genesis was the story of the Caucasian race as originated by Adam and Eve.[67] Agassiz constantly used cultural and temperamental differences to reenforce his belief that the races of mankind represented distinct species. The Chinese and Japanese had produced almost identical cultures because they were members of the same race, whereas that of the Malay was strikingly different. Racial differences in temperament were so great as to preclude any advantageous commingling among them, Agassiz argued. This was especially noticeable among the "colored races" which, in fact, were three separate species: "The indomitable, courageous, proud, Indian—in how very different a light he stands by the side of the submissive, obsequious, imitative Negro, or by the side of the tricky, cunning and cowardly Mongolian." [68]

The pluralistic position was dealt a fatal blow by Charles Darwin. But Americans were too religious to find polygenesis very attractive anyway, and the degree to which the scientific community embraced this theory is much in dispute. John Higham's conclu-

sion that it was never significant is challenged by Stanton's assertion that the "bulk of scientific opinion" was clearly on the side of
polygenesis.[69] If only by implication, Edward Lurie and Earl
Count appear to side with the position taken by Stanton.[70] As
far as the medical profession is concerned, it would appear that
Higham's interpretation is more valid. Although J. C. Nott enjoyed an excellent professional reputation among his colleagues,
his work in ethnology was contemptuously dismissed in one medical journal as "folly." [71] Of forty-nine private medical libraries
assembled by famous practictioners during the second half of the
nineteenth century, only two contained the works of Nott and
Glidden on race and one of these collections belonged to Nott
himself.[72]

More important for this inquiry is the fact that both sides in
the controversy, the pluralists and monists, accepted the inferiority
of the colored races.[73] The debate not only heightened American
consciousness of racial differences but left an important by-
product in the germ theory of culture which grew in influence
during the last quarter of the nineteenth century among social scientists and historians. According to Edward Saveth, "The belief
that American institutions were peculiarly racial products made
the disciples of the new historical school especially conscious of
supposed racial differences between the old . . . and the new
immigrants. . . . American institutions, they reasoned, were designed by and for Teutonic peoples, and it was doubtful whether
others could carry on in the traditional conception of freedom, individual liberty, local self government and federalism." [74]

The germ theory of culture had been expressed before the ethnologists articulated a relationship between biological factors and
social institutions. When Theodore Parker refused to concede any
capacity for cultural progress to the colored races, he expressed the
essence of this relationship. He indicated surprise that H. T.
Buckle in his *History of Civilization in England* should deny "any
original differences in the faculties of different races of men."
Parker then used cultural attainments as indices of natural superi-
ority and concluded, "It seems to us, that the difference in the
natural endowment of different races is enormous. All great, permanent, and progressive civilizations are Caucasian." [75]

When Nott made his first concessions to the Darwinists in 1866,
he still insisted that racial instincts changed so slowly as to be
immutable for all contemporary purposes. Earlier, a key argument
in the pluralist position was that great racial differences could not

have evolved in the time span of the brief Biblical chronology. When Darwin and the geologists destroyed this chronology, Nott shifted to the new, longer chronology and argued that racial instincts would take as long to change as they had taken to evolve into their present state. These instincts had permitted the Chinese and Asian Indians to attain only a semicivilized state, while American Indians and Negroes were unable to rise above "savagism." [76] This theory was carefully developed on the pages of the *Anthropological Review* of London, to which Nott was a frequent contributor. Typical of the type of assertions that appeared in this journal was the explanation of one contributor that China's despotism derived from the nature of the Mongolian race and that despotism in ancient Egypt developed only after members of her ruling classes began to intermarry with "African aborigines." [77] One writer asked rhetorically, "And why is a Chinese pagoda the only response to . . . the Parthenon, and Saint Peter's? Why is chivalry utterly unknown in the farther East, and gallantry perfectly inconceivable? And the reply of the anthropologist is, that the Mongolic type is utterly incapable of producing these things. . . ." [78] China's earlier accomplishments had to stem from "alien germs," the same author explained, which were transmitted from generation to generation as an "educational heirloom" rather than being the product of an "inherent proclivity" in the Chinese. But, as "a naturally non-progressive race," the Chinese must sooner or later exhaust or vitiate these foreign cultural gifts: "The Chinaman has not a sufficiency of 'blood' to effectually develope the idea of hereditary refinement, delicacy, sensibility, or spirit. . . . His vaunted civilisation, when examined from our immeasurably higher standpoint, is a sham and a pretence; it leaves him gross, sensual, grovelling, a liar, a trickster, and a cheat." [79]

An editorial in the same journal explained that physiologically the structure of the Mongolian was "infantile," while that of the Negro was "foetal." The language, government, literature, and art of China were also childish, the editor argued, and reflected the racial character of the Chinese, as did their "beardless" condition. This article was partially a response to John Stuart Mill's expressed fear that Europe would become another China through excessive organization. Obviously, Mr. Mill did not understand the racial basis of all social institutions, a failure which this editor attributed to "pseudophilanthropy." [80]

One of the best examples of the germ theory of culture applied to Chinese immigration appeared in *Popular Science Monthly* in

1882. The author advanced the view that social characteristics were as "fundamental and as immutable as are the physical characteristics of races." It would be absurd to expect the Chinese to adjust to American institutions when the Indian and Negro could not, he argued. Moreover the author warned of the grave dangers of "commingling" between races. When two races exist side by side, acculturation takes place in favor of the longest established traits, not necessarily the superior ones. Thus, Chinese culture which was institutionalized in the dawn of history would become dominant, a victory that could hardly be considered an "exemplification of the survival of the fittest," he concluded.[81]

Such fears were expressed more crudely in the popular press. Since "the Asiatics are cunning, treacherous and vicious, possessing no conception of American civilization," adjustments to their increasing number in California would have to be "disastrous" to our way of life, it was reasoned on the pages of the *New York World*. Indeed, the western states were in 1876 already "degenerating into Chinese colonies," the editor warned.[82] Many of the eastern newspapers examined oscillated between such extreme fears and a Darwinian optimism that as a superior race Americans had nothing to fear in a contest with the Celestials, who were after all "one of the debased races of the earth." [83] The general editorial consensus, however, was that while the Chinese were not biologically suitable for America's melting pot, it would be foolish not to exploit their cheap labor before shipping them back to China. The cultural and biological dissimilarity of the Chinaman, coupled with his intense national pride, militated against his desiring to remain in the United States on a permanent basis. They were birds of passage who would return to China once they earned enough money to live well in their natural habitat, it was comfortably assumed by these editors.[84]

In Congress, concern over assimilation and fears of a vague cultural threat were frequently expressed during the debates over Chinese immigration. "They are of a different race and possess an entirely different civilization, and in my opinion are incapable of being brought into assimilation in habits, customs, and manners with the people of this country," Senator Saulsbury of Delaware declared. Congressman McClure of Ohio virtually repeated Saulsbury's words in the lower chamber. In reluctantly giving up the industrial advantages of such "cheap and docile labor," Connecticut's Joseph Hawley indicated he would vote in favor of exclusion only because he thought the Chinese unassimilable.[85]

One of the best indicators of assimilation fears about Chinese immigration, on a national rather than a sectional level, was the defeat of Senator Sumner's proposal in 1870 to remove the word *white* from all Congressional acts pertaining to naturalization. The ensuing debate made it clear that his intention was to extend naturalization rights to the Chinese. It was defeated, twelve ayes to twenty-six nays, with thirty-four absent.[86] Obviously shocked, Trumbull of Illinois introduced a second proposal stipulating that the Chinese were eligible for naturalization. He pleaded with his colleagues: "I do hope that now the Senate will not act so inconsistently as to vote down this amendment. . . . We have struck the word 'white' out of the naturalization laws so far as it applies to the Hottentot, to the pagan from Africa. Now it is proposed to deny the right of naturalization to the Chinaman who is infinitely above the African in intelligence, in manhood, and in every respect." The plea went unheeded, however, and the proposal was defeated, nine ayes to thirty-one nays, with thirty-two absent. The pattern of this vote was clearly national. While all four senators from the west who were present voted against the motion, seven easterners also voted against it and only three for it. Twelve southern (including border states) senators voted no and four yes. Among the midwestern contingent eight opposed Trumbull and two supported him.[87] This vote is particularly important because the issue of citizenship neatly separates cultural fears from the economic advantages of continued Chinese immigration, and the national pattern certainly supports the thesis of this study that anti-Chinese sentiment was not merely a West Coast sectional phenomenon before 1882.

The fourth new theme developed between 1850 and 1882 was that Chinese filth and disease endangered the safety and welfare of American society. During the three decades of unrestricted Chinese immigration, the medical profession not only became deeply interested in racial factors in disease, but by 1870 had made Americans highly conscious of dirt as a threat to the health of a community. During the next decade the germ theory of disease was developed, and the medical profession played an important role in feeding the fears of American journalists over Chinese germs.

In 1851 the American Medical Association appointed a committee to study the "physiological peculiarities and diseases of the Negroes," which Lurie characterized as a "primary forum for the pluralistic-unitarian debate." [88] Nott, to whom Walter Reed gave credit "for having first suggested that yellow fever could only be spread by an intermediate host," [89] also believed that susceptibility to yellow fever was directly proportional to the fairness of the skin. Thus Italians, Spaniards, Mongols, mulattoes, and Negroes were progressively less susceptible. This peculiar immunity was not the result of climate but a function of race, which "was originally made to suit the climate in which nature placed it." [90] Conversely, the darker races were more vulnerable to "cholera, typhoid fever, plague, smallpox, and all those diseases arriving from morbid poisons. . . ." Nott cited as the leading authority on such racial aptitudes and immunities Jean Boudin in Paris, who wrote a brief article that was widely discussed in American medical journals. It is interesting that Boudin in this article continually cited Nott as the leading authority on the subject.[91]

Out of this developed a theory on the part of Nott and his clique that transferring an "alien" race to a new environment in which they had no natural immunities would heighten their susceptibility to sickness to epidemic proportions which might threaten the indigenous race. Such fears were not new, of course. The yellow fever epidemic of 1798 in Philadelphia was attributed to ships returning from foreign ports, of which Canton was the most suspect.[92] Canton was thought to offer a particularly unhealthy environment. In 1853 the Royal Navy investigated the high incidence of disease in its East India squadron and reported that China was fraught with ubiquitous and "formidable maladies": "Bowel complaints, dystentery, diarrhaea, cholera morbus, and worst of all Asiatic cholera" were among the most frequent ailments. One dissenting opinion in the report, however, attributed the oversized sick list to the quantities of alcohol consumed by the tars.[93]

Missionaries also helped create the impression that China was rotten with disease. Their reports were full of comments on the wretched climate and high incidence of epidemics that had claimed the health and lives of Milne, Abeel, Tracy, Morrison, and a good many missionary wives. One medical missionary would have it that the Chinese shake hands with themselves upon greeting a person because of the prevalence of cutaneous diseases among them! [94]

The first sensational effort to represent Chinese immigrants as a medical threat to the United States was Dr. Arthur B. Stout's *Chinese Immigration and the Physiological Causes of the Decay of a Nation*. Stout was a prominent physician in California who had national connections with the American Medical Association. His 1862 report was an incredible potpourri of medical lore, ethnology, religion, and plain nonsense. The main threat to society was the "hereditary diseases" which he listed as "phthisis or consumption, scrofula, syphilis, mental alienation and epidemic diseases." These in turn were aggravated by opium smoking among the Chinese. Stout hinted that there was a higher incidence of syphilis among the Chinese; but since this disease caused sterility and the Chinese were so prolific, he could not be sure. Stout was never really clear on the mechanics of the threat, but insisted, unabashed, that the introduction of Chinese and Negroes into America would be like "a cancer" in "the biological, social, religious and political systems." There was nothing to be gained by such an infusion and everything to be lost. Improvements on the "Divine excellence" of the Anglo-Saxons seemed unlikely. "Until Islamism and Paganism alike sink into oblivion, and Christianity enters, like sunlight into chaos, to illuminate and revivify this ancient world . . . we cannot permit Asiatics to enter," he concluded.[95]

Stout's report was perhaps less shocking than the evaluation it received by Thomas M. Logan, former president of the AMA and permanent secretary of the California Board of Health. In 1871, he enlisted Stout to investigate "the evils likely to result from the combined intermixture of races and the introduction of habits and customs of a sensual and depraved people in our midst . . . with hereditary vices and engrafted peculiarities." He praised Stout's earlier report, but urged him to be even more specific: "you have already . . . cited the opinions of the learned and scientific, and from this vast research have drawn certain conclusions and defined certain laws, which ages will never be able to controvert; but . . . changes occurring in the civil states of the Mongolian . . . may prompt you . . . to qualify your inferences."

Logan suggested that great attention be given to the medical threat arising from the fact that the Chinese came from another climate, enhanced by their alleged propensities for filth and vice. "In view of such inducements to disease and enemies to health, it is a matter of astonishment that a relentless pestilence does not arise every year and spread dismay and desolation throughout our land." [96]

The ensuing report of Stout was largely a rehash of the one made nine years earlier except that it now relied on Charles Darwin rather than J. C. Nott and Abbé Huc. But Stout did not believe that the fittest could survive this racial encounter. For here was no normal conflict on a manly level but an underhanded subversive battle involving unseen germs and horrible contagions:

Better it would be for our country that the hordes of Genghis Khan should overflow the land, and with armed hostility devastate our valleys with the sabre and the firebrand than that these more pernicious hosts in the garb of friends, should insidiously poison the well-springs of life, and spreading far and wide, gradually undermine and corrode the vitals of our strength and prosperity. In the former instance, we might oppose the invasion with sword and rifled cannon, but this destructive intrusion enters by invisible approaches. . . .[97]

Medical endorsement of popular fears was to be found throughout the profession and not just in California. No less a figure than J. Marion Sims of New York, president of the AMA and world-famous gynecologist, sounded the tocsin on Chinese syphilis in 1876. In his official address at the centennial jubilee of the AMA, Sims warned that the spread of syphilis had already reached epidemic proportions. He indicted the "Chinese slave" used for the purpose of prostitution, who "breeds moral and physical pestilence" on the West Coast. There, "even boys eight and ten years old have been syphilized by these degraded wretches. . . . Cholera has a permanent home [Asia] where it is perpetually generated." But cholera burns out after a brief "flourish," while syphilis remains lurking in "the haunts of ignorance, poverty, squalor, filth and vice." Sims urged the government to terminate the importation of people who represented such risk to the national health.[98]

The fear that the nation's bloodstream was being poisoned by Chinese prostitutes had caused a formal study of the problem by the AMA in 1875. The report of this committee, which Sims evidently chose to ignore, revealed nothing startling beyond the conclusion that syphilis among the Chinese was transmitted in much the same manner as it was among Europeans.[99] The editor of the *New York World* asked, "If Chinese prostitutes are inoculating the gilded youth of San Francisco with the terrible diseases of Asia does not the fault lie with the gilded youth?" [100]

By leaving diseases nameless, they were rendered mysterious and more terrifying to many persons. Chinese afflictions were considered to be the result of thousands of years of beastly vices, resistant to all the efforts of modern medicine. American children were pictured as the most likely potential victims. In an editorial on the "scourge of the hordes of China," Bennett warned that John Chinaman's "beastliness" could have such far-reaching effects; and in an analogy that reflects this hysteria, he compared the Chinese presence in California to the "introduction in our schools and

nurseries of some new and horrible diseases that defied treatment." [101] The "frightful consequences" alluded to in such warnings of strange and devastating diseases could be found in "ethnol-
ogies of Orientalism," another editor suggested.[102] Syphilis was
generally the disease implied, but in such a manner that the reader
was left with the impression that "Chinese syphilis" was more
potent, ravaging, and impervious to treatment. "This disease
which is spoken of under different names in medical works, for
convenience we will designate 'the foul contagious disease',," an
editorial in the *Medico-Literary Journal* explained in 1878; one
that Chinese prostitutes were infusing into "the Anglo-Saxon
blood." [103] Apparently this fear was an old one; at least, the *Encyclopaedia Britannica* in 1810 mentioned the dreaded "Canton
ulcer" among the venereal diseases to be found in China.[104]

The fear of leprosy became much more pronounced after 1872.
Dr. O'Donnell, one of Kearney's lieutenants, received as much
coverage in New York newspapers as his chief for his exposure of
Chinese lepers on the street corners of San Francisco. Even the
New York Times, which strongly supported continued Chinese
immigration, showed concern over O'Donnell's charges.[105] A report that whites had also contracted the disease on the West Coast
thoroughly shocked editors in the east. Under a huge headline,
"White Lepers in San Francisco—A Pest Brought from China,"
the *New York Herald* reprinted the testimony of a sailor who had
caught leprosy in a "Chinese den" while on a "spree" and of another Californian who attributed his affliction to cigars wrapped
by Chinese workers. Bennett demanded a Congressional investigation before leprosy became "naturalized" in California.[106] It was
even asserted that Anson Burlingame had died of leprosy! [107]

There was some debate and more confusion over the nature of
this disease in professional circles of the 1870s, for little was known
of its etiology. Thus, early in the decade, dermatologists concluded
that leprosy was transmitted by heredity.[108] One specialist conjectured that only the "primeval races" were really affected. The
meaning of this observation was no more clear-cut than his after-
thought, "hence certain obvious inferences," but in all probability
it was directed at the Chinese.[109] By 1880, however, new theoreti-
cal developments in medicine had opened up such disputes to re-
examination. Spurred by the allegations of Dr. O'Donnell, the
president of the American Dermatological Association, Dr. James
Hyde of Chicago, requested that Dr. John Foye of San Francisco
conduct a careful examination of the possibilities that leprosy was

contagious and could spread across the country. In this case, it was the California doctor who calmed his midwestern colleague, insisting that leprosy was "less general than is supposed" on the West Coast, and that only one "non-Mongolian had it." [110] In 1880, a Dr. Janeway diagnosed a case as leprosy among New York's Chinese which received far more sensational treatment in the press than did its denial nine months later.[111]

In 1866 a rash of books on disinfectants had made Americans more conscious of the relationship between dirt and disease.[112] Five years later an editorial on "The Germ Theory of Epidemics" appeared in the *New York Herald* in which Bennett explained that the new theory conceived of disease as spreading "not by diffusion, but by living infusoria." [113] In 1878, *Appleton's Cyclopedia* ran an article on "The Germ Theory and Spontaneous Generation," [114] and American opinion leaders were becoming increasingly conscious of germs. When a Chinese in Nevada fought off a gang of young tormentors, it was reported that the scratches inflicted on one of the gang never healed. This led to speculation over whether the Chinese had deposited a mysterious poison under his fingernails or whether strange germs had been responsible.[115] A correspondent for *Scribner's* who was exceptionally friendly to the Chinese admitted that he could not stand to be touched by their "tawny fingers," while his companion could hardly wait to throw away the cigar given him by "China Sam's wife," fearing the germs with which it was probably contaminated.[116] An epidemic of cholera in 1871 provoked such headlines as "The Asiatic Cholera Again upon its Travels from East to West" and "Asiatic Pestilence," which enhanced the uneasy feelings over Chinese immigration as a threat to the country's health.[117] In 1877 the editor of the *New York Times* predicted that medical fears would play a crucial role in restricting Chinese immigration, though protesting that if the Chinese were as "loathsome" as popularly believed, their death rate would be much higher.[118]

In Congress, West Coast representatives skilfully exploited these popular fears. Oregon's Senator Slater warned that "filth and frightful and nameless diseases and contagions" were a part of the package when one imported cheap Chinese labor.[119] California's Johnson characterized the Chinese immigrants as "a multitude bearing pestilence in their garments and reeking with filth and decay." [120] In an appeal that foreshadowed the far-reaching implications of Chinese immigration restriction as well as questioning the nation's basic melting-pot concept, Senator Sargent of California asked, "Can we stand all the vices, all the diseases, all the mischief that infect humanity the world over and retain our American civilization?" [121]

In view of developments in the urban, East Coast intellectual center of the country, it seems obvious that eastern "capitulation" to the western demands for Chinese exclusion in 1882 must be considered in the broadest possible perspective. It cannot be explained solely in terms of the unfavorable image traced in this study. The commentaries of traders and missionaries were replete with references to Chinese stagnation, slavishness, inferiority, and dirt; but it was the interaction of these conceptions with popular considerations and anxieties dealing with industrialization, slavery and civil war, racial assimilation, and disease that proved to be crucial. Eastern regional fears that a new system of slavery was being instituted in the United States and concern over possible dangers in admitting a totally dissimilar racial and cultural group, even on a temporary basis, were patently influential in the successful passage of the exclusion laws. The germ theory of disease provided an explanation of the manner in which an obviously inferior group might best a superior one, contrary to the natural law of the social Darwinists. Such a means of conquest was compatible with the older stereotype of Oriental cunning and with the belief that the Chinese would never confront the West in a manly fashion. They were the people who, in the words of Sir John Bowring, fought wars with poison and arson. The hidden nature of germs and "primeval" racial traits enhanced the belief in sinister Chinese characteristics and magnified the Chinese threat in the eyes of American editors and their audiences.

Th' time may come, Hinnessy, whin
ye'll be squirtin' wather over Hop
Lee's shirt while a man named
Chow Fung kicks down ye'er sign
an' heaves rocks through ye'er
windy. The time may come, Hinnessy. Who knows?

. . . th' Chinymen have been on
earth a long time, an' I don't see
how we can push so manny iv thim
off iv it. Annyhow, 'tis a good thing
f'r us they ain't Christyans an'
haven't larned properly to sight a
gun.

Peter Finley Dunne, *Mr. Dooley:
Now and Forever*, ed. L. Filler,
p. 139.

8

East Coast Reaction to Chinese Immigration, 1850-1882

In view of the evolution of American images of the Chinese up to
the middle of the nineteenth century, one could almost predict
certain well-defined East Coast reactions to the news that Celestial
immigrants were arriving in significant numbers on the West
Coast. Some eastern opinion makers would simply chuckle at the
thought of these ludicrous human specimens in the New World.
"Decidedly it is hard to imagine a great, and glorious Chinaman,"
a writer in *Putnam's* explained in 1857. "There is something essentially ridiculous in all the pertainings of this outlandish creature. For myself I think I could with less embarrassment, with a
more successful air of indifference to the grins of the crowd, stand

shaking hands on Broadway, with a veritable tailed gentleman from the interior of Africa . . . than I could do the same by any impulse of cosmopolitan affability, with Chu-Jin-Sing of the 'Forest-of-Pencils Society.' " [1] This was essentially the early trader's view of the Chinese, one of good-natured derision from which both moral indignation and respect were absent. On the other hand, Bayard Taylor's response in 1855 to large-scale Chinese immigration was closer to the perceptions of the Chinese associated with missionaries and diplomats:

It is my deliberate opinion that the Chinese are, morally, the most debased people on the face of the earth. Forms of vice which in other countries are barely named, are in China so common, that they excite no comment among the natives. They constitute the surface-level, and below them there are deeps on deeps of depravity so shocking and horrible, that their character cannot even be hinted. . . . Their touch is pollution, and, harsh as the opinion may seem, justice to our own race demands that they should not be allowed to settle on our soil.[2]

Still other easterners would nostalgically view the Chinese as representatives of a noble race and great civilization that had of late suffered from a stagnation for which the returning immigrant from America might be just the catalyst needed to restore greatness. Such was the sentiment of the editor of *North American Miscellany* in 1852, in which a good deal of the older, eighteenth-century respect for the Chinese was tempered by an awareness of recent decline and some "social decay." [3]

Almost immediately in the early 1850s two features in the eastern editorial response to Chinese immigration were discernible. First of all, newspaper editors were primarily interested in the economic value of the Celestial immigrants. Labor shortages and high wages had hampered the economic development of California, they reasoned, and the Chinese would be to this newly acquired territory in the West what the Celt was to the East and the African to the South.[4] This was most crassly expressed in the *Nation* by E. L. Godkin who explained that the chief virtues of these Chinese "barbarians" were "their fitness for servile duties and their want of social ambition." If this were "a severe blow" to America's "social ideal," industrialization was rapidly terminating the era when workers were of a higher caliber and eligible to move up the social ladder, Godkin argued.[5]

Many editors attempted to soften this exploitative emphasis, and simultaneously to assuage their own fears of a permanent, servile class in America, by stressing the fact that the Chinese would not remain in the country, but would return to China once he saved sufficient money to live comfortably there. He would not only take back some capital, but also the seed of Christianity and a taste for American goods. Hence, the flow of Chinese workers back and forth across the Pacific would have short- and long-range benefits for both nations. For a Milwaukee editor, history had come the full circle in 1852 with "the banner of the cross and the banner of commerce . . . repaying to Asia the debt of civilization, learning and faith purified from the errors and superstitions which belong measurably to their Asiatic origin." [6] Indeed, returning immigrants from America would benefit China even more than did the Opium War, the *New York Times* proclaimed in 1852.[7] Anyone who questioned the wisdom of this arrangement was, in James Gordon Bennett's eyes, "a free soiler, abolitionist, or worse." [8]

The second feature immediately evident in the eastern editorial response to Chinese immigration was the social unacceptability of these immigrants. The bird-of-passage argument was stressed not simply to assuage fears of a caste system, but also cultural and racial concerns. The unfavorable image of the Chinese had preceded them to America, and few editors could consider them an addition to the country's melting pot. The Celestials were, after all, "a semi-barbarous and sickly people," *Graham's Magazine* warned in 1854.[9] Eastern editors were clamoring for legislation that would preclude any possibility that the Chinese might become citizens, almost two decades before the Senate in 1870 officially denied them the right of naturalization.[10] "The great mass of those who come are Coolies, heathenish, slavish and in every sense degraded," the *New York Courier* explained in 1854; and "no American" would want to "elevate these Pagan idolators to the rank of American citizen," however valuable their cheap labor was to the development of the West Coast.[11]

Chinese immigration was already "a fertile topic of private conversation" in the East in 1854, according to the *New York Tribune*.[12] Horace Greeley admitted to "grave fears" over admitting such people to the United States. "The Chinese are uncivilized, unclean, and filthy beyond all conception without any of the higher domestic or social relations; lustful and sensual in their dispositions; every female is a prostitute of the basest order," Greeley declared in 1854, decades before Kearney and Sargent were making similar declarations on the street corners of San Francisco and in the halls of Congress. Greeley also conceded that the Chinese were "industrious people, forbearing of injury" which enhanced their economic value. But only the "Christian races" or "any of the white races" were welcome as permanent settlers, he insisted, since only they "assimilate with Americans." "Thank heaven" Californians were ready to end this "flood of ignorant, filthy idolators" with an "exclusive policy," the editorial concluded.[13]

Greeley's list of grievances is interesting in view of its early date. His charges in 1854 of filth, sin, lecherous perversions, slavery, and even "secret societies and secret deaths" [14] indicate that such fearful conceptions of the Chinese are much older on the East Coast than has been believed. They also demonstrate the efficacy of the reports of traders, missionaries, and diplomats in shaping the unfavorable image of the Chinese, without which Californian reports on the nature of this immigration could never have struck such a sympathetic response in the East. Indeed, some of the first sinophobic outbursts in eastern newspapers occurred almost simultaneously with those on the West Coast.[15]

Moreover these fears were also expressed by editors who were strongly comitted to the continuation of Chinese immigration for economic reasons. The editor of the *New York Times* consistently justified the use of Chinese labor on the West Coast in spite of his serious reservations about the alleged social and racial dangers involved. In an 1865 editorial on "The Growth of the United States Through Emigration—The Chinese," the *Times* declared,

Now we are utterly opposed to the permission of any extensive emigration of Chinamen or other Asiatics to any part of the United States. There are other points of national well-being to be considered beside the sudden development of material wealth. The security of its free institutions is more important than the enlargement of its population. The maintenance of an elevated national character is of higher value than mere growth in physical power. Dr. Draper himself admits that with Oriental blood will necessarily come Oriental thoughts and the attempt at Oriental social habits; and he even anticipates the establishment of the institution of polygamy on a large scale.

. . . We have four millions of degraded negroes in the South . . . and if there were to be a flood-tide of Chinese population—a population befouled with all the social vices, with no knowledge or appreciation of free institutions or constitutional liberty, with heathenish souls and heathenish propensities, whose character, and habits, and modes of thought are firmly fixed by the consolidating influence of ages upon ages—we should be prepared to bid farewell to republicanism and democracy.[16]

In essence, these editors were willing to continue the practice as long as the Chinese remained in California. The Rockies would act as a natural barrier, they hoped, which would keep the coolies dammed up on the Pacific slope whence they would be more apt to return to China once their economic function was fulfilled.[17] Few of these editors thought in terms of exclusion before 1870. If Greeley did in 1854, he changed his mind several times during the next two decades.[18] If Americans would only keep in mind that their country was merely a "temporary home" for the Chinese, there would be less anxiety over the subject, counseled Boston's *Evening Traveller*.[19] Meanwhile, the *New York Times* suggested, it would be wise to carefully segregate the Chinese on the West Coast:

Although they are patient and reliable laborers, they have character-istics deeply imbedded which make them undesirable as a part of our permanent population. Their religion is wholly unlike ours, and they poison and stab. The circumstance would need be very favorable which would allow of their introduction into our families as serv-ants, and as to mixing with them on terms of equality, that would be out of the question. No improvement of race could possibly result from such a mixture.[20]

Reports from correspondents in California and China on the nature of the Chinese, however, continually undermined the con-fidence of these editors in the wisdom of permitting the Chinese to make even a temporary home in the United States. A missionary who described how girls in China prostituted themselves at four and five years of age provoked an Albany, New York, editor to blurt out, "Can you imagine anything good coming from such a place?" [21] But forced to reexamine his stand on Chinese immigra-tion, he once more fell back on the bird-of-passage rationale to assure himself that no permanent damage could result.[22] One cor-respondent in California submitted an impressive array of statis-tics on wages and profits to demonstrate that Chinese immigration was still imperative for the economic well-being of that state. But the next day he conceded that the dirt, disease, and wanton lewd-ness of the Chinese in their "fever nests" were part of the price California was paying for this cheap labor. "If it were not for these blessed winds," he warned, "I am convinced that they would have originated pestilence long since." [23]

Such reports were chilling warnings to eastern editors and kept alive the discussion of Chinese immigration. But before 1870 these

editors generally agreed with Greeley that "so far the benefits
. . . have decidedly overbalanced the evils." The strongest threat
to this editorial confidence was China's huge population which
could flood the nation with inferior types and result in a new form
of slavery before Congress could legislate the necessary restrictions.
"But what has hitherto been a rivulet may at an early day become
a Niagara," Greeley worried, "hurling millions instead of thousands upon us from the vast, overcrowded hives of China and India, to cover not only our Pacific slope but the Great Basin, and
pour in torrents through the gorges of the Rocky Mountains into
the vast, inviting valley of the Mississippi . . . and result in . . .
a novel and specious Serfdom but little removed in essence from
old-fashioned Slavery." [24]

With the general optimism over Sino-American cooperation
that was generated by the Burlingame Treaty in 1868, these fears
gave way to a renewed confidence by 1869 that Chinese immigration could only benefit the nation. California's Senator Casserly
was dismissed as an "Irish Know Nothing" by several New York
editors for attacking the Chinese immigrants, although his castigations were scarcely distinguishable from their own sinophobic editorials of a year earlier.[25] In a new buoyant mood, eastern editors
were willing to let the Chinese cross the Rockies, mix freely with
the Caucasian population, and test the Darwinian laws of natural
selection. "If the Anglo-Saxon is inferior, it is time he made way
for his betters; if he be superior, as he certainly is, then all other
races which he absorbs in America will only help to do his inferior
work for him," the *New York Times* boasted in 1869. But even in
his most confident mood this editor had no intention of offering
the ballot to the Chinese in this struggle to determine the fittest.
Since the Celestials were unfamiliar with such a tool, it would be
unbecoming to afford them the vote, he rationalized.[26]

Full of the same confidence, the editor of the *Evening Transcript* in Boston assured his readers that, "destitute of that strength
and toughness of moral fiber, . . . the Chinese may be welcomed
as assistants in colonization; they need not be feared as the dominant race of the future." [27] The *Albany Evening Journal* headlined "Let the Chinese Come . . . He Won't Paganize Us." [28] As
Bennett bumptiously expressed it, "the Anglo Saxon, Celtic-
American or Anglo-American races were never born to be absorbed by Blackamoors or pagans." [29]

Except for a few initial doubts in 1852, the *New York Herald*
was unusually consistent up to 1869 in its support of unlimited

Chinese immigration. Bennett's major concern was that some abolitionist type would want to give these coolies the vote. He even taunted the "nigger worshipping radicals" in California that they were likely to become the next victims of "a political and social monster" of their own creation.[30] With the Sino-American cooperation promised by the Burlingame Treaty, Bennett's optimism grew boundless. Upon meeting a Chinese on Vesey Street in New York, he was inspired to speculate over the world power that the United States could generate from his cheap labor: "Our word will be law. 'I am an American citizen' will be a boast which has nothing to compare with it since Rome was in the zenith of her glory." [31] But Bennett made it explicit in a series of editorials that this Sino-American collaboration was not to be one of equals. "Accepted as a freeman," the Chinese would "eventually become a voter," he warned. "We have liberated the African and absorbed both the Caucasian and the Teuton. What will become of the Asiatic, or of our race with the Mongolian?" he asked.[32] Americans should bear in mind, Bennett insisted, that "on the Caucasian element only can we hope to build up such an empire as the world has never seen. . . . Chinese may be all very good, but Europeans are at least ten times better." [33]

The Burlingame Treaty was followed, however, by a series of new, unprecedented, and disturbing events. On July 13, 1869, a convention of manufacturers and planters was held in Memphis, Tennessee, to explore the possibility of using Chinese labor in cotton fields and factories. A "Committee on Transportation" reported that coolies were available in lots of more than 500 at $47.50 per head and could be shipped anywhere in the United States. Lest this sound too crudely commercial, the report added:

If God, in His providence, has opened up the door for the introduction of the Mongolian race to our fields of labor, instead of repelling this class of population as heathens and idolators, whose touch is contaminating, would we not exhibit more of the spirit of Christians by falling in with the apparent leadings of Providence, and whilst we avail ourselves of the physical assistance these pagans are capable of affording us, endeavor at the same time to bring to bear upon them the elevating and saving influence of our holy religion, so that when those coming among us *shall return to their own country*, they may carry back with them, and disseminate the good seed. . . .[34]

The legislature of Tennessee remained unconvinced by this altruistic rationale, however, and immediately prohibited the importation of Chinese workers into that state by a vote of 53 to 15.[35] Nor did many northern editors see the plan as anything but a commercial venture. Only Dana in the *New York Sun* agreed that it would be unchristian to exclude any "children of one common Father" from "His Bounty." [36]

Considering the widespread concern over coolies in the South expressed in 1867,[37] there was surprisingly limited protest in the press over the Memphis proposal. The lack of a stronger reaction was undoubtedly a function of the optimism created by the Burlingame Treaty. At any rate it is clear that most editors in the East perceived the South as the destination of these shipments of coolies. Hence even the pro-labor *New York World* was content to let the coolies replace Negroes in the cotton kingdom. "That will force the freedman either to starvation or to industrious rivalry; and thus we may hear less talk about suffrage and more news of honest work," the editor advised.[38] To prevent Americans from using Chinese labor anywhere would be on a par with attempts to destroy newly introduced machinery, the *New York Times* now insisted in 1869.[39]

Strangely enough, Bennett joined Greeley in protesting against the plans laid at Memphis to import coolies to other sections of the country. But whereas the *Tribune* was morally opposed to anything that resembled a new form of slavery, the *Herald* was uneasy over the possibility that a future civil war was in the making. At least the "Yankee slave-traders" could ship coolies to the South "without soiling their irreproachable consciences on the nigger issue," Bennett scoffed.[40] But Bennett also was unhappy over the possibility that coolies could be imported into the eastern section of the country. The delegates had been "too eloquent" in their praise of John Chinaman, he complained. "They know very little about him, or they are anxious to get cheap labor meanwhile, no matter what the future consequences may be to the country." [41] As Bennett brooded over all the implications of the Memphis convention, he concluded for the first time since 1852 that, perhaps, no Celestial immigrants should be allowed to emigrate to the United States: "The prejudice against Chinese immigration may be partly accounted for by the fact that, notwithstanding its demonstrable material advantages . . . , not only the vices of the Chinaman, but his apparent incapacity for moral improvement, his stereotyped habits . . . and the manifest inferiority of his political and industrial capabilities make it still an open question whether it should be encouraged or discouraged." [42] But typically, Bennett reversed himself a few weeks later when he apparently convinced himself that cotton plantations were the main targets of the delegates at Memphis. "Sambo must make up his mind to work or starve," he agreed.[43]

In view of the highly publicized proceedings in Memphis in 1869, one would have expected the East to be adequately prepared for the importation of Chinese workers in June 1870 to work in a North Adams, Massachusetts, shoe factory. A trade publication for shoe manufacturers had already served notice that coolies would be used to break the power of the Crispins.[44] A long editorial in the *New York Times* in March expressed some concern over the imminent arrival of Oriental contract workers at a number of eastern locations.[45] A scare headline in April warned that "The Chinese are Coming," [46] and several newspapers in Massachusetts traced the cross-country route of the Celestials headed for Calvin Sampson's factory in North Adams.[47] Nevertheless, when the Chinese actually materialized in June, they precipitated angry headlines, emotional editorials, and strong protest meetings in Boston, New York, Philadelphia, Rochester, Albany, Troy, Astoria, Newark, and as far away as Hamilton, Ohio.[48]

In part, this exaggerated response to seventy-five Chinese workers in North Adams was due to the sensational treatment of their arrival in both friendly and hostile newspapers. "They are with us! The 'Celestials'—with Almond eyes, pigtails, rare industry, quick adaptation, high morality, and all . . . ," announced the friendly *Boston Commonwealth*.[49] "We Are Coming, Father Mississippi, 100,000 Strong," chanted a headline in the undecided *New York Herald*.[50] "Coolie Slavery. Why Are Not the Laws Prohibiting Coolie Importation Enforced by President Grant," screamed another headline in the *New York World*.[51]

The arrival of more Chinese in September 1870 to work in a laundry in Belleville, New Jersey, together with constant rumors that coolies were headed for the potato fields of Long Island, a railroad company in Mauch Chunk, Pennsylvania, and cigar factories in New York City, developed a sense of crisis among labor leaders and those easterners with racial or cultural anxieties concerning Chinese immigration. A headline in the *New York Herald* succinctly captured the mood: "Cheap Chinese Labor. How New Jersey Accepts the Coming Revolution. The Pigtailed People from the Flowery Land—What They Are Doing and What the White Trash Threaten to Do—Ku Klux vs Chop Sticks—Belleville in a Dilemma." [52]

Protest meetings were presided over in the main by labor leaders and public figures sympathetic to the labor movement. At one "largely attended meeting" in Boston, "the blasphemy and exhibition would have been highly creditable to the American Congress," the *New York Herald* ridiculed. Judge Cowley was "handsomely applauded" when he "intimated that the Chinese must be wiped out by force," Bennett reported disapprovingly.[53] At a rally in New York City, Sheriff O'Brien personally offered $5,000 "to fight the coolies." [54] In Newark, New Jersey, a Dr. Vail took advantage of the contemporary Chinese atrocities at Tientsin to remind his audience that "the Chinese race are the only people who lift the dagger to plunge it into Christian missionaries." [55] Jennie Collins told a crowd in Boston that Calvin Sampson was to the workingman what "Judas was to Christianity . . . what Jefferson Davis was to the freedom of the slaves." [56]

Some very important political figures in the Northeast also addressed these anticoolie rallies, among them generals Butler and Banks, Senator—and soon to be Grant's running mate—Wilson in Massachusetts, and Horatio Seymour in New York, that state's former governor and the Democratic party's standard bearer in the presidential election of 1868. Seymour sent a statement to a sinophobic meeting in Rochester which denounced the importation of Chinese into the United States. European immigrants do not "overthrow" American customs or bring in "strange blood," he explained. "We do not let the Indian stand in the way of our civilization so why let the Chinese barbarian?" Seymour demanded.[57] Mayor Hall misinformed a New York audience that Massachusetts Bay Colony was the first to institute Negro slavery in North America and now it was the first to import Chinese who were just as "debased in race." [58] Ben Butler and Joseph Hawley publicly debated the issue after the Massachusetts legislature failed to pass restrictions against the use of "coolies." [59] Albany also turned down Senator Tweed's proposal to outlaw Chinese labor in New York.[60] And in Washington the Honorable William Mungen of Ohio proposed that a joint congressional committee be created "to inquire into the dangers" of importing Chinese "from the crowded, filthy and narrow alley of their rat-breeding and rat-catching homes to work in a large boot and shoe manufactory." [61]

The North Adams affair brought confusion and dismay to radical ranks, as Godkin sardonically recorded. He himself was far from happy with the prospects but concluded that the law of supply and demand would soon diminish the number of Chinese arriving.[62] The anguish caused by the coolie issue is perhaps best revealed by the tortured reasoning of Wendell Phillips on the pages of the *National Standard*. He was not against the Chinese workers on racial grounds, Phillips explained, but on the grounds that it was not "spontaneous immigration." Sampson could even control their votes should they be enfranchised, he warned. "Chinese immigration of labor was an unmixed good," he insisted, but "importation of human freight is an unmixed evil." He went on to laud the Chinese as "a painstaking, industrious, thrifty, inventive, self respected and law abiding race," but only a few sentences later commented that "the Chinaman works cheap because he is a barbarian." [63]

In a similar manner Russell H. Conwell twisted and turned in his popular book on Chinese immigration, without coming to any clearly stated position. Yet it is difficult to escape the impression that he favored exclusion of the Chinese. Whereas European immigrants recognized at least some parts of the American system when they arrived, the coolies emigrated from a social condition that closely resembled slavery, Conwell argued. Already they had instituted female slavery on the West Coast, and much worse will follow, he predicted. Citing the works of missionaries, Conwell asserted that the national character of the Chinese made them wholly undesirable as immigrants. "Pride, Fear and Cunning" were characteristics of all Chinese, he charged, but the lower classes were also "turbulent" and "bloodthirsty." Only a few pages earlier he had characterized the Chinese as "timid and docile" and "deficient in active courage," but few Americans were consistent in describing the Chinese at this time. Conwell's concluding pages left little doubt that the country was in danger of being inundated with the dregs of China. On the cover of his book, running Chinese in peasant dress depicted above the words "We Are Coming" could only have been designed to inflame American fears of invading Asiatic hordes.[64]

If Conwell was reluctant to specify his conclusions, his readers were not. The *New York Herald* allocated six full columns to a summary of it under the headlines: "That 'Heathen Chinese' . . . The Coolie Merchants and Their Victims. Who is Responsible for the Asiatic Inundation . . . The Traffic in Human Flesh." [65] Bennett recommended Conwell's book as required reading for every American and appears to have been converted to the exclusionist position himself as a result of reading it. Of course, Bennett's opinions were not very stable. But Conwell's book also provoked the first doubts in several editors who had consistently supported Chinese immigration on the grounds of its economic necessity. These editors generally associated exclusionist arguments with organized labor, the Democratic party and the Irish— often lumping the three together. But Conwell did not fall into any of these categories, and his esteem as an author and lecturer enhanced the influence of his book on Chinese immigration.[66]

By 1870, however, it was becoming increasingly difficult to categorize the anti-Chinese mood in terms of political or class affiliations. The editor of the *Springfield Republican* expressed dismay over former friends who had joined the sinophobic camp.[67] In explaining the obviously bipartisan and national character of the vote in the Senate to deny naturalization rights to the Chinese, Boston's *Evening Traveller* complained that too many Republicans had "taken up the old democratic 'oligarchy of the skin' idea." [68] William Lloyd Garrison was "startled" by the opposition to Chinese labor on the part of eminent Republican party leaders and former abolitionists. Throughout the 1870s Garrison exchanged missives with these "renegade radicals," and in 1879 he dueled with the eastern exclusionist champion, James G. Blaine, on the pages of the *New York Tribune*. The debate was more than a little confused, however, by Garrison's insistence on using the terms "slavery" and "racism" interchangeably. Hence, opposition to Chinese immigration in his eyes was "the slavery question all over again," while his opponent was classifying the Chinese immigrants as "slaves." [69]

Perhaps William Cullen Bryant's quiet fears were more typical of eastern opinion makers in the 1870s than were the blatantly stated positions of Butler, Blaine, Wilson, Garrison, and Greeley. Bryant refused to comment publicly on the issue; but in rejecting an article on the Chinese submitted to his journal, he wrote, "We shall be obliged to have closer relations with our pig-tailed brethren . . . ere long, but I do not contemplate it with any pleasure; I prefer the Caucasian race. The Negroes among us are a source of trouble, and there is no knowing what might yet happen as a consequence of the mutual jealousy of races." [70] The editor of the *Springfield Republican* readily conceded that no one was particularly happy about the arrival of Chinese on the East Coast. He described Sampson's crew as "the van of the invading army of Celestials seen in a vision by Wendell Phillips, greatly feared by all democrats, and not particularly welcomed by anybody except in dire necessity." [71]

Editorial reaction to North Adams was mixed but generally negative in a sample of fifteen newspapers representing Albany, Utica, and New York City in the Empire State and Springfield, Newburyport, and Boston in Massachusetts. Eight of these editors were clearly outraged by Sampson's action, while the other half supported it. But three of these supporters were somewhat equivocal in endorsing open Chinese immigration and, by the end of 1870, expressed enough concern over its cultural threat to infer that they would have accepted some restrictions on it. The editor of the *Albany Evening Journal* furiously battled with the *Utica Observer* and the *Albany Argus,* whose "democratic" editors he accused of being racists on the Chinese question.[72] But only four months later this editor himself succumbed to racial fears over large-scale Chinese immigration.[73] In a similar manner, the *Springfield Republican* attacked the *Newburyport Herald* and New York's *Evening Post* for confusing a labor question with racial issues.[74]

All three Boston papers examined cheered the North Adams experiment, although the editor of the *Evening Transcript* did confess to some uneasiness over the use of Chinese to break the strike, which had "portents of a somewhat disturbing nature." The "exclusiveness, arrogance and domineering of workingman's associations" had brought it upon themselves, he agreed, but wondered if "native strikebreakers from Maine" could not have been used instead. It was "unwise to incorporate such an element" as the Chinese into American society, he thought.[75] Less than a month later, however, this same editor chided "the alarmed opponents of Chinese immigration" with the reminder that "Providence does not work by an eight hour clock." Undoubtedly God had a higher purpose in mind in bringing such inferior types as the Negroes, Chinese, and Irish into the country, he suggested. At any rate, the superior American institutions affected these groups more than our culture is affected by them, he confidently concluded.[76] All three Boston editors along with their colleague in Springfield were strongly antilabor and anti-Irish, and they saw in Sampson's action an opportunity to give the "Crispins" and "Paddies" their long overdue comeuppance.

Similar hostility to labor and to the Irish was expressed in the reaction of the *New York Times* to North Adams. Months before Sampson's Celestial crew arrived, this editor was upset that such immigrants would not be "free";[77] but once they were in Massachusetts, he concluded that the arrogant Irish workers had left employers with no other choice. General Butler and "Governor" Hawley missed the point in "debating principles," he asserted, while ignoring the fact that "Paddy" was "slovenly" and "impudent" and "Biddie" was a bad cook. "John Chinaman is to rid us of the old plague of domestic life." [78] There were plenty of jobs for people willing to work for "sensible wages," the *Times* insisted in another editorial on North Adams. Besides, all the hysteria was unnecessary since the Burlingame Treaty not only precluded Chinese exclusion but also ruled out the citizenship for Celestials which everyone feared. How could the Chinese imperil republican institutions, the editor asked in another dig at the Irish, when "he does not stay long enough, and is not sufficiently civilized to take a very lively interest in naturalization frauds, primary meetings, or the mystery of ballot box stuffing . . . ?" He did concede to Sampson's critics, however, that slavery was always a "potential danger" in importing Chinese workers, although he rejected the *New York Star's* hysterical insistence that the Celestials in North Adams were "outright slaves." [79]

Initially the *New York Tribune* denounced Sampson's action and warned that a new form of slavery and the makings of another civil war could be the consequences. "The results of the introduction of this element there [North Adams] are likely to be very deplorable . . . , dangerous to the society in which such a system of labor is permitted." [80] Two weeks later another *Tribune* editorial disarmingly confessed that "we by no means contemplate the present aspect of this immigration with unmixed satisfaction," as it proceeded to list a host of cultural, racial, and population fears in almost hysterical tones. It observed that "scattered attempts at the introduction of Chinese labor on Southern plantations and railroads" were also being made. China's population and frequent famines made this emigration far more dangerous than Ireland's. "For every Irishman ready and able to emigrate there is a score of Chinamen. Any slight propelling force may suddenly precipitate them upon us by thousands for every score now coming," [81] the editorial concluded.

Greeley also made his front page available to writers whose denunciations of Chinese immigration evoked a strong rebuke from the *New York Times* for such flagrant racism.[82] One such article by John Swinton warned that "Mongolians will gradually incorporate themselves into the blood and being of the country." There was a "vast preponderance of females in Massachusetts," Swinton pointed out, among whom perverted and lecherous Chinese were arriving with "their foul and mortifying vices." But he left "others to draw such deductions as they please" from this frightening situation. While the *Times* denounced Swinton's article as flagrantly "racist," it provoked Greely to conclude that "this Chinese problem is really one of the gravest questions of the age." [83]

But Greeley's hostility to the Irish also tempered his anticoolie position, so that on other occasions he agreed that the Chinese could supply "the wholesome corrective of competition" for the indolent Irish who made up "a class of laborers more tyrannous to employers and less skillful in their crafts than any others." [84] He also endorsed an article on his front page in which a correspondent suggested that the Chinese immigrants could "become the understratum of American society and lift every class above them to a higher level." [85]

The tone of the editorial pages of the *New York World* quickly escalated to hysteria on the subject of North Adams. These Chinese workers would not return to China as everyone seemed so certain they would, the editor argued, for the simple reason that they were pariahs for having left their homeland in the first place. By way of illustration he recounted how one Celestial who was educated at Yale—and even learned to read Horace and translate Aeschylus—was ostracized and ridiculed in China. Chinese vices would corrode and finally destroy American institutions the longer the Chinese remained, the editor warned. *"Polyandry* we know is an Oriental though not exactly a Chinese institution, with all its frightful consequences of virtual prostitution and sure sterility," he added.[86] The exact intent of this non sequitur is unclear, but it reflects this editor's almost irrational alarm over North Adams. A few days later he sobered up sufficiently to admit sheepishly that his reaction was, perhaps, out of proportion to the small number of coolies who actually arrived at Sampson's shoe factory, but he explained that his concern was over the precedent being established in North Adams. If the workers' just demands against coolie labor were settled by his editorial emotion it was well worth it, he concluded.[87] The *World* was taunted by others for having contradicted its free trade position by demanding restrictions on Chinese immigration. An editorial in answer explained that there was no inconsistency in these two positions. Free trade, the editor argued, provided the community with cheaper goods, whereas coolie immigration only lined the pockets of the Sampsons and threatened the very nature of society.[88]

Charles Dana, who only a year earlier was highly altruistic about sharing God's bounty in America with all comers, now fussed and fumed over North Adams in the *New York Sun*.

Finally, he exploded into a tirade against those who "treat the question whether or not some millions of barbarian Asiatics shall be suddenly brought and placed alongside as many intelligent Americans, as if it were purely a calculation of dollars and cents." And just as bad, Dana argued, were "the sentimentalists" who would "bring the whole world here to share in the advantages of our superior civilization, and rescue it from barbarism. In the excess of their benevolence they would have Americans starve and die in order that everybody else might grow fat. To them, too, one man is as good as another and birth, education, morality, and intellectual power count for nothing at all." Dana concluded that Chinese exclusion was only "simple justice" for the workingmen, and those who opposed it were "neither good Americans, good economists, good philanthropists, nor sensible men." [89] Thereafter, Dana favored restrictions on Chinese immigration, if not always total exclusion.

Bennett displayed his usual mercurial oscillation in discussing North Adams. At first his main concern was still over the possibility that new abolitionists would threaten another civil war over the coolie issue. The proximity of North Adams to the "home of abolitionism" triggered bitter memories for Bennett, which he expressed in his own inimitable style: "The 'hub' can never be quiet as long as there is a wooly-headed nigger or a pig-tailed coolie to be provided with that 'inestimable boon of freedom'—the right to vote." [90] But Bennett decided, a few days later, that cheaper shoes were perhaps worth the risk of some abolitionists going beserk again, as well as any cultural and racial dangers attendant upon this immigration. Having survived the "depraved, slothful and brutal African in its midst," Bennett thought that American society could manage the Chinaman.[91] As his mood became more sanguine over the prospects, Bennett decided that the "coolie" would be America's "Hindu" and thus "the Anglo Saxon race" would jointly exploit the "Asiatic" or "heathen race." [92]

Within a month, however, Bennett was stricken with fresh doubts, and he became more pessimistic over Chinese immigration: "They are a people who are our antipodes in all social and intellectual regards; it is not possible to imagine civilizations more widely at variance than their's and our's; and varying civilizations never harmonize side by side. There will be conflict and . . . other revolutions besides that in the relations of labor." [93] A series of editorials on opium dens, lewd females, dirt, and disease in Californian Chinatowns provoked Bennett to blurt out, "Compared with these base Chinese, the vilest dregs that come into New York from the vilest holes in Europe are refined and attractive people." [94]

By the end of July, the announcement that China had agreed to slow down her emigration in order to assuage American fears was sufficient to placate Bennett. Wendell Phillips's conditions had been met, he insisted, and Horatio Seymour was merely "beating a dead horse." [95] But two months later Bennett was in possession of reports from California that, as soon as these coolies learned the shoe or cigar making trades, they went into business for themselves. As entrepreneurs, the Chinese were more efficient than Americans in exploiting coolie labor. This disturbing news, coupled with Conwell's book, was sufficient to permanently topple Bennett into the anti-Chinese camp, a position more consistent with his ethnocentric and racist predilections. It was no longer a simple question of "labor vs. capital," Bennett warned. If the Chinese first displaced the Negro and then the Irish, he asked, where would it end? "We may soon see them building our ships and houses, digging our canals, driving our city railroad cars . . . it will thus be seen that the Chinese question interests all classes of the community . . . because there is absolutely no limit to the supply of oriental laborers, except the capacity of ships and railroads to transport them." [96]

Bennett's alarm over the news that Chinese coolies were developing an entrepreneurial spirit was by no means unique. It was discussed by several eastern editors with some excitement, perhaps because such a turn of events was so unexpected. Editorial reaction was stronger in those newspapers which had continued to support Chinese immigration. The *New York Times,* for example, published a series of editorials on the "sharp practice" of those coolies who worked only to learn the trade and put their former bosses out of business with unfair competition.[97] "Employers are getting to be more and more disgusted with the hapless Mongolian every day . . . that presumptuous individual, having faithfully served out the period for which he contracted, now wishes to turn his skill to account by engaging in the manufacturing of goods for his own benefit." This editor was at least honest enough to recognize that such entrepreneurial initiative was in the best American tradition, adding, "With this purpose no fault could be found, if the opposition were carried on in a 'legitimate' manner, but as John Chinaman's notion of the legitimate is not quite clear, he begins by so greatly underselling his former employer that the latter

speedily loses a considerable amount of custom." [98] In this climate
of opinion, even laissez-faire economics was un-American as far as
the Chinese were concerned.

By 1875 a sufficient number of Chinese had arrived on the East
Coast to establish miniature Chinatowns in New York, Boston,
and Philadelphia. For almost a century before this a trickle of Chinese had found its way into the eastern United States. The first
group arrived in Baltimore as part of the crew of the *Pallas* in
1785 and spent a winter as wards of the city of Philadelphia before
being sent home. Chinese sailors, jugglers, circus riders, and students drifted into eastern cities throughout the nineteenth century.[99] In 1856, excited reports of "idol worshipping on Cherry
Street" sent a *New York Times* reporter to investigate a Chinese
settlement that already numbered 150. These were mostly ma-
rooned sailors under a leader whose unlikely name was reported as
"Mr. Chimpo Appo." The interviewing reporter sounded disappointed to find no idols, and only "sundry Chinese ornaments
which are undesirable." Indeed, Mr. Appo was a Methodist who
offered his services as a missionary to the Chinese in New York. It
was also reported that the Chinese lived "fraternally," neither
feasted on rats and dogs nor smoked opium, and occasionally married Irish ladies. While the queries of the reporter reflected the
popular stereotype of the Chinese, the report produced was more
typical of the friendly curiosity that greeted the early stray arrivals
from China on the East Coast.[100]

Seventeen years later the *New York Times* produced another
full page report on the city's Chinatown, which had grown to ap-
proximately 500. In contrast with the earlier profile, the story in
1873 featured denizens continuously gambling, feasting on ro-
dents, living in filth, and worshipping hideous idols. "In the midst
of a great Christian city like New-York, the theatre of the last
meeting of the Evangelical Alliance, it is very strange, but none
the less true, that such an abode of idolatry exists." Still more evil
practices were implied in the article: "To the reporter's inquiry
about "a handsome but squalidly dressed young white girl"
present in an opium den, the owner "replied with a horrible lear,
'Oh, hard time in New York. Young girl hungry. Plenty come
here. Chinaman always have something to eat, and he like young
white girl, He! He!'" The reader was warned that this was no
empty boast; many white girls were lured into these opium
dens.[101]

The belief that the Chinese had perverted sexual proclivities was by now firmly entrenched in the American mind. An 1876 article on Chinese servants in *Scribner's* warned: "No matter how good a Chinaman may be, ladies never leave their children with them, especially little girls." [102] Three years later Elbridge T. Gerry wrote a plea to the president on behalf of the New York Society for Prevention of Cruelty to Children to intervene in China to save the children of some defeated rebels who were to be turned over to the soldiers "for uses and practices unhappily too common in the East, but which Lord Coke says, 'are not so much as to be named among Christians.' " [103]

The absence of Chinese females among the Chinese workers who arrived on the East Coast in 1870 enhanced these sexual fears. A Boston editor recounted the uncomfortable joke making the rounds of his city: "Will the Chinese 'takkee wifee'?" And the *New York Tribune* hinted at frightful consequences in store for Caucasian maidens in Massachusetts.[104] When some Chinese attended Sunday school, it was rumored that they were not motivated by any interest in Christianity but at best by a desire to learn English and at worst to debauch their white, female teachers. One such teacher, who apparently escaped the experience with her virtue intact, had "her health . . . broken down" from the smell of her Chinese pupils—another martyred missionary.[105] When some Celestials married their Sunday school teachers, it caused a scandal in several churches. The father of one such bride insisted that his daughter had been drugged by her suitor.[106]

The fear of the Chinese laundry as the site of evil assignations on the West Coast, mentioned by Oscar Handlin, was by no means absent in other sections of the country as he implied.[107] In 1889 a Chinese laundry in Milwaukee, Wisconsin, was demolished by an angry mob of two thousand after its two owners were indicted for ravaging more than twenty young white girls between the ages of 9 and 13 in the back room. Such incidents provoked sensational stories in the eastern press. Under the headline "Two Mongolian Minotaurs—Shocking Debauchery of Innocents," the *New York World* reported in detail the testimony of the young victims in court.[108] In Brooklyn two seventeen-year-old prostitutes, Lizzie Kane and Minnie Brennan, claimed that Chinese laundrymen had started them on their "shameful life" at a very tender age. Mrs. Brennan tried to choke the nearest Chinese spectator in the court when she heard this, and Mr. Kane threatened vengeance on all Chinese.[109] The fear of perverted sexual proclivities on the part of the Chinese immigrants, in and out of their laundries, neither originated in California nor was it confined to that state. Its origin would be more accurately traced to Protestant missionaries in China and to the descriptions of the Chinese to be found in American magazines before the arrival of the first immigrant. The myriad reports that emanated from California after 1852 merely corroborated and reenforced this older definition of Chinese behavior.

One Celestial arrival on the East Coast told a reporter that he left California to escape the "Ilishman," but he astutely added, "Bimby hab got more Chinaman come, mi thinkee this side alla same San Flancisco." [110] With the influx of Chinese immigrants, New York papers began to report on dark doings in that city's Chinese quarter. The Chinese New Year festival, which has since become so attractive to New Yorkers, provoked such headlines in 1874 as "Idolatry in Baxter Street—Feasting and Smoking Opium—The Great Idol 'Fo.'" [111] Chinese funerals, banquets, and picnics were the occasion for additional unfavorable reports. Even a Chinese celebration in the basement of the Spring Street Presbyterian Church was the subject of some suspicious speculation. And, of course, there were frequent eyewitness reports of the Chinese feasting upon the neighborhood dogs and cats to supplement their alleged diet of rats. By 1883, some Mott Street leaders threatened lawsuits for such slander.[112] In 1876, Bennett warned that the Chinese spreading across the nation were seriously endangering "the highest interest of society and civilization." Bennett in particular was fond of medical metaphors and explained that "the leprosy which comes into the country with every ship from China will taint and corrupt not alone the body politic but the sanctities of society and the sacredness of religion." [113]

The *New York Times* was one of the few big dailies left in the East that was still in favor of totally unrestricted Chinese immigration after 1875. Its defense of Celestial immigrants was a bit left-handed, however, arguing that "John" was a better addition to our society than was "Paddy," a point implicitly made in sarcastic editorials. For example, the *Times* agreed that the Chinese were terribly "degraded" after observing one of their picnics in Belleville, New Jersey, in which "nothing stronger than tea" washed down "their puppy dog stew." Not even during the display of fireworks did whiskey cross their lips and not a single Celestial was stabbed, the editor mockingly complained. "They occasionally twitched each other's pigtails in a way so obviously good-natured as to excite the disgust of every civilized spectator who saw such admirable opportunities for an enlivening riot so utterly thrown away," he jibed. But everyone knows how "imitative" these "barbarians" are, the readers were assured, so "John" will soon learn to get drunk and knock down his wife between stabbing matches, and "we can feel that the example of civilization has not been wholly in vain." [114] Needless to say, such sarcasm was not lost on the Irish, and it neither endeared the Chinese nor the *New York Times* to the editors of Irish newspapers in the city.[115]

Even favorably disposed Americans experienced difficulty under conditions of increasing contacts with the Chinese. When a Chinese commissioner took up residence in Providence in 1877 with his wife and sister-in-law, the leading citizens were determined to demonstrate that they had none of the vulgar prejudices of their compatriots elsewhere. They took the local minister to task for referring to their distinguished visitors as "pagans." The Celestial official accepted their presents of sparrows' nests good-naturedly, but became somewhat indignant over the offerings of wharf rats. The birth of the commissioner's first child was eagerly awaited, but when his sister-in-law turned out to be instead a "two piece wife" and, four months later, was also delivered of a son, the good citizens of Providence were horrified to realize that polygamy was being practiced in their Christian city.[116]

A parallel case was that of the Chinese philosopher Wong Ching Foo, who arrived in 1874 and had the effrontery to think that he could convert Bostonians and New Yorkers to Buddhism. In a series of lectures, he castigated American missionaries, whom he accused of painting false pictures of "Chinese degradation, immorality and idolatry" in order to wring more money from the American people. "The Heathen Among Us. His Horrible Heterodox views of Christian missions in China," the indignant *New York World* headlined a story on Wong Ching Foo.[117] Even the more cosmopolitan editor of the *New York Times,* who had warmly welcomed the Chinese philosopher in 1874, by 1877 had had enough of his "deprecatory" remarks concerning Christianity and Christian missionaries.[118]

In 1876 the report of a joint congressional committee sent to California to investigate the Chinese problem received a great deal of publicity in the American press. Although the 1200 pages or more of testimony produced included some few endorsements of Chinese immigration by businessmen and ministers, the great bulk of it was composed of the hostile testimony of lawyers, judges, doctors, journalists, labor leaders, and self-styled sociologists who

repeated all the negative themes thus far developed. It could
hardly have been otherwise. Senator Oliver P. Morton was too ill
to journey to the West Coast and relinquished the chair to California's Sargent, who was flanked by Piper from his own state and
Cooper of Tennessee after Mead and Wilson of New York and
Iowa, respectively, had withdrawn from the committee.[119]

In spite of the loaded composition of the committee and the
rank prejudice and patently hysterical nonsense promulgated in
the report, eastern editors treated it with far more respect than it
deserved. The committee's report, in fact, provoked the first
doubts in the *New York Times* since 1873 about the wisdom of
continuing immigration from China. "It may be admitted that the
Chinese immigrants are wholly undesirable, and that their coming is a misfortune," the editor confessed.[120] Other editors responded to the report with demands that immediate action be
taken to rid the country of such social evils, although Bennett cautioned the government to institute a remedy that would "guard
ourselves against the influx of semi-barbarous Chinese while not
losing the increasing advantages of our trade with China." [121]
Editorials and magazine articles on the congressional investigation
of the Chinese in California bore such titles as the "Asiatic Invasion" and the "Mongol Problem," [122] and the editor of the *New
York World* declared that he "shudders at the consequences of this
invasion." [123] Bennett asked his readers and members of Congress
to read the "loathsome details" of this report very carefully. It
provided Americans, he contended, with the "authentic and in-
contestable truth of what has been so often related to the beastliness, the filth, squalor, leprosy, venereal diseases; the lawlessness,
perjury and violence; the corruption of youth and the injury to
the laboring classes that make the Chinese quarter of San Francisco a huge festering ulcer which is eating into the morals of the
country." Congress had to act on this report, Bennett declared, or
"bear the odium of shirking a plain duty." [124] Even the more
sober *New York Times* headlined the story of the Joint Congressional Report on Chinese Immigration when it was finally published: "Immorality Unmentionable—A Startling Array of facts."
The editor concluded that "upon the point of morals, there is no
Aryan or European race which is not far superior to the Chinese as
a class." The "safety of the state" called for some action, he decided.[125]

A famine in 1878 also fanned the fears that China would flood
the United States with immigrants. It further shook the belief of
the *New York Times* that the law of supply and demand would

regulate and curtail this immigration.[126] Articles on how the starving Chinese were being driven to cannibalism and the tales of Chinese officials who behaved like "a class of human hyenas . . . thrills the civilized world with horror," Bennett wrote.[127] Remembering the effects of the potato famine in Ireland on migration, editors speculated fearfully about Chinese immigration; and as the *New York World* had expressed it, the beginning of the "inevitable tide of an illimitable sea, of which the first billow has as yet not broken upon our shores." [128] An article in the *North American Review* utilized statistics from the Irish famine, along with some Malthusian arguments, to conclude that 100 million Chinese would arrive in the United States by 1900. Once America was as overcrowded as China, the same article warned, "the characteristics of the Chinese which we despise . . . make him a most formidable rival for the ultimate survival as the fittest." Finally, the author asked, "Is not the Mongol a thistle in our field? Shall we pluck it up, as does the wise husbandman, or shall we withdraw the intelligence of artificial selection from the environment and leave the battle to the chances of natural selection alone?" [129]

Once the fear of massive Chinese immigration into all sections of the country had taken hold, the country was ripe for some kind of restrictive measures. In Washington, the leadership and prodding for such legislation was by no means restricted to California's senators and representatives. It is impossible to rank in order of demogogic effectiveness the efforts of Sargent of California, Blaine of Maine, Willis of Kentucky, Cameron of Wisconsin, Browne of Indiana, or Speer of Georgia to secure a law that would limit or exclude the Chinese. All of them were outspoken sinophobes who harangued their colleagues with almost identical arguments that exploited fears of Chinese numbers, stagnation, slavery, diseases, and immorality. True, the western and southern contingents voted unanimously for the various restrictive and exclusionist measures that were proposed, but the easterners and midwesterners who opposed these measures in Congress were very much in the minority among the delegates from their sections. For example, the first successful exclusion law in 1882 passed the House of Representatives with 201 yeas, 37 nays, and 51 absent. While all 7 representatives on the floor from the western section of the nation voted for the measure, as did all 82 Southerners on hand, 53 from eastern states also voted for it in contrast to 24 in opposition, and the midwesterners answered the roll call with 59 yeas and 13 nays.[130]

Senator Sargent was, in fact, fond of citing encouraging letters that he received from important eastern opinion leaders. He acknowledged that Horatio Seymour was the originator of his plan to limit the number of passengers on arriving vessels as one means of restricting Chinese immigration.[131] Andrew D. White, president of Cornell University, wrote to Sargent in 1876, "I confess to a very deep-seated dread of this influx of Asiatics of a type which it seems to me can never form any hopeful element in this nation." [132]

It is also a mistake to interpret President Hayes' veto of the first restrictive measure against the Chinese as indicative of American attitudes outside of the West and South. Too often this veto has been used to illustrate the argument that the demands for exclusion were California inspired and supported by the South in opposition to the wish for open immigration in the rest of the nation. In fact, President Hayes recorded in his diary in 1879, "I am satisfied that the present Chinese labor invasion (it is not in any proper sense immigration—women and children do not come) is pernicious and should be discouraged. Our experience in dealing with the weaker races—the Negroes and Indians, for example,—is not encouraging. . . . I would consider with favor any suitable measures to discourage the Chinese from coming to our shores." [133]

Upon his return to the United States in 1876, Samuel Wells Williams expressed shock at the amount of hostility in the eastern states to Chinese immigration and began a speaking tour in an attempt to correct the situation.[134] An interesting editorial in the *New York Times* in 1880 also testified to the widespread fear of Chinese immigration throughout the nation. "Never in the history of this country has so much been made from so little as in the case of the Chinese in the United States. . . . The prodigious hullabaloo which has been raised over the 'invasion of the Asiatic hordes' is childish." [135] Both Williams and the author of this editorial were impervious to the roles played by themselves in nurturing this hysteria. The missionary had only to pick up his still popular text on China, *The Middle Kingdom,* to locate an important source of ammunition for the sinophobes; and the journalist did not have to go back very many issues in his own *New York Times* to locate evidence of editorial fright over immigration from the Celestial Empire. Indeed, in the very same editorial he conceded that "the general character of the Chinese is as bad as has been charged by the 'Chinaphobists.' " His argument was that a mere 92,327 Celestials were hardly "hordes . . . devouring the land." [136]

How listless, stagnant, unprogressive are the Chinese. No improvement in language, literature, modes of agriculture or mechanical arts—still reading books and practicing the arts of antiquity, without the genius to invent, or energy to execute anything new or give any evidence of progress.

Hon. Harlow S. Orton, Annual Address, State Historical Society of Wisconsin, Feb. 23, 1869, p. 14.

We are accustomed to think of the Chinese as belonging to a degraded race, ignorant of civilized life. . . .

Atlantic Monthly (Boston), XXIII (1869), 747.

I do not see how any thoughtful lover of his country can countenance this Mongolian invasion, involving as it does the subversion of our civilization.

Montgomery Blair in *New York Times*, March 6, 1882.

9

Chinese Exclusion in Historical and National Perspective

The accepted interpretation of the Chinese exclusion laws, referred to in Chapter 1 as the "California thesis," does not stand up under close scrutiny and should be substantially modified, if not completely altered. To view the policy of exclusion simply as a victory for the obsessive prejudice of Californians is neither accurate nor fair. Although that state unquestionably catalyzed and spearheaded the movement for exclusion, there were much more potent national and historical forces at work than the mere accident of evenly balanced political parties. Not even a very enthusiastic tail of such small dimensions could have wagged a dog that was less than willing to be wagged.

The fear of creating a permanently servile class, which motivated respectable elements in California to oppose Chinese immigration, was a national not a sectional fear, for which the center of gravity was much farther East. Opinion leaders in the East were just as concerned over what Mary Coolidge called the "coolie fiction," and not all of them can be easily dismissed as ambitious politicians eager to please California in close balance-of-power situations. President Grant was neither a Californian nor a candidate for office in 1874 when he appealed to Congress to terminate Chinese immigration on the grounds that the Celestials were not voluntary immigrants but absolute slaves.

Cultural anxiety over the admission of such an unfamiliar and dissimilar migrant as the Chinese was not confined to any one section of the country either. Eastern editors articulated such fears at least as early as they were expressed in California. Americans have generally assumed that the theory of the melting pot involved a two-way process whereby immigrants contributed to the cultural matrix in the process of becoming "Americanized." Until the coming of the Chinese, however, no immigrant group had differed sufficiently from the Anglo-American root stock to compromise basic social institutions such as Christian religion and ethics, monogamy, or natural rights theory, not to mention the doctrine of material progress for the individual. Faced with the concrete possibility that it might become necessary to sacrifice substantial elements of these axiomatic beliefs in the name of a melting-pot hybrid "Americanization," many editors and legislators frankly shifted their ground. Social foundations were not negotiable. The immigrant had to become a convert and shed his foreign, heathen ways. The alternative was total exclusion of culturally distant groups, and a melting pot that was limited rather than infinite in scope. Thus, the Chinese Exclusion Act of 1882 marks a revolutionary shift in the course of American immigration history, full of disturbing implications for the future.

Cultural pluralists have long contended that the melting pot is mythical, and that Americans always had in mind a cauldron in which the immigrant was cleansed of his foreign ways. There is a serious need for a study of the historical meanings given to the melting-pot concept. As far as the Chinese were concerned, it would appear that American opinion leaders did have a real melting pot in mind prior to their arrival, albeit one which already excluded Indians and Negroes. As immigrants, the Chinese posed the first serious threat to this concept. They had little of value to contribute to any evolving American culture, in the eyes of most opinion makers, and they were believed to be immutable, tenaciously clinging to old customs and recalcitrantly opposing "progress" and "moral improvement." Thus, the great cultural disparity created by Chinese immigration was rendered even more menacing. The discussion of the "Chinese question" played a significant role in transforming America's conception of the melting pot, from one which amalgamated the best from all the donor cultures into a new synthesis, to one that achieved Anglo conformity.

The modern racist theory that evolved during the three decades of unrestricted Chinese immigration added a biological dimension to the Chinaman's lack of cultural fitness. The germ theory of culture hypothesized by racists helped to validate the cultural fears provoked by the arrival of the Chinese and placed the rejection of these immigrants on a seemingly more scientific basis. "Oriental blood" determined the "Oriental thoughts" and "Oriental habits" which precluded any possibility that the Chinese could be "Americanized." The Burlingame Treaty of 1868 and, two years later, the defeat of the Sumner and Trumbull amendments to the naturalization laws in the Senate officially recognized this in denying citizenship to Chinese immigrants. The strongest supporters of unrestricted Chinese immigration made it clear that they could not conceive of the Chinese as a permanent part of American society.

What made easterners move beyond the simple denial of citizenship to acquiesence in, and often active support for, a termination of this immigration? After all, the Chinese had not yet arrived on the East Coast in substantial numbers. As "birds of passage" they would not remain in the country, presumably, but would return to China after helping fill the West Coast's need for cheap labor. Businessmen and Protestant clerics, who were the most ardent supporters of Chinese immigration, argued that the Chinese would carry back to China the seeds of Christianity and a taste for American goods, thus continuing to serve the interests of the United States and God.

Several factors help to explain why easterners abandoned this obviously advantageous situation. Many of them shared Horace Greeley's fear that "the rivulet" of sojourners could become "a Niagara" spilling Chinese over the Rockies and the great plains to flood the nation with Celestial immigrants. Crucial to the passage of the first exclusion law was the fear of China's huge population, without which one wonders if the East would not have been more content to simply let California assume the "burden" of Chinese immigration in order to gain its commercial and spiritual rewards.

A second factor that caused the East to give active support to the decision to exclude the Chinese was the fear that these sojourners offered a serious threat to the nation's health. By 1870 Americans had become sensitive to the relationship between dirt and disease. During the next decade they grew concerned over specific Chinese germs that would afflict the nation with syphilis, cholera, leprosy, and, much worse, nameless contagions spawned in the fleshpots of Oriental lechery. Concern over China's potential for exporting both large numbers of people and devastating diseases caused some American opinion leaders to speculate that an inferior people might well overcome a superior group, in a blind Darwinian struggle for the survival of the fittest. By intelligent interference with natural law, they argued, such a contest could be avoided and American civilization made more secure.

The year 1870 was a crucial one in crystallizing anti-Chinese sentiment on the East Coast. While editors in this section had expressed considerable anxiety over the nature of Chinese immigration, they were, in the main, content with restricting the Celestials to the Pacific slope, denying them citizenship, and encouraging them to return to China after having filled their economic function here. Following the Burlingame Treaty, a Darwinian optimism ran high in many eastern newspapers, whose editors were confident that the Anglo-American stock would best the Chinese in any racial contest. In such a mood, these editors were willing to let the Chinese migrate anywhere in the United States and mix freely with the Caucasian population. But this mood shifted rapidly with the arrival of Chinese workers in Massachusetts in June 1870, and a number of eastern editors began to call for Chinese exclusion.

Although the fear that the handful of Celestials in North Adams was but the advance guard of an army that could easily number in the millions was clearly the crucial factor in crystallizing anti-Chinese sentiment in the East, other events during the summer of 1870 also encouraged these editors to advocate exclusion. Only weeks after their debut in North Adams, Chinese immigrants were denied naturalization rights on the floor of the Senate, an action that seemed to confer official sanction to the cultural and racial fears expounded on in the press. This was quickly followed by news that Christian missionaries were being tortured and butchered at Tientsin. The rest of the summer was filled with rumors and spurious reports of new arrivals of Chinese work crews at various eastern locations. Finally one did materialize in New Jersey September along with the news that Chinese coolies in Peru had staged a bloody uprising. It was this unfortunate combination of events over a four-month period, rather than simply Sampson's action in Massachusetts, that caused many eastern editors to add their voices to the cry for Chinese exclusion during the closing months of 1870.

Interestingly enough, historians who have examined the Chinese issue in California have also underlined the year 1870 as one in which the anti-Chinese forces achieved a high degree of organization and a larger measure of popular support. This further supports the interpretation that sinophobia was a national rather than a purely sectional sentiment. That the successful passage of an exclusion law still had to wait another decade is a tribute to the powerful economic and religious interests that supported Chinese immigration as well as to the inertial power of America's commitment to open immigration at this time.

To discover the mechanics by which the anti-Chinese movement was organized on a national level, it would be necessary to consider the role of organized labor and possibly the Irish press and Roman Catholic clergy within the evenly balanced political situation. Ira Cross chronicled the important role played by organized labor in the anti-Chinese movement in California.[1] Robert Seager demonstrated that in California the Roman Catholic clergy and press was sympathetic to the demands that the Chinese must go, while Protestant clerics generally opposed exclusion.[2] This may have been a function of the ethnic character of the leadership in both the Church and organized labor. At least Mary Coolidge and many of the nineteenth-century opponents of exclusion charged the Irish with instigating, organizing, and leading the anti-Chinese movement in California. But labor organizations and the Church transcended state boundaries and sectional divisions, as did their essentially Irish leadership.

It would not be difficult to indict organized labor as the backbone of the anti-Chinese movement on a national level. Labor leaders in every section of the country attacked the coolie issue with the monomania of men whose backs are to the wall. Their fear that the Chinese worker would be used to create an industrial feudalism was not without foundation. "These 'Celestials' belong to no striking organization—do not care to be out nights—don't worry about their pay—do not presume to dictate to their employers," one editor explained in justifying the use of Chinese in

North Adams.[3] Indeed, only their hostility to organized labor permitted some editors with sinophobic and racist inclinations to support, albeit uneasily, Calvin Sampson's use of Chinese strikebreakers.

The siege mentality produced in labor leaders by such antiunion sentiment led to violently racist denunciations of the Chinese. Even A. C. Cameron, who enjoyed a reputation for being much more liberal than his colleagues on the Negro issue, demanded that the Chinese be banished and threatened "sterner measures, which the founders of the Republic resorted to when argument and appeal failed to convince, and when wrongs inflicted were too grievous to be borne." [4] With the news of the Memphis convention in 1869, Cameron kicked off labor's anti-Chinese campaign in the *Workingman's Advocate* and demanded racial loyalty from all Americans to destroy "the Mongolian blight." [5]

If Cameron did not get this loyalty from the population at large, he certainly got it from labor leaders. The most prominent labor spokesmen of the time—George McNeil, John Swinton, John P. Irish, T. V. Powderly, Samuel Gompers, Eugene Debs, Henry George, and William J. McLaughlin—were outspoken sinophobes.[6] Virtually every labor newspaper and organization opposed Chinese immigration after 1870. Even the Negro delegates at the first Colored State Labor Convention in Baltimore in December 1869 passed a plank in favor of Chinese exclusion.[7] Nor were the more radical groups and leaders exempt from this obsession with the Chinese. The International Workingman's Association succumbed in 1873, passing an anticoolie resolution only one year after it had called for "complete political and social equality for all, without distinction of sex, creed, color or condition" at its first convention in Cleveland.[8] Publications such as the *Socialist* in New York and the *National Socialist* in Cincinnati opposed Chinese immigration.[9] The anarchist Joseph Buchanan explained that although he believed in the equality of man he had to draw the line at the Chinaman, and preferred to call his scheme "Brotherhood of Man Limited." [10]

When Richard Trevellick attempted to stipulate that labor's opposition was "to the importation but not the free immigration of the Chinese" in his presidential address to the National Labor Union's convention in Cincinnati in 1870, he ran into stiff opposition. Those historians who feel it necessary to uncover a Californian behind every national expression of sinophobia before 1882 could make much of the fact that W. W. Delaney of San Francisco chaired the "Committee on Coolie Labor" at this convention. But the committee on Trevellick's address also opposed this distinction between coolie and immigrant and the entire convention upheld them.[11] Labor was in no mood for such hair-splitting. When Wendell Phillips and other contributors to the *Socialist* attempted to make the same distinction that Trevellick did, they were roundly taken to task by readers. "I believe in race, and on this point I am supported by many prominent socialists and enlightened thinkers of the day," one subscriber protested.[12] John Swinton was closer to the temper of the worker when he took a frankly racist position in his column in the *New York Tribune* in 1870 against all Chinese, coolie or free immigrant: "The Mongolian blood is depraved and debased blood. The Mongolian type of humanity is an inferior type—inferior in organic structure, in vital force or physical energy, and in the constitutional conditions of development. On this point all anthropologists and ethnologists are agreed." [13] Charles Bergman was warmly applauded when ten years later, in 1881, he demanded at the American Federation of Labor's convention in Pittsburgh that Congress prohibit Chinese immigration "absolutely," a resolution that passed with a single dissenting vote.[14] As A. C. Cameron explained it, "there is no such thing as Chinese *emigration*. It would be just as proper to say that the cured beef of Buenos Ayres [sic] emigrated to Great Britain." [15]

There were a few dissenters, of course, to this almost unanimous stand taken by organized labor against Chinese immigration. A few, mostly intellectuals, attempted to maintain the distinction between coolie and free immigrant, while others simply remained silent on the issue. The New England Labor Reform League refused to discuss the Chinese question at a meeting in 1871 and the Socialist Labor party managed to avoid an anticoolie resolution at their convention in 1878.[16] When the *American Socialist* dared to criticize Kearney for advocating violence as a means of getting rid of the Chinese, it was attacked by the *National Socialist*.[17] It is also possible to infer from his total silence on the subject that William Sylvis was not happy with the growing obsession with the Chinese in the ranks of labor just before his death in August 1869.

Labor propaganda skilfully exploited all the popular fears related to Chinese immigration; periodicals and pamphlets referred to Chinese filth, disease, and vice and presented inverted Darwinian arguments that on occasion reached yellow peril proportions.

Such themes appeared a good deal more often than economic issues such as cheap Chinese wages. Indeed, the latter complaint was rarely presented without fortification from an assertion that the wages depressed by coolies sent the women in white families into prostitution—usually selling their flesh to Chinamen who infected them with "the leprosy of the Chinese curse." [18] When John P. Irish declared that the veto by Hayes insulted every female in America, his working-class audience knew exactly what he meant.[19]

Often the evils posed by Chinese immigration were left deliberately vague in these sources, with references to "Asiatic horrors" and "the blighting curses of Oriental life," so that the reader might enhance the dangers with his own imagination. Medical metaphors were employed so often that it is difficult to always tell whether these writers were referring to social habits or physical afflictions when they spoke of Chinese "leprosy" and "spreading ulcers" in American cities.[20]

On other occasions the exact nature of the threat was made most explicit. The *Workingman's Advocate* in 1873 carefully catalogued the various means by which the Chinese were corrupting the nation's bloodstream. The "innumerable hells" burrowed beneath every Chinese settlement held captive white girls for "crimes that cannot be named." As servants, the Chinese were bringing their "debasing habits" and "loathesome diseases" right into the American home. There, they were permitted "to wash and dress little white girls." Beguiled by the childish quality of these Chinese houseboys, the mothers innocently undressed in front of them. Through harmless looking cigars the Chinese imported more disease into American families. "With ulcerated hands they wrap the fallen leper scales with the tobacco, and the smoker sucks it into his system, which may break out in one year, or in ten years, and children may inherit the disease from the careless father." [21]

These labor journalists also hammered away at the economic threat of the Chinese entrepreneurial spirit. Coolies wrapped cigars and made shoes only long enough to learn the business. "John is entirely too smart to work for $1.25 if he sees an opportunity to do better," Cameron warned white employers.[22] With the profits earned on coolie wages in the cigar and shoe industries, these Celestial businessmen were looking to expand economically and geographically so that banking in New York could be his next venture. This was an effective argument which stirred fears in a number of antilabor editors who supported Chinese immigration.[23]

The most effective of these articles in labor periodicals were reproduced many times during the 1870s, often in the same journal or separately as part of a pamphlet, to convince readers who needed little convincing that the Chinese bring "moral destruction, pauperism and disease in their train." [24]

If the five most prominent Irish newspapers in New York City during the 1870s are at all typical of this genre, then Irish editors were unanimously opposed to Chinese immigration. Ironically, the sinophobic arguments to be found in the Celtic press frequently resemble the ones directed at Irish immigrants by nativistic editors. Opium smoking took the place of whiskey drinking, of course, but otherwise these Irish editors complained that the Chinese were unfamiliar with democracy, subverted Christianity, committed crimes, and were immoral.[25] Such "degraded races" as "Niggers and Chinamen" were "incapable" of understanding the democratic principles for which the Irish had continually fought, *McGee's Illustrated Weekly* declared in 1877.[26] "You cannot stop short in the course you have set out upon, you philanthropists," the editor of the *Irish Citizen* taunted Republicans in 1870. "Either the Declaration of Independence requires this nation to open its doors to 300 million obscene yellow rascals, or else does *not* require it to admit the three or four million malodorous fetish-worshipping black fellows." He reminded them that "reasonable people wanted to keep these Negroes in their proper places. . . ." [27] In contrast to the Chinese, immigrants from the Emerald Isle had greatly benefited the United States, this editor reminded his readers—lest there be any bigoted Anglo-Saxons among them, one must presume. But he only demanded that a racial rather than ethnic discrimination form the basis of American immigration policy: "We want white people to enrich the country, not Mongolians to degrade and disgrace it." [28]

Compared to the labor press, however, Irish ethnic newspapers in New York City were far less obsessed with the Chinese question. Celestial immigrants had to share Hibernian wrath with England, Negroes, atheistic public schools, the Orange Lodge, and that scourge of mankind, the Seventh Regiment, which was habitually used to protect Protestant marchers, celebrating the Battle of the Boyne each July 12th, from Celtic justice.

A case against the Catholic clergy and press outside of California is more difficult to make unless one wishes to infer anti-Chinese sentiment behind their almost total silence on the issue. This omission is in sharp contrast to the incessant demands for greater justice for the Indian, as well as the struggle against any restrictions on European immigration, to be found in official and semi-official Catholic sources at this time. One history of a famous newspaper, the *Catholic Telegraph*, concluded that its editors "assumed a different attitude" on Oriental immigration.[29] When a Church official in New York reprimanded Denis Kearney in 1878, it was for preaching socialism, not his rabid sinophobia.[30]

In 1878 the *American Catholic Quarterly Review* briefly broke the silence with some bitter attacks on Chinese immigration. "Is it our duty to convert them [the Chinese]?" one anonymous contributor asked. "Yes, if they will be converted but they will not. . . . They are unclean, indescribably unchaste, intolerably dirty; shall we reform them? If it were possible but it is not." The author was careful to disassociate himself from the vulgar "Know-nothingism" of Kearney, however. He wanted to exclude the Chinese quietly.[31] The famous liberal Catholic historian, James Gilmary Shea contributed another article to this publication in 1880 on "The Rapid Increase of the Dangerous Classes in the United States" in which he demanded that the Chinese be removed from the country—along with paupers, lechers, Mormons, and utopian socialists. Most of the nation's problems would be solved by such an extirpation, Shea contended, along with putting God into the Constitution. He did concede that some crime and vice existed among Irish immigrants, but this was a result of poverty. By nature the Irishman was "pure, virtuous and healthy," Shea insisted, while the faults of the Chinaman were "hereditary," he explained.[32]

Shortly after the enactment of the first exclusion law, Bryan Clinche summed up the Chinese question "as regards American Catholics" in this same Catholic journal. He carefully condemned Kearney's brand of sinophobia and promised a "fair evaluation" of the issue. "To describe the Asiatic immigrants as a body of lepers or slaves" was just as "absurd" to Clinche as it was to insist that the American "crucible" could "hold all the Chinese who wanted to come." Yet Clinche turned out to be only a more refined Kearney. In more temperate language, he raised all the standard population, economic, cultural, and racist arguments against Chinese immigration. His frank espousal of the germ theory of culture had interesting implications for the evangelical mission of Christianity. He argued that history has taught us that only Europeans have a natural basis for Christianity; this is why it was so easy to convert the Germanic tribes that overran Rome while it was impossible to Christianize the Moors and Arabs in Spain. Three centuries of failure for European missionary efforts in Asia and Africa forced him to conclude that it was "childish" to even hope for conversion among nonwhites. The Chinese in America could neither become Christians nor develop the "feeling of patriotism, the love for political liberty . . . common to all the races of Europe." But Clinche stipulated that the Indians and Negroes could remain since they had a "natural right" to be here, whereas the Chinese did not.[33]

One Catholic official, Samuel Becker, a former University of Virginia professor and secretary to the bishop of Wilmington, Delaware, wrote a witty lampoon of the political circus put on by the joint congressional committee investigating the Chinese problem in California in 1876. In the preface to his pamphlet, however, Becker conceded that Catholics "joined as a body in hounding down the Chinese." [34] If the clergy were as annoyed as Becker over the role being played by their flock in the anti-Chinese movement, they left little evidence of it and greeted Becker's complaint with silence.

A more systematic study of labor and the Catholic clergy outside of California, giving special attention to the role of the Irish on the Chinese question, is needed. The poor state of preservation and chaotic organization of the records of the Irish press and Catholic newspapers that enjoyed at least a semiofficial status offer formidable but not insurmountable obstacles to such an undertaking.

The last and most crucial factor in the success of the anti-Chinese movement on a national level was the historical one, that is, the unfavorable image of the Chinese that preceded them to the United States. This, of course, is the special concern of this study. Californians did not have to expend much effort in convincing their compatriots that the Chinese would make undesirable citizens. The existing image of the Chinese in America had already done it for them. For decades American traders, diplomats, and Protestant missionaries had developed and spread conceptions of Chinese deceit, cunning, idolatry, despotism, xenophobia, cruelty, infanticide, and intellectual and sexual perversity. This negative image was already reflected in American magazines and geography textbooks before 1840, a fact that is at variance with the assumption made by many diplomatic historians that Americans respected the Chinese and sympathized with them during the Anglo-Chinese wars. These wars—in conjunction with the Taiping Rebellion, the Burlingame mission, Tientsin Massacre, and emigration of Chinese "coolies" to the western hemisphere—coincided with the development of the first recognizably modern mass media in the United States. The immediate result was a notable jump in American awareness of China, if the greatly increased coverage given to that nation in the mass media after 1840 is any index. It was the unfavorable, previously developed, trader-diplomat-missionary view of the Chinese that was available to the editors for popularization during this period in which occurred a chain of sensational events in China.

The main task of the sinophobes was to convince fellow Americans that the now familiar cultural threat of Chinese immigration outweighed any possible economic and religious gains to be derived from it. The warm glow of national pride that characterized the post-Civil War era rendered this task less difficult, and it was facilitated by all the old charges against the Chinese plus new fears of slavery, alien genes, mysterious germs, unfair competition from an unexpected Chinese entrepreneurial spirit, and inverted Darwinian arguments that anticipated the yellow peril fears more clearly articulated a decade later.

Once an exclusion law was passed, it exerted its own effect on the American image of the Chinese. A casual glance at the mass media after 1882 indicates that familiar themes and fears about the Chinese reached hysterical proportions by the end of the century. This illustrates the functional interrelationship between cognitive images and institutional change. The government's action made the unfavorable image of the Chinese the official definition of these people, and journalists eagerly supplied more illustrative material drawn from America's Chinatowns to justify that decision continually. Those who had opposed exclusion before 1882 would have suffered a certain amount of cognitive dissonance after it became official policy. This dissonance could have been alleviated by changing the policy of exclusion or by adjusting one's image to justify belatedly the decision to exclude the Chinese. Judging from the higher incidence of criticism of the Chinese after 1882 from sources that previously opposed exclusion—Protestant clerics, some businessman, and the *New York Times*—it would seem that many Americans chose the latter means of cognitive adjustment.

The exaggerated reaction to Chinese immigrants in nineteenth-century America may also illustrate another relationship hypothesized by E. C. Tolman as a result of his experiments on "cognitive

maps." Tolman suggested that "the three dynamisms called respectively, 'regression,' 'fixation' and 'displacement of aggression
onto outgroups' are expressions of cognitive maps which are too
narrow and which get built up in us as a result of too violent motivation or of too intense frustration." [35]

In developing their cognitive image of the Chinese in the nineteenth century, Americans repeatedly experienced a pattern of
unrealistic expectation followed by bitter disappointment. From
the beginning of the China trade, Americans expected rewards
that never materialized. It was fully expected that a handful of
missionaries, or perhaps the Lord, would effect a rapid, miraculous
mass conversion of the Chinese. The failure to realize these gains
before 1840 was attributed to China's unreasonable restrictions on
the activities of traders and missionaries, the removal of which by
the war was the occasion for newly inflated hopes. Proselytism, a
favorable balance of trade—if no longer fabled wealth—and normal diplomatic relations were to follow the Treaty of Wanghia in
1844. But every time American hopes reached unrealistic levels
they were followed by more frustration. The bitterness caused by
this disappointment can be readily seen in the belated justification
of the Opium War by 1850 on the part of some of England's severest critics during the conflict.

The Taiping Rebellion quickly revived hopes for a Protestant,
commercially oriented China, full of gratitude for America's neutrality in the first Anglo-Chinese war and for the victorious Hung's
conversion at the hands of an American missionary. Once more
these expectations were rendered illusory by the revelations of
Taiping blasphemy and xenophobia. British policy was justified
all over again in the bitter conclusion that bombardment was the
only way to deal with the Chinese. Thanks to the "wisdom" exercised by the Royal Navy, we got a new treaty in 1858 to remove the
"loopholes" in the earlier one, which prevented our harvest in
profits and souls. These new hopes proved more ephemeral than
the others, however, when the Chinese "treacherously ambushed"
a Franco-British task force at Taku and humiliated the American
envoy in Peking. Actually, this cycle happened too fast to permit
American optimism to get out of hand, and the threatening Civil
War in the United States cut short any ensuing bitterness.

By 1869 American opinion leaders once more waxed enthusiastic over our prospects in China, thanks to Anson Burlingame.
Our special friendship with that nation would permit us to
monopolize the Chinese market for American manufacturers and
to exploit her cheap labor in the United States. There was less in-

terest in Chinese souls, perhaps because American missionaries remained dubious about the benefits of the Burlingame Treaty. A year later, the news of Tientsin and new xenophobic outbursts in China demolished these hopes on the rocks of despair.

The cycle of sublime hope, frustration, and bitter disappointment which is so clearly patterned in the reports of missionaries is also discernible, although less pronounced, in most of the press that commented on China. When American ministers to China, Humphrey Marshall in 1853 and J. Ross Browne in 1869, attempted to check the rising tide of optimism provoked by the Taiping Rebellion and Burlingame Treaty, respectively, they were vilified by editors who later felt obliged to apologize to them when subsequent events in China destroyed their optimism. This pattern of hope and despair may also help to account for the great inconsistency of American editors when they discussed our China policy or Chinese immigration. It is exceedingly dangerous to generalize about a newspaper's position regarding the Chinese without following the editorial twists, turns, and reversals over many months. When one historian of the North Adams incident concluded in 1947 that "Horace Greeley and his New York *Tribune* . . . were solidly behind Calvin Sampson and his Chinamen" on the basis of a single editorial which he cited secondhand from the *Nation,* he committed an egregious error.[36] Opposed to what he considered to be Celtic arrogance on the part of the workers in North Adams, Greeley would naturally have supported Sampson's action against the Crispins. But Greeley and his editorial staff were also subject to the same social, cultural, racial, and medical fears concerning Chinese immigration that affected other editors in the East. These fears had been expressed by Greeley, personally, and by his newspaper for decades before the arrival of Celestials in North Adams. Hence the *New York Tribune* in 1870 vacillated between endorsement and almost hysterical condemnation of Sampson's action, just as it had vacillated between hope and despair for decades in its editorial discussions of Sino-American relations.[37]

Very possibly our contemporary bitterness toward China may be yet another phase of disillusioned reaction to the unwarranted expectations that grew out of the highly romanticized special Sino-American friendship in the 1930s and during the Second World War. China, in a sense, has been the least successful commercial and spiritual part of America's "Manifest Destiny."

Notes

1. THE CALIFORNIA CONSPIRACY AND CHINESE EXCLUSION

1. Most nineteenth-century works on the subject are highly partisan. Of these the most important are Rev. Otis Gibson, *The Chinese in America* (Cinn., 1877); George F. Seward, *Chinese Immigration in Its Social and Economic Aspects* (New York, 1881); James A. Whitney, *The Chinese and the Chinese Question* (New York, 1888); Rev. Ira M. Condit, *The Chinaman as We See Him* (Chicago, 1900). The twentieth-century scholarly treatments are Mary Coolidge, *Chinese Immigration* (New York, 1909); Elmer Sandmeyer, *The Anti-Chinese Movement in California* (Urbana, 1939); Tien-Lu Li, *The Congressional Policy of Chinese Immigration* (Nashville, 1916); R. D. McKenzie, *Oriental Exclusion* (Chicago, 1928). The Coolidge work is the most comprehensive treatment, to which little of substance had been added until the publication of Gunther Barth's *Bitter Strength* (Cambridge, 1964). But Barth's work stops at 1870, over a decade short of the first exclusion law, and focuses almost entirely on California.

2. Coolidge, *Chinese Immigration*, pp. 15–25; Sandmeyer, *Anti-Chinese Movement*, pp. 12, 79; R. W. Paul, "The Origins of the Chinese Issue in California," *Mississippi Valley Historical Review*, XXV (1938), 181–196.

3. Coolidge, *Chinese Immigration*, p. 364.

4. Sandmeyer, *Anti-Chinese Movement*, p. 48.

5. Coolidge, *Chinese Immigration*, pp. 250–251; R. D. McKenzie, *Oriental Exclusion*, pp. 24–29.

6. Richmond Mayo-Smith, *Emigration and Immigration* (New York, 1890), pp. 235–237; Prescott F. Hall, *Immigration* (New York, 1906), pp. 327–331; Henry Pratt Fairchild, *Immigration* (New York, 1913), pp. 98–101; Frank Julian Warne, *The Immigrant Invasion* (New York, 1913), pp. 298–299; George M. Stephenson, *A History of American Immigration* (Boston, 1926), pp. 258 ff.; Roy L. Garis, *Immigration Restriction* (New York, 1927), pp. 287–291; Lawrence G. Brown, *Immigration* (New York, 1933), pp. 266–296; Bertram Schrieke, *Alien Americans* (New York, 1936), pp. 3–22; George E. Simpson and J. Milton Yinger, *Racial and Cultural Minorities* (revised edition; New York, 1958), p. 127; Carl Wittke, *We Who Built America* (Cleveland, 1939), pp. 474–475; W. S. Bernard, *American Immigration Policy* (New York, 1950), pp. 11–12; John Higham, *Strangers in the Land* (New Brunswick, 1955), pp. 167–170; Oscar Handlin, *The Americans* (Boston, 1963), pp. 303–304; Marion Bennett, *American Immigration Policies* (Wash., D.C., 1963), pp. 15–17.

7. Marcus Hansen, "The Second Colonization of New England," *New England Quarterly*, II (1929), 556.

8. Wittke, *We Who Built America*, pp. 474–475; Brown, *Immigration*, p. 266.

9. Carey McWilliams, *Brothers Under the Skin* (revised edition, Boston, 1951), pp. 97–98, 100–104.

10. Handlin, *The Americans*, p. 304.

11. Higham, *Strangers in the Land*, p. 170.

12. Maldwyn A. Jones, *American Immigration* (Chicago, 1960), p. 249. Italics added.

13. Leonard Pitt, "The Beginnings of Nativism in California," *Pacific Historical Review*, XXX (1961), 28.

14. Higham, *Strangers in the Land*, p. 167.

15. Barth, *Bitter Strength*, p. 131.

16. *Ibid.*, pp. 131 ff.

17. Coolidge, *Chinese Immigration*, pp. 49–50.

18. Sandmeyer, *Anti-Chinese Movement*, p. 26.

19. *Ibid.*, p. 47.

20. Walter Lippmann, *Public Opinion* (New York, 1922), p. 81.

21. Such a construct skirts the pitfalls to which the historian is vulnerable when tracing public opinion in its formal sense as conceived of by social scientists. For a good discussion of this problem, see Paul Lazarsfeld, "The Obligation of the 1950 Pollster to the 1984 Historian," *Public Opinion Quarterly*, XVI (1950), 617–638, and Joseph Strayer's reply, "The Historian's Concept of Public Opinion," *Common Frontiers of the Social Sciences*, ed. Mirra Komarovsky (Glencoe, 1957), pp. 263–278. For an excellent discussion of the role of cognitive images in human behavior, see Kenneth Boulding, *The Image* (Ann Arbor, 1956).

22. Harold Isaacs, *Scratches on Our Minds: American Images of China and India* (New York, 1958), pp. 72–73.

23. The *New York Tribune* (Aug. 13, 1905, Pt. IV, p. 1) reported as fact that the city's Chinatown was "honeycombed with underground tunnels and passageways that lead from sub cellar to sub cellar."

24. See "Rescuing Angel of the Little Slaves of Chinatown," *New York Times*, April 30, 1905, Pt. IV, p. 4; "Donaldine Cameron and the Chinese Slave Trade in America," *Everybody's Magazine*, XI (1904), 40–48. For an example of such articles in more sophisticated magazines, see Charles F. Holder, "Chinese Slavery in America," *North American Review*, CLXV (1897), 288–294. For testimony of this sort before a Congressional investigating committee, see Samuel Gompers, *Meat vs. Rice; American Manhood Against Asiatic Coolieism. Which Shall Survive?* (A.F. of L., 1902), pp. 25 ff; *Senate Reports*, no. 776, 57th Cong., 1st Sess., Feb. 15, 1902, Pt. II, pp. 442–447.

25. J. Torrey Connor, "A Western View of the Chinese in the United States," *Chautauquan*, XXXII (1900–1901), 373–378. Magazines and dime novels were also filled with such conceptions of Chinatown during the first decade or so of the twentieth century.

26. Dorothy B. Jones, *The Portrayal of China and India on the American Screen, 1896–1955* (Cambridge, Mass., 1955), p. 31.

27. Isaacs, *Scratches On Our Minds*, p. 71.

28. *Ibid.*, pp. 63–71. Gordon Allport attributed these conflicting themes to a "fading effect" as stereotypes change over a period of time. See his *The Nature of Prejudice* (New York, 1958), pp. 185–199.

29. David Katz and Kenneth Braley, "Racial Stereotypes of 100 College Students," *Journal of Abnormal and Social Psychology*, XVIII (1933), 280–290.

30. Bruno Lasker, *Race Attitudes in Children* (New York, 1929), pp. 140–141; G. H. Greene, "Racial Prejudice in Children of School Age," Ninth International

Congress of Psychology, *Proceedings and Papers* (1929), pp. 192–193. A composite of American student views of China compiled by a Chinese exchange student in *Literary Digest,* May 12, 1927, and T. Lew's "China in American School Text-books," *Chinese Social and Political Review,* VII, supplement, produced similar conflicting impressions.

31. Beekman Papers, MSS., Box 25, folder 2, New York Historical Society.

32. Donald F. Lach, *Asia in the Making of Europe* (Chicago, 1965), Vol. I.

33. William Appleton, *A Cycle of Cathay* (New York, 1951), pp. 1–20.

34. This was a compilation by Fathers Couplet, Intorcetta, *et al.,* of translations from Confucius published in Goa in 1669. For good discussions of the influence of the works of Confucius on the Enlightenment, see Virgile Pinot, *La Chine et la formation de l'esprit philosophique en France* (Paris, 1932), *passim;* Adolph Reichwein, *China and Europe* (New York, 1925), pp. 75–98; Arnold Rowbotham, "La Mothe le Vayer's *Vertu des payens* and Eighteenth-Century Cosmopolitanism," *Modern Language Notes,* LIII (1938), 10–14; Donald Lach, "Leibnitz and China," *Journal of the History of Ideas,* VI (1945), 436–455; Lewis Maverick, *China: A Model for Europe* (San Antonio, 1946), pp. 15–19; S. Y. Teng, "The Predispositions of Westerners in Treating Chinese History and Civilization," *Historian,* XIX (1957), 307–327.

35. Paul Honigsheim, "Voltaire as Anthropologist," *American Anthropologist,* XLVII (1945), 112.

36. Appleton, *Cycle of Cathay,* p. 47. See also Ch'ien Chung-shu, "China in the English Literature of the Eighteenth Century," *Quarterly Bulletin of Chinese Bibliography,* II (1941), 7–48, 113–152.

37. Ely Bates, *A Chinese Fragment, Containing an Enquiry into the Present State of Religion in England* (London, 1786), p. 4. Italics in original. See also *An Irregular Dissertation Occasioned by the Readings of Father Du Halde's Description of China* (London, 1740), *passim.* Published anonymously, the latter is now credited to the Reverend Joseph Huttner. See also Edmund Gibson, *The Bishop of London's First Pastoral Letter . . . Occasioned by some Late Writings in Favor of Infidelity* (London, 1727), *passim.*

38. See Appleton, *Cycle of Cathay,* pp. 62–64; Tsen-Chung Fan, *Dr. Johnson and Chinese Culture* (London, 1945), pp. 2–7, 10, *passim;* "Sir William Jones' Chinese Studies," *Review of English Studies,* XXII (1946), 304–314; Ch'en Shou-yi, "Daniel Defoe, China's Severest Critic," *Nankai Social and Economic Quarterly,* VIII (1935), 511–559; Rev. Joseph Spence, *Anecdotes, Observations, and Characters, of Books and Men. Collected from the Conversation of Mr. Pope and Other Eminent Persons of his Time,* ed. S. W. Singer (London, 1820), pp. 52, 68, *passim;* A. H. Rowbotham, "A Brief Account of the Early Development of Sinology," *Chinese Social and Political Science Review,* VII (1923), 113–138. For the best eighteenth-century summary of this debate, see the review of de Guignes' work in *Monthly Review,* LXII (1780), 505–511.

39. James Boswell, *Life of Johnson* (1791), ed. George B. Hill (New York, 1887), III, 386.

40. As cited in *Monthly Review,* LXII, (1780), 522.

41. The library lists examined by Louis Wright, Carl Bridenbaugh, Frederick Tolles, and Daniel Boorstin in their attempts to reproduce the literary atmosphere of the colonial period were perused for any mention of works on China, with almost no success. See Boorstin, *The Americans* (New York, 1959), Pt. V, pp. 269–273, for a good bibliographic discussion of the problem of reconstructing colonial literary interests.

42. Louis Wright, "The Classical Tradition in Colonial Virginia," Bibliographic Society of America, *Papers*, XXXIII (1939), 85–97.

43. Louis Wright, "The 'Gentleman's Library' in Early Virginia: The Literary Interests of the First Carters," *Huntington Library Quarterly*, I (1937–38), 3–61.

44. Frederick B. Tolles, "A Literary Quaker: John Smith of Burlington and Philadelphia," *Pennsylvania Magazine of History and Biography*, LXV (1941), 300–333.

45. Lawrence C. Wroth, *An American Bookshelf, 1775* (Phila., 1934), *passim*.

46. Frederick B. Tolles, *Meeting House and Counting House* (New York, 1963), pp. 147, 174–175 n. 38.

47. The Du Halde volume was a 1735 edition but did not appear on Jefferson's personal list of books in 1783. Grosier was not published until 1785, and comments by Jefferson date all these as having been purchased in Paris between 1783 and 1789. See E. Millicent Sowerby, *Catalogue of the Library of Thomas Jefferson* (Wash., D.C., 1952–1959), I, 132, 147–149; IV, 94, 141–149. It is not clear when Jefferson obtained his copy of Père Le Comte's *Nouveaux mémoires* (third edition; Paris, 1697), but it is probably safe to assume that it was also purchased in Paris.

48. For example, see Tolles, *Meeting House*, p. 160; Wright, *Huntington Library Quarterly*, I (1937–38), 55; Wroth, *American Bookshelf, 1755*, pp. 24, 35, 97; Carl Bridenbaugh, "The Press and the Book in Philadelphia," *Pennsylvania Magazine of History and Biography*, LXV (1941), 26.

49. *Diary and Autobiography*, ed. L. H. Butterfield (Cambridge, Mass., 1961), II, 247.

50. *The Papers of Alexander Hamilton*, ed. H. C. Syrett (New York, 1961), I, 384.

51. See letter from Jefferson to Benjamin Vaughn, May 17, 1789, *The Papers of Thomas Jefferson*, ed. Julian Boyd (Princeton, 1955–1958), XV, 133; *Jefferson's Garden Book, 1766–1824*, ed. E. M. Betts (Phila., 1944), pp. 125, 321, 325, 394, 424.

52. *The Works of Benjamin Franklin*, ed. Jared Sparks (Boston, 1840), II, 241, 243, 247–248.

53. Letter from Madison to Jefferson, April 27, 1785, *Letters and Other Writings of James Madison* (Phila., 1867), I, 146.

54. Letter from Washington to Tench Tilghman, Aug. 29, 1785, *Writings of George Washington*, ed. John C. Fitzpatrick (Wash., D.C., 1938), XXVIII, 239.

55. *American Magazine and Historical Chronicle*, I (1744), 615–632.

56. *Boston News-Letter*, March 24, 1749.

57. *Ibid.*, Feb. 20, 1735; [Philadelphia] *Pennsylvania Gazette*, Jan. 25–Feb. 1, 1739.

58. See for example, *Boston News-Letter*, May 18, 1719, and Jan. 24, 1753; *Pennsylvania Gazette*, Nov. 4–11, 1736; [Williamsburg] *Virginia Gazette*, Dec. 2, 1735, Nov. 17, 1738.

59. See Bernard Berelson, "Communications and Public Opinion," *Reader in Public Opinion and Communication*, eds. Bernard Berelson and Morris Janowitz (2nd ed.; Glencoe, 1953), p. 455.

60. See *Ibid.*, p. 454, for a discussion of the role of events in the formation of public opinion.

2. THE AMERICAN TRADER'S IMAGE, 1785–1840

1. Harold Isaacs, *Scratches on Our Minds: American Images of China and India* (New York, 1958), p. 71.

2. Kenneth Latourette, "History of the Early Relations Between the United

States and China," Connecticut Academy of Arts and Sciences, *Transactions*, XXII (1917), 124; Tyler Dennett, *Americans in Eastern Asia* (New York, 1922), p. 61.

3. George H. Danton, *The Culture Contacts of the United States and China* (New York, 1931), p. 82; Foster Rhea Dulles, *China and America: The Story of Their Relations Since 1784* (Princeton, 1946), pp. 5–6; Thomas A. Bailey, *A Diplomatic History of the American People* (6th ed.; New York, 1958), pp. 302–303.

4. Latourette, Conn. Academy of Arts and Sciences, Trans., XXII, 124.

5. Danton, *Culture Contacts*, pp. 83 ff.

6. S. Y. Teng, "The Predispositions of Westerners in Treating Chinese History and Civilization," *Historian*, XIX (1957), 326.

7. Rose Hum Lee, *The Chinese in the United States of America* (Hong Kong, 1960), p. 354.

8. Dennett, *Americans in Eastern Asia*, p. 65 n. 14.

9. Bailey, *Diplomatic History*, pp. 302–303. The fact that W. W. Wood was contemptuous of the Chinese underscores the fallacy of inferring respect for China from a collection of Chinese artifacts or the display of a Celestial lady with bound feet. See his *Sketches of China* (Phila., 1830) for an exceedingly hostile report on the Chinese.

10. Dulles, *China and America*, p. 5.

11. Dennett, *Americans in Eastern Asia*, p. 102; Bailey, *Diplomatic History*, p. 302.

12. Danton, *Culture Contacts*, pp. 13–15.

13. William C. Hunter, *The "Fan Kwae" at Canton Before Treaty Days, 1825–1844* (London, 1882), p. 115.

14. This was an article signed "Mercator" in the *New-York Gazetteer*, May 24, 1785. See also [New York] *Daily Advertiser*, May 16, Sept. 2, 1785; *New-York Packet*, May 16, 1785; *Newport Mercury*, May 21, 1785; *Freeman's Journal*, June 22, 1785; [Providence] *U.S. Chronicle*, Aug. 25, 1785; *Pennsylvania Gazette*, May 18, 1785.

15. John K. Fairbank, *The United States and China* (Cambridge, Mass., 1948), p. 325.

16. Grover Clark, "Changing Markets," *Empire in the East*, ed. Joseph Barnes (New York, 1934), pp. 127–128.

17. Latourette, "Voyages of American Ships to China, 1784–1844," Connecticut Academy of Arts and Sciences, *Transactions*, XXVIII (1923), 239–271; Dennett, *Americans in Eastern Asia*, pp. 17–18.

18. *Ibid.*, p. 8. For a detailed list of these concessions see Latourette, Conn. Academy of Arts and Sciences, *Trans.*, XXII, 78–79.

19. Clark, *Empire in the East*, pp. 126–127. See also Report of the Secretary of the Treasury, *House Documents*, No. 248, 26th Cong., 1st Sess. (July 1, 1840) for a review of the trade between 1785 and 1840.

20. See Edmund Fanning, *Voyages and Discoveries in the South Seas* (Salem, 1924), pp. 322–330, for a good firsthand account of these adventures and trials. See also "Instructions to Capt. Samuel Hill," June 30, 1815, in T. H. Perkins Papers, MSS, Massachusetts Historical Society, Boston, Mass.

21. Randall to Hamilton, Aug. 14, 1791, in Arthur H. Cole, *Industrial and Commercial Correspondence of Alexander Hamilton* (Chicago, 1928), pp. 129–141.

22. See Lui Kwang-Ching, *Americans and Chinese* (Cambridge, 1963) for an excellent bibliographical guide to these sources. In addition to these, there are many untouched logs that occasionally contain long, chatty passages on China squeezed in between the records of navigation and business transactions. On the whole, how-

ever, these logs are not a fruitful source for such commentary, and working with them can be frustrating.

23. See Waln's notebooks dated 1808 and 1813 in Waln Family Papers, MSS, Library Company of Philadelphia.

24. Erasmus Doolittle, "Recollections of China," in [Silas Holbrook], *Sketches, by a Traveller* (Boston, 1830), p. 256. Doolittle was probably influenced by Sir John Barrow, F.R.S., *Travels in China* (London, 1804), pp. 48–50. This work is discussed in Chapter III with the works of diplomats.

25. As quoted in *American Quarterly Review*, IX (1831), 53.

26. L. W. Jenkins, ed., *Bryant Parrott Tilden of Salem, at a Chinese Dinner Party, Canton, 1819* (Princeton, 1944), p. 23. The names of the hong merchants were Western versions of their real names. For example, "Houqua" was Wu Ping-ch'en. See Joseph Downs, *The China Trade and Its Influences* (New York, 1941), p. 15.

27. Jenkins, *Bryant Parrott Tilden*, p. 10.

28. Letters dated Jan. 29 and Aug. 16, 1816 (both in the hand of M. P. Cushing) in Carrington Family Papers, MSS, Rhode Island Historical Society, Providence, R.I.

29. Letter dated Aug. 3, 1816, Carrington Family Papers, MSS.

30. Jenkins, *Bryant Parrott Tilden*, pp. 23–24.

31. Peter Auber, *China: An Outline* (London, 1834), p. 365; letters between Heard and Russell & Co. dated May 15, 1832, Aug. 21, 1832, Heard Collection, MSS, Baker Library, Harvard University, Cambridge, Mass.

32. W. W. Wood, *Sketches of China* (Phila., 1830), pp. 141–142.

33. Hunter, *"The Fan Kwae" at Canton*, pp. 31, 16 ff.

34. *Diplomatic Correspondence* (Washington, 1855), III, 789.

35. [Holbrook], *Sketches, by a Traveller*, p. 42.

36. *Ibid.*

37. See *Niles' Weekly Register* XVI (1819), 297 and LII (1837), 240, for typical examples of "box scores" on British and American tonnage out of Canton. Invariably these published comparisons were to demonstrate that the United States was catching up to England although they always did lag well behind.

38. See Benjamin Goodhue Papers, MSS, Log of the ship *Margaret*, MSS, and Nathaniel Silsbee, Jr., Sea Journal to Batavia and China, MSS, all in the Essex Institute, Salem, Mass.; Hunter, *The "Fan Kwae" at Canton*, p. 146; Augustine Heard to J. S. Armory, Sept. 27, 1841, Heard Collection, MSS.

39. George W. Heard, Jr., Diary, typescript copy, pp. 31–32, Heard Collection, MSS.

40. Dennett, *Americans in Eastern Asia*, p. 51.

41. See Hsin-pao Chang, *Commissioner Lin and the Opium War* (Cambridge, Mass., 1964), pp. 31 ff, for a recent appraisal of the important role played by Americans in the opium trade.

42. William Hickey, *Memoirs, 1749–1809*, ed. Alfred Spencer (London, 1919), I, 198; Danton, *Culture Contacts*, p. 95. Major Shaw expressed annoyance over the failure of the Chinese to distinguish fully between the two English-speaking nations. See *Diplomatic Correspondence* (Washington, D.C., 1855), III, 763. See also Benjamin Hoppin to E. C. Carrington, Dec. 27, 1805, Carrington Family Papers, MSS. Jefferson mentioned this failure to Gallatin in a letter dated Aug. 15, 1804, in *The Writings of Thomas Jefferson*, ed. Andrew Lipscomb (Washington, D.C., 1903–1904), XII, 134.

43. "For the Port-Folio on China," *Port Folio* (Philadelphia), s. 5, VII (1819), 111.

44. Doolittle, *Sketches, by a Traveller,* p. 253.

45. Nathaniel Appleton, Journal of a Voyage from Salem to Canton, 1799–1802, MSS, Essex Institute, Salem, Mass. See Robert E. Peabody, ed., *The Log of the Grand Turks* (Boston, 1926), pp. 27, 85–86, for the best description of the "cumshaw" ritual. The term is still used by sailors to cover any subtle bribe involving goods rather than money. Its origin is not clear although it has been suggested that it was a Chinese corruption of the word "commission."

46. Samuel Shaw, *The Journals of Major Samuel Shaw, the First American Consul at Canton. With a Life of the Author by Josiah Quincy* (Boston, 1847), pp. 184–185.

47. Wood, *Sketches of China,* p. 232.

48. For a good description of this affair, see Earl Pritchard, *The Crucial Years of Anglo-Chinese Relations, 1750–1800* (Pullman, Washington, 1936), pp. 225–230.

49. B. C. Wilcocks to John Quincy Adams, Nov. 1, 1821, in *House Executive Documents,* no. 71, 26th Cong., 2nd Sess., p. 13. See *ibid.,* pp. 7–16, for the full report and firsthand description of Terranova's hearing.

50. [Holbrook], *Sketches, by a Traveller,* pp. 42–45.

51. Shaw, *Journals,* p. 11.

52. Amasa Delano, *A Narrative of Voyages and Travels* (Boston, 1817), p. 542.

53. *American Quarterly Review,* IX, 57, 59; Wood, *Sketches of China,* p. 150.

54. *American Quarterly Review,* IX, 56.

55. Wood, *Sketches of China,* pp. 120–121, 238–239; Edmund Roberts, *Embassy to the Eastern Courts* (New York, 1837), p. 152.

56. W. S. W Ruschenberger, *A Voyage Round the World* (Philadelphia, 1838), p. 431.

57. Hunter, *The "Fan Kwae" at Canton,* pp. 41–42.

58. *Ibid.,* p. 41; Tilden alone seems to have been cosmopolitan enough to admire the Chinese cuisine. See Jenkins, *Bryant Parrott Tilden,* pp. 21–22.

59. Wood, *Sketches of China,* pp. 224, 155–156.

60. Doolittle, *Sketches, by a Traveller,* p. 256.

61. Wood, *Sketches of China,* p. 74.

62. Doolittle, *Sketches, by a Traveller,* pp. 254–255.

63. *Ibid.,* pp. 259–260.

64. Ping Chia Kuo, "Canton and Salem: The Impact of Chinese Culture upon New England Life During the Post-Revolutionary Era," *New England Quarterly,* III (1930), 439.

65. Thomas Knox, *John; or Our Chinese Relations* (New York, 1879), p. 13.

66. Kuo, *New England Quarterly,* III, 439.

67. William Bently, *Diary* (Salem, 1905–1914), III, 68, 328.

68. See Ebenezer Townsend, "Diary," New Haven Colony Historical Society, *Papers,* IV (1888), 93, 101 for descriptions of these frauds that were so popularized that they were reported in the fourth edition (1810) of the *Encyclopaedia Britannica* (VI, 36–37) and in numerous English and American geography texts (see p. 93).

69. See entry for Jan. 1, 1793, in John Boit's Sea Journal, MSS, Massachusetts Historical Society, Boston, Mass

70. E. B. Hewes, "Thomas Handasyd Perkins, Super cargo of the *Astria* of Salem," Essex Institute, *Historical Collections,* LXXI (1935), 210.

71. Delano, *Narrative,* p. 537. In all fairness to the Chinese it should be pointed out that cheating was not in a single direction. One hong merchant suffered losses

in excess of one million dollars by extending credit to Americans. See Dennett, *Americans in Eastern Asia*, p. 86. One Englishman reported a lively business in defective clocks sold to unsuspecting Celestials. See J. Johnson, *Oriental Voyager* (London, 1807), p. 209. The purpose of this study, however, is not to correct such impressions but merely to report them.

72. Sarah Forbes Hughes (ed.), *Letters and Recollections of John Murray Forbes* (Boston, 1899), I, 86.

73. Hunter, *The "Fan Kwae" at Canton*, p. 40.

74. Shaw, *Journals*, p. 183.

75. Townsend, New Haven Colony Society, *Papers*, IV, 86, 94.

76. Log of the *Ann* and *Hope*, 1799–1800, MSS, Rhode Island Historical Society, Providence, R.I.

77. Boit, Sea Journal, MSS. Entry for Jan. 1, 1793.

78. Fanning, *Voyages*, p. 226.

79. Hunter, *The "Fan Kwae" at Canton*, pp. 27–28. One historian suggested that since the Chinese devil, or "qui," had red hair and blue eyes it was only natural for them to call the first Dutch traders "foreign devils." See *Journal of American Folk-Lore*, V (1892), 322.

80. Delano, *Narrative*, p. 537.

81. For good examples of this reaction, see Wood, *Sketches of China*, p. 98 note; Shaw, *Journals*, p. 184; Charles Forbes, "Remarks by an Ordinary Seaman, 1815–1817," MSS, Essex Institute, Salem, Mass.; John Gibson, *Observations on the Trade with China* (Phila., 1807), p. 38.

82. Shaw, *Journals*, p. 195.

83. Fanning, *Voyages*, p. 191. Captain Fanning himself was extraordinarily superstitious, and recounted several mysterious happenings. See *ibid.*, pp. 194–196.

84. Wood, *Sketches of China*, pp. 157–158.

85. Shaw, *Journals*, pp. 195–196.

86. Goodhue Papers, MSS, Essex Institute, Goodhue never personally visited China, but was engaged in the trade and based this observation on frequent conversations with captains and supercargoes returning from Canton.

87. Hewes, Essex Institute, *Historical Collections*, LXXI, 209.

88. *American Quarterly Review*, IX, 56.

89. Delano, *Narrative*, pp. 539–540.

90. *Ibid.*, p. 533.

91. Doolittle, *Sketches, by a Traveller*, pp. 274–276.

92. Hunter, *The "Fan Kwae" at Canton*, pp. 152–153.

93. Doolittle, *Sketches, by a Traveller*, p. 262.

94. Wood, *Sketches of China*, pp. 191, 118–119.

95. C. Toogood Downing, *Fan-Qui in China, 1836–37* (London, 1838), I, 293–295.

96. Doolittle, *Sketches, by a Traveller*, p. 262.

97. Wood, *Sketches of China*, pp. 143–144.

98. Fanning, *Voyages*, p. 22.

99. J. R. Morrison, *A Chinese Commercial Guide* (London, 1834), glossary.

100. Townsend, New Haven Colony Historical Society, *Papers*, IV, 91.

101. Delano, *Narrative*, p. 542.

102. Roberts, *Embassy to Eastern Courts*, p. 152.

103. Gideon Nye, *The Morning of My Life in China, 1833–1839* (Canton, 1873), p. 4.

104. [Holbrook], *Sketches, by a Traveller*, p. 1.

105. *Ibid.*

106. See the article on Dobell's *Travels in Kamchatka and Siberia; With a Narrative of a Residence in China* (London, 1830) in *American Quarterly Review*, IX (1831), pp. 52–81. Since Wood and Dobell were both natives of Philadelphia, the generous estimates of the popularity of their works in this Philadelphia magazine may have been exaggerated.

107. See Bernard Berelson, "Communications and Public Opinion," *Reader in Public Opinion and Communications*, ed. Berelson and Morris Janowitz (Glencoe, 1950), p. 452.

108. Dorothy S. Hewes, "To the Farthest Gulf. Outline of the Old China Trade," Essex Institute, *Historical Collections*, LXXVII (1941), 142.

109. Dennett, *Americans in Eastern Asia*, p. 16.

110. See *The Autobiography of Benjamin Rush; His "Travels Through Life" Together with His "Commonplace Book," for 1789–1813*, ed. George W. Corner (Princeton, 1948), pp. 175–176.

3. THE DIPLOMATIC IMAGE, 1785–1840

1. See John King Fairbank, "Tributary Trade and China's Relations with the West," *Far Eastern Quarterly*, I (1942), 129–149. See Li Chien-nung, *Political History of China* (Princeton, 1956), pp. 12–26, for a succinct account of China's negotiations with Western nations before the Opium War.

2. See Earl Pritchard, *The Crucial Years of Early Anglo-Chinese Relations, 1750–1800* (Pullman, Wash., 1936), pp. 272–284, for a description of the Macartney embassy.

3. Aeneas Anderson, *A Narrative of the British Embassy to China, in the Years 1792, 1793, and 1794* (London, 1795), p. xix.

4. Helen H. Robbins, *Our First Ambassador to China* (New York, 1908), p. 436.

5. Anderson, *Narrative*, p. 327.

6. Jean Baptiste Grosier, S.J., *A General Description of China* (London, 1788), II, 56.

7. Anderson, *Narrative*, p. 114.

8. *Ibid.*, pp. 114, 133, 120–127, 327–333, 201–202.

9. *Ibid.*, pp. 217, 182, 333–334.

10. *Ibid.*, pp. 87–88, 195–196.

11. Robbins, *Our First Ambassador to China*, p. 436.

12. [Philadelphia] *Aurora*, May 7 and 12, 1796.

13. William Winterbotham, *An Historical, Geographical, and Philosophical View of the Chinese Empire* (Phila., 1796), prefatory advertisement. Rather than deny the charges of China's critics, as Anderson did, Winterbotham attempted to mitigate them in the same manner that Grosier and even Du Halde had done: Most exposed infants were rescued by wealthier families to be raised as servants; China's scientific primitiveness was a function of her great age, so that remarkable innovations of a millennium earlier were by 1795 "a little obsolete and primitive" (pp. 380–81, 422). To Winterbotham, China's only serious flaw was her anticommercial values which were being "corrected" through contact with the West (p. 392).

14. Sir George Staunton, *An Authentic Account of an Embassy from the King of Great Britain to the Emperor of China* (London, 1797), I, title page.

15. Sir George Staunton, *An Abridged Account of the Embassy to the Emperor of China* (London, 1797), p. 190; *Authentic Account*, II, 65.

16. Staunton, *Abridged Account*, pp. 286–287, 356–357. The British army surgeon, Dr. Scott, also witnessed the Chinese diagnosis and treatment of a member of Macartney's embassy, and reported to Benjamin Rush, during a subsequent visit to Philadelphia, that the Chinese believed that the arteries were filled with air which had to be kept moving or would stagnate. See *The Autobiography of Benjamin Rush; His "Travels Through Life" Together with His "Commonplace Book," for 1789–1813,* ed. George W. Corner (Princeton, 1948), pp. 245–246. Ilse Veith contends that this popular misconception was the result of mistranslating the Chinese character for "essence of life" into "air." This was stated in response to my questions following Professor Veith's lecture on the history of Chinese medicine at the Medical Center, University of California, San Francisco, March 31, 1964.

17. Robbins, *Our First Ambassador to China,* p. 287.

18. Staunton, *Abridged Account,* pp. 198, 318–319.

19. *Ibid.,* pp. 275–281.

20. Robbins, *Our First Ambassador to China,* pp. 321, 307.

21. *Ibid.,* pp. 386, 394–396.

22. William Appleton, *A Cycle of Cathay* (New York, 1951), pp. 169 n. 29, 170.

23. In the preface to his second edition Anderson acknowledged heavy criticism on such points; and in spite of his claim that only "literal errors" were corrected, the second edition omitted the "interviews" described in the first. See Aeneas Anderson, *A Narrative of the British Embassy to China* (2nd ed.; London, 1795), pp. 2–3.

24. William Jardine Proudfoot, *Barrow's Travels in China; an Investigation into the Origin and Authenticity of the Facts and Observations in a Work Entitled Travels in China by John Barrow, F.R.S.* (London, 1861), p. 48.

25. Staunton, *Authentic Account,* I, 41.

26. John F. Davis, *The Chinese* (London, 1836), I, 241.

27. John Barrow, *Travels in China* (London, 1804), pp. 178–179, 184, 48–50.

28. *Ibid.,* pp. 167–171. Olaf Torreen was an eighteenth-century visitor to China.

29. *Ibid.,* pp. 31, 187.

30. *Ibid.,* pp. 4, 151.

31. *Ibid.,* pp. 224–225, 313–323.

32. *Ibid.,* pp. 73–74, 77, 460, 462.

33. See C. L. Boxer, "Isaac Titsingh's Embassy to the Court of Ch'ien Lung (1794–95)," *T'ien Hsia Monthly,* VIII (1939), 9–33; J. J. L. Duyvendak, "The Last Dutch Embassy to the Chinese Court," *T'oung Pao,* XXXIV (1938), 98–107, for accounts of this mission.

34. Barrow, *Travels in China,* pp. 9–10, 210–211.

35. Staunton, *Abridged Account,* p. 190.

36. Boxer, *T'ien Hsia Monthly,* VIII, 8, 28. See also André Everard Van Braam-Houckgeest, *An Authentic Account of the Embassy of the Dutch East-India Company* (London, 1798), I, 261 ff.

37. Boxer, *T'ien Hsia Monthly,* VIII, 28 ff.

38. Thomas La Farque, "Some Early Chinese Visitors to the U.S.," *T'ien Hsia Monthly,* XI (1942), 131; Edward R. Barnsley, "History of China's Retreat," *Bristol* [Penn.] *Courier,* May 9, 10, and 11, 1933. Among the more famous émigrés who visited Van Braam, according to tradition, were Moreau, Casenove, Lafayette, Talleyrand and even Louis Phillippe. The evidence to support such claims is weak, however, and Talleyrand returned to France before "China's Retreat" was completed.

39. Van Braam, *Authentic Account of the Embassy of the Dutch East-India Company*, I, 192.

40. *Ibid.*, II, 38, 65–66, 78–79, 85–86.

41. *Ibid.*, I, 244, 209, 261.

42. Boxer, *T'ien Hsia Monthly*, VIII, 10.

43. Van Braam, *Authentic Account*, I, 211.

44. Sir Henry Ellis, *Journal of the Proceedings of the Late Embassy to China* (London, 1817), p. 144.

45. George T. Staunton, *Notes of Proceedings and Occurrences, During the British Embassy to Pekin, in 1816* (London, 1824). I was unable to find a single review or reference to this work, although the author's treatise on Chinese law had been well received over a decade earlier.

46. Captain Basil Hall, RN, *A Voyage to the Eastern Seas in the Year 1816* (New York, 1827). American editors showed interest in Hall's description of the "Loo Choo" islanders which comprised a major portion of his book. See for example the review in *North American Review*, XXVI (1828), 514–538.

47. Clarke Abel, *Narrative of a Journey in the Interior of China* (London, 1818), Introduction, pp. 197, 235.

48. John M'Leod, *Narrative of a Voyage, in His Majesty's Late Ship Alceste to the Yellow Sea, Along the Coast of Corea, and Through Its Numerous Hitherto Undiscovered Islands to the Island of Lewchew* (London, 1817), pp. 106–109.

49. *Ibid.*, p. 122.

50. *Ibid.*, pp. 123–125.

51. *Atheneum; or, Spirit of the English Magazines*, II (1817), 385.

52. *American Monthly Magazine and Critical Review*, II (1818), 430–445.

53. Ellis, *Journal*, pp. 74, 86.

54. *Ibid.*, p. 430.

55. *Ibid.*, pp. 408, 340, 388.

56. *Ibid.*, p. 134.

57. *Ibid.*, p. 440.

58. George Timkowski, *Travels of the Russian Mission Through Mongolia to China, and Residence in Peking, in the Years 1820–1821* (London, 1827), I, 1–4, 341–348, 369–372; II, 187.

59. See *Southern Review*, IV (1829), 204; *North American Review*, XXV (1827), 1–19. The latter was a joint review with another Russian account, Captain Krusenstern's description of a world cruise in 1803–1805. This work was exceedingly critical of the Chinese, but was mentioned so rarely by Americans that it cannot be considered important to this study.

60. Li Chien-nung, *Political History of China*, p. 18.

61. Davis, *The Chinese*, I, 92, 94, 196, 237.

62. Tyler Dennett, *Americans in Eastern Asia* (New York, 1922), p. 133.

63. See *North American Review*, XLVII (1838), 395–422.

64. Edmund Roberts, *Embassy to the Eastern Courts* (New York, 1837), p. 152.

65. *Ibid.*, pp. 79, 150.

66. W. S. W. Ruschenberger, M.D., *A Voyage Round the World; Including an Embassy to Muscat and Siam, in 1835, 1836, and 1837* (Phila., 1838), p. 398.

67. *Ibid.*, pp. 371, 387–388, 424.

68. *Ibid.*, p. 431.

69. See for example, Barrow, *Travels in China*, pp. 456–463; Ellis, *Journal*, pp. 438, 487, for comments of these two harsh critics on Chinese religious practices.

4. THE PROTESTANT MISSIONARY IMAGE, 1807–1870

1. Kenneth S. Latourette, *A History of Christian Missions in China* (New York, 1929), pp. 209–227. Actually the most famous of these missionaries, Samuel Wells Williams, was not an ordained minister but a printer.

2. *Ibid.*, p. 436.

3. F. L. Mott, *American Journalism: A History of Newspapers* (New York, 1950), p. 370.

4. *General Conference of the Protestant Missionaries of China Held at Shanghai, May 10–24, 1877* (Shanghai, 1878), p. 4.

5. *North American Review*, LXVII (1848), 267.

6. At least a comparison of the *Missionary Herald* published in London with the periodical of the same title published in Boston would indicate that the English journal allocated far greater space to India and Africa and that the tone of its editorial comment on these areas was one of greater excitement and expectation than was true for China.

7. *Memoirs of the Life and Labors of Robert Morrison*, comp. Mrs. Morrison (London, 1849), I, 64, 106.

8. *Ibid.*, I, 136–137. See Allen T. Price, "American Missionaries and American Diplomacy" (unpub. Ph.D. dissertation, Harvard University, 1934), p. 4, for a good discussion of Morrison's reception in America.

9. *Niles' Weekly Register*, XXI (1822), 405.

10. *Ibid.*, XLIV (1833), 119.

11. For a good summary of this alliance between commercial and missionary interests in China before 1850, see American Board of Commissioners for Foreign Missions, *Memorial Volume of the First Fifty Years* (Boston, 1863), pp. 240–242 ff. The missionaries in turn insisted that "a free commercial intercourse" between China and the West was a necessary step toward the conversion of China. See *Missionary Herald*, XXIX (1833), 181–182.

12. William W. Sweet, *Religion in the Development of American Culture, 1765–1840* (New York, 1952), pp. 146–149.

13. Ray Allen Billington, *The Protestant Crusade* (Chicago, 1964), p. 41.

14. American Board of Commissioners for Foreign Missions, *China* (Boston, 1868), p. 4.

15. *A Legacy of Historical Gleanings*, comp. by Mrs. C. V. Bonney (Albany, New York, 1875), II, 225.

16. Raymond Dawson calls the reports of these missionaries "the Protestant view of China" with no national or denominational distinctions. See his "Western Conceptions of Chinese Civilization," *The Legacy of China* (Oxford, 1964), p. 22.

17. George H. Danton, *The Culture Contacts of the United States and China* (New York, 1931), p. 82.

18. Of 111 male missionaries in China in 1867 only 14 were lay missionaries, according to the *Methodist Quarterly Review*, XLIX (1867), 434.

19. Rev. John L. Nevius, *Demon Possession and Allied Themes* (New York, 1895), p. v. It is interesting that Latourette was critical of Catholic missionaries for exploiting the Chinese belief in demon possession to acquire converts in the nineteenth century while ignoring Nevius' work which was widely quoted in Protestant circles and went through five editions by 1915. See his *History of Christian Missions in China*, pp. 194–195. Although a valuable and comprehensive work on missionaries in China, Latourette's book has a strong Protestant bias.

20. Nevius, *Demon Possession*, pp. 285, 290.

21. *Missionary Herald*, LXXV (1879), 77–80.

22. Rufus Anderson, *The Theory of Missions to the Heathen* (Boston, 1845), p. 3.

23. *Chinese Repository*, I (1832), 149.

24. *Missionary Herald*, XXVI (1830), 279–280.

25. Letter from Williams to his father, Nov. 6, 1833, in Frederick Wells Williams, *The Life and Letters of Samuel Wells Williams* (New York, 1899), p. 64.

26. "The Church and China," *Methodist Quarterly Review*, XXXII (1850), 593.

27. See *Missionary Herald*, LXXII (1876), 30–32, for an excellent example of Chinese idolatry described in sexual metaphors.

28. *Chinese Repository*, I (1832), 126.

29. Samuel Wells Williams, *The Middle Kingdom* (New York, 1848), II, 96.

30. Rev. R. S. Maclay, *Life Among the Chinese* (New York, 1861), pp. 136–137.

31. "China," *Presbyterian Monthly*, II (1857), 226–230.

32. American Sunday School Union, *The People of China* (Philadelphia, 1844), p. 73.

33. *Chinese Repository*, I (1832), 59.

34. Rev. David Abeel, *Journal of a Residence in China, and the Neighboring Countries* (New York, 1836), p. 81.

35. Arthur Christy, *The Orient in American Transcendentalism* (New York, 1932), pp. 29–34, 123–125.

36. *Journals and Miscellaneous Notebooks of Ralph Waldo Emerson*, ed. William Gilman *et al.* (Cambridge, Mass., 1961), II, 224, 228–229, 378. See also *The Letters of Ralph Waldo Emerson*, ed. Ralph L. Rusk (New York, 1939), I, 140.

37. Proclus, "On the Genius of the Chinese," *Port Folio*, s. 3, V (1811), 426. Italics in original.

38. Rev. Robert Morrison, *A View of China* (Macao, 1817), I, 207–208.

39. Rev. M. Simpson Culbertson, *Darkness in the Flowery Land* (New York, 1857), pp. 27–28.

40. "Confucius," *Christian Examiner*, LXXXIV (1868), 167.

41. Henrietta Shuck, *Scenes in China* (Phila., 1853), p. 55.

42. *Christian Examiner*, LXXXIV (1868), 177, 180.

43. Rev. John L. Nevius, *China and the Chinese* (New York, 1869), pp. 46–48, 49–54.

44. "For Young People: Confucius and His Son of the Seventieth Generation," *Missionary Herald*, LXXXV (1889), p. 219.

45. William Medhurst, *China: Its State and Prospects* (London, 1838), pp. 194–195.

46. *Missionary Herald*, XXIX (1833), 273.

47. *Christian Examiner*, LXXXIV (1868), 167, 174.

48. F. W. Williams, *Life and Letters of Samuel Wells Williams*, p. 446.

49. Maclay, *Life Among the Chinese*, pp. 88–89.

50. *Missionary Herald*, XXIV (1828), 327.

51. Rev. J. B. Jeter, *A Memoir of Mrs. Henrietta Shuck, the First American Female Missionary to China* (Boston, 1846), p. 87. See also Abeel, *Journal*, pp. 141–142; *Missionary Herald*, XIX (1823), 56; XXIV (1828), 326–327.

52. *Missionary Herald*, LXXXV (1889), 219.

53. This was Rev. Ellinwood's statement in the *New York Evangelist* as reprinted in the *Missionary Herald*, LXXII (1876), 30.

54. Medhurst, *China*, p. 195.

55. James Legge, *The Chinese Classics* (London, 1861–1872), I (1861), 107, 109, 113.

56. Ralph Waldo Emerson, "What Books to Read," a Lecture delivered at Howard University, Jan. 7, 1872 (Washington, D.C., 1957), p. 9; Corliss Lamont, *The Philosophy of Humanism* (New York, 1957), pp. 40–41.

57. Legge, *Chinese Classics* (2nd ed.; London, 1893–95), I, 111.

58. Medhurst, *China*, pp. 45–46.

59. Abeel, *Journal*, pp. 134–135.

60. Nevius, *China and the Chinese*, pp. 252–253.

61. "Chinese Infanticide," *Presbyterian Monthly*, III (1868–69), 13–14; *Missionary Herald*, LVI (1860), 41.

62. Williams, *Middle Kingdom*, II, 260; Abeel, *Journal*, p. 134.

63. Rev. Justice Doolittle, *Social Life of the Chinese* (New York, 1867), p. 207; *Presbyterian Monthly*, III (1868–69), 15.

64. Williams, *Middle Kingdom*, II, 161.

65. Morrison, *View of China*, p. 121. One exception to this rule was Rev. J. G. Wood, M.A., F.L.S., *The Uncivilized Races* (Hartford, 1870), II, 800.

66. "The Condition of the Heathen Females," *Baptist Missionary Magazine*, XX (1840), 35–37, is an excellent summary of missionary opinion on this subject before 1840. See also *Chinese Repository*, I (1832), 149; *Missionary Herald*, LVI (1860), 41–42; Williams, *Middle Kingdom*, II, 63; Nevius, *China and the Chinese*, pp. 238–239; an article by Henrietta Shuck from *Mother's Journal* reproduced in Jeter, *Memoir of Mrs. Henrietta Shuck*, pp. 209–210.

67. See minutes of the American Female Moral Reform Society, in *New York Morning Herald*, May 15, 1839.

68. Mrs. Shuck, *Scenes in China*, p. 168.

69. The statistics on conversion published by missionary organizations were not very encouraging. *The General Conference of the Protestant Missionaries of China* (Shanghai, 1890) claimed that only six converts were made before 1842 and 350 over the next decade (p. lvii). Comparative figures on Protestant conversions in Africa and India published by the London Missionary Society indicate that China was far less fruitful a field for harvesting souls for Christ. See *Missionary Herald*, LXXII (1876), 95.

70. *Missionary Herald*, XXIX (1833), 16.

71. Abeel, *Journal*, p. 143.

72. Morrison, *View of China*, p. 121.

73. For example, see the account of such a junket by Medhurst during which he claimed that thousands of Christian tracts were distributed and eagerly received each day by Chinese villagers. Medhurst, *China*, pp. 370–521.

74. Morrison, *Memoirs*, I, 79–80; *Missionary Herald*, XIX (1823), 158.

75. Williams, *Middle Kingdom*, II, 142–143.

76. Letter from Williams to his father, Nov. 23, 1835, in F. W. Williams, *Life and Letters*, 80.

77. *Chinese Repository*, III (1834–35), 41.

78. Medhurst, *China*, p. 441.

79. *Missionary Herald*, XLI (1845), 31.

80. *Christian Examiner*, L (1851), 365.

81. Medhurst, *China*, p. 441.

82. *Missionary Herald*, XXIX (1833), 318.

83. Doolittle, *Social Life of the Chinese*, II, 420. Italics in original. A heated debate took place in Protestant missionary circles over the translation of "God" and "spirit" into Chinese which was similar to one that took place among Catholic missionaries about two centuries earlier. See *Records of the General Conference* (Shanghai, 1890), p. 31. For description of the earlier "Shang-ti controversy," see George H. Dunne, S.J., *Generation of Giants* (South Bend, 1962), pp. 282–301; Arnold Rowbotham, "The Jesuits at the Court of Peking," *Chinese Social and Political Science Review*, V (1919), pp. 297–324.

84. *Methodist Quarterly Review*, XXXII (1850), 598.

85. *Missionary Herald*, XLI (1845), 156; Williams, *Middle Kingdom*, II, 367.

86. American Board of Commissioners for Foreign Missions, *Historical Sketch of China* (Boston, 1880), p. 8.

87. *Methodist Quarterly Review*, XXXII (1850), 598; Medhurst, *China*, p. 380; Nevius, *China and the Chinese*, pp. 74–76; Williams, *Middle Kingdom*, I, 388–389.

88. Rev. William Speer, *The Oldest and Newest Empire* (Hartford, 1870), p. 453. See also his "Democracy in China," *Harper's* XXXVIII (1868), 839–849. Of course, Speer was very active in defending Chinese immigrants against the charges of the sinophobes, one of which was that they could never adjust to democratic institutions.

89. Rev. Charles Gutzlaff, *The Journal of Two Voyages Along the Coast of China, in 1831 and 1832* (New York, 1833); *Report of Proceedings on a Voyage North* (London, 1833).

90. *Missionary Herald*, XXIX (1833), 452.

91. *Baptist Missionary Magazine*, XVII (1837), 176.

92. Medhurst, *China*, pp. 370–521. Two of the vessels upon which Gutzlaff traveled, the *Lord Amherst* and the *Sylph* were engaged in the opium trade according to William Hunter, *The "Fan Kwae" at Canton Before Treaty Days, 1825–1844* (London, 1882), p. 70, and corroborated by Medhurst, *China*, pp. 363–364, 366.

93. *Chinese Repository*, II (1833), 312, I (1832), 146; *Missionary Herald*, XXXI (1835), 69; *Christian Examiner*, LXIII (1857), 63–64, 206.

94. Maclay, *Life Among the Chinese*, p. 80.

95. Williams, *Middle Kingdom*, II, 98.

96. Morrison, *View of China*, pp. 124–125.

97. Milne, in the *Missionary Herald*, XXIV (1828), 326–327.

98. Rev. M. Simpson Culbertson, *Darkness in the Flowery Land* (N.Y., 1857).

99. Morrison in the *Missionary Herald*, XVII (1821), 197.

100. Williams, *Middle Kingdom*, II, 98-99.

101. Maclay, *Life Among the Chinese*, p. 19.

102. Letter from Rev. Titus Coan to his wife, Aug. 29, 1837, in Titus Coan Letters, 1836–1845, MSS, New York Historical Society.

103. *Missionary Herald*, XLI (1845), 156.

104. *Ibid.*, XXVIII (1832), 13.

105. *Biblical Repertory*, n.s., XI (1839), 171.

106. Anderson, *Theory of Missions to the Heathen*, pp. 1–22.

107. One gets the impression, however, that some of these missionaries would not have been above just that. At least Morrison explained that Chinese mythology "is perhaps quite as ridiculous as those of the Greeks and Romans, though certainly not so offensive to good morals as some parts of those 'elegant' systems." *View of China*, p. 112.

108. *Chinese Repository*, II (1833), 509; III (1834–35), 7, 51.

109. Maclay, *Life Among the Chinese*, pp. 45–47.

110. *Ibid.*, p. 20; *Chinese Repository*, II (1833), 3–4; Medhurst, *China*, p. 120; Culbertson, *Darkness in the Flowery Land*, p. ix.

111. *Baptist Missionary Magazine*, XVII (1836), 57; *Chinese Repository*, I (1832), 326–333.

112. *Methodist Quarterly Review*, XXXII (1850), 593, 602.

113. Williams, *Middle Kingdom*, I, 297; II, 52–53.

114. *Missionary Herald*, XXXI (1835), 269.

115. J. G. Wood, *The Uncivilized Races*, frontispiece; see II, 800–819, for his low estimation of Chinese culture.

116. See for example, American Board of Commissioners for Foreign Missions, *China* (Boston, 1868), p. 4.

117. *New York Observer*, April 7, 1864.

118. Letter from S. W. Williams to Dr. Blodget of the American Board, Aug. 9, 1883, in F. W. Williams, *Life and Letters*, pp. 457–458.

119. Maclay, *Life Among the Chinese*, p. 18; *Methodist Quarterly Review*, XLIV (1862), 212; *Missionary Herald*, XXIX (1833), 452.

120. Culbertson in *Methodist Quarterly Review*, XLIV (1862), 208.

121. *Christian Examiner*, LXIII (1857), 206.

122. *Missionary Herald*, LXXVI (1880), 292.

123. Chao-kwang Wu, *The International Aspects of the Missionary Movement in China* (Baltimore, 1830), pp. 239–240; S. Y. Teng, "The Predispositions of Westerners in Treating Chinese History and Civilization," *Historian*, XIX (1953), 319.

124. Dawson, *Legacy of China*, p. 22.

125. For early examples of such attacks, see *Chinese Repository*, I (1832), 3; II, (1833), 3–4; IV (1835), 105–118; *Missionary Herald*, XXVII (1831), 245; *Baptist Missionary Magazine*, XVII (1837), 227; Williams, *Middle Kingdom*, I, 421–453.

126. American Board of Commissioners for Foreign Missions, *Historical Sketch of the Missions of the American Board* (Boston, 1880), p. 8.

127. Oscar Handlin, *The Americans* (Boston, 1963), p. 304. Italics in original. For a national expression of these sexual fears, see pp. 168–171, 180–186, 242n106.

128. See, for example, the remarks of S. W. Williams to Rufus Anderson in F. W. Williams, *Life and Letters*, p. 91; Bridgman, in *Home Missionary*, IV (1831), 97–98; Medhurst, *China*, pp. 71–73; Abeel, *Journal*, pp. 141–142; *Missionary Herald*, XXX (1834), 334; XXXI (1835), 69–70.

129. *Missionary Herald*, XXIX (1833), 273.

130. Évariste Régis Huc, *The Chinese Empire* (London, 1855), I, 103; II, 88, 174, 344–346.

131. *Methodist Quarterly Review*, XXXVII (1855), 623–624.

132. W. W. Wood, *Sketches of China* (Phila., 1830), pp. 141–142. Cf. *ibid.*, pp. 71–73, 76–79, 83, 86.

133. Maclay, *Life Among the Chinese*, p. 121. Cf. *ibid.*, p. 80. See also Morrison, *View of China*, p. 124, for another example of the missionary's unawareness of the effect his own harsh criticism might have on Western opinion of the Chinese.

134. *McColloch's Geographical Dictionary* (New York, 1853), I, 605.

135. Williams, *Middle Kingdom*, II, 140.

136. Rev. Gilbert Reid, *The Social Relationship of Missionaries with the Chinese* (Shanghai, 1905), pp. 1–8.

137. Bernard Berelson, "Communication and Public Opinion," *Reader in Public Opinion and Communication,* eds. Bernard Berelson and Morris Janowitz (Glencoe, 1953), pp. 449–450, 453–454.

138. Laurence C. Wroth, *An American Bookshelf, 1755* (Phila., 1934). For examples of some of these reading lists and bibliographies for China, see the publisher's preface to G. T. Lay, *The Chinese as They Are* (Albany, New York, 1843); Howard Malcolm, *Travels in South Eastern Asia* (Boston, 1839), II, 188–190. The latter went through ten editions by 1853 and picked up the significant works on China to be added to the author's recommended list of books each year. See also the bibliographies in E. C. Wines, *A Peep at China in Mr. Dunn's Collection* (Phila., 1839); *10,000 Things on China and the Chinese . . . Barnum's Chinese Museum* (New York, 1850). Caleb Cushing was reputed to have one of the finest private libraries on China in the United States up to 1879, which contained the trader, diplomat, and missionary accounts stressed in this study. See *Catalogue of the Private Library of the Late Honorable Caleb Cushing* (Boston, 1879). One list prepared for missionaries at the end of the nineteenth century still contained the works of Du Halde, Barrow, Staunton, Dobell, W. W. Wood, Williams, Huc, Maclay, etc. See George W. Bailey, *"Tank Kee" A List of Works on China* (Marshalltown, Iowa, 1893). Latourette in 1929 still recommended the works of Barrow, Davis, Malcolm, Staunton, and Timkowski in his *History of Christian Missions in China,* pp. 845–899.

5. THE OPIUM WAR POPULARIZES THE UNFAVORABLE IMAGE, 1839–1850

1. Carl Bode, *The Anatomy of American Popular Culture, 1840–61* (Berkeley, 1959), p. x.

2. *New York Herald,* March 23, Nov. 24, 1840.

3. *Boston Evening Transcript,* June 11, 1840.

4. [Providence] *United States Chronicle,* June 16, July 21, 1785. For similar reports see [Philadelphia] *Pennsylvania Gazette,* May 18, 1785; [Philadelphia] *Freeman's Journal,* June 22, 1785; *Providence Gazette,* May 18, 1785; *New-York Packet* [Loundon's], May 16, 1785; *New-York Daily Advertiser,* May 16, 1785; *Newport Mercury,* May 21, 1785.

5. [Baltimore] *Maryland Journal,* Aug. 12, 1785. According to one local editor, Noah Webster journeyed from Hartford to interview the crew. See [Baltimore] *Maryland Gazette,* Oct. 16, 1785. But Webster's diary indicates that he was already in Baltimore on other business when the *Pallas* arrived. See E. E. F. Ford (comp.), *Notes on the Life of Noah Webster* (New York, 1912), I, 141.

6. *Salem Mercury,* May 29, 1787.

7. *Pennsylvania Gazette,* July 23, 1785.

8. *Boston Magazine,* March 1786. Perhaps nowhere was this editorial preference more clearly expressed than in the erroneous report that the hapless gunner on the *Lady Hughes* was generously acquitted, instead of being executed, which provoked a Providence editor to sing paeans to China's "most excellent laws." See *United States Chronicle,* June 9, 1785.

9. *American Apollo,* I (1792), 21; *New-York Magazine, or Literary Repository,* III (1792), 602.

10. *Massachusetts Magazine, or Monthly Museum,* IV (1792), 40.

11. *American Museum, or Universal Magazine,* XI (1792), 99.

12. William Stanton, *The Leopard's Spots: Scientific Attitudes Toward Race in America, 1815–59* (Chicago, 1960), pp. 19–22.

13. Proclus, "On the Genius of the Chinese," *Port Folio*, s. 3, V (1811), 343–346, 418–420, 432; VI (1811), 115, 120.

14. See *American Monthly Magazine and Critical Review*, II (1818), 437–444; *Atheneum; or Spirit of the English Magazines*, II (1817), 288–289, 329–331, 382–385; *Analectic Magazine*, X (1817), 435–436.

15. *American Monthly Magazine and Critical Review*, II (1818), 437, 431, 438.

16. *Port Folio*, s. 5, VII (1819), 101.

17. *American Quarterly Review*, III (1828), 255.

18. *Atheneum*, IV (1818–1819), 156. The possibility that the Chinese might have been highly creative in the kitchen was rarely considered. Even the revelation that Napoleon had a Chinese cook failed to arouse this editor's suspicion that the Chinese cuisine could be anything but bizarre, grotesque, and repulsive. See *ibid.*, XIV (1823), 285. See also *The Lady's Book (Godey's)*, I (1830), 34 f for examples of this stress upon the bizarre and ludicrous in Chinese behavior.

19. *Albany Farmers', Mechanics', and Workingmen's Advocate*, April 10, 1830.

20. *Niles' Weekly Register*, XXXV (1828), 4; XLI (1831), 238; XLVII (1835), 358.

21. *New York Mirror*, VII (1829), 84. See also *The Punishments of China, Illustrated by 22 Engravings* (London, 1830).

22. *American Monthly Magazine and Critical Review*, II (1818), 439. See *Ladies' Literary Cabinet*, VI (1822), 53; *Casket*, I (1826), 34–35; *Ariel*, IV (1830), 107.

23. *Atkinson's Casket*, X (1835), 448–449.

24. *New England Magazine*, VIII (1835), 275.

25. *North American Review*, XVII (1823), 11–12.

26. *Ibid.*, XXVI (1828), 514–528.

27. *Ibid.*, pp. 533, 538–540, 561–562.

28. *Southern Review*, IV (1829), 201.

29. *Free Enquirer*, I (1828), 2.

30. *North American Review*, XXXVIII (1834), 528–529; XL (1835), 58; *American Magazine of Useful and Entertaining Knowledge*, I (1835), 478; *Museum of Foreign Literature*, XXVI (1835), 239–240; *Niles' Weekly Register*, XLVII (1835), 358; XLVIII (1835), 259.

31. *North American Review*, XLII (1836), 272–273. Cf. *ibid.*, XXVII (1828), 561.

32. *Ibid.*, XLVII (1838), 399–401, 405–406.

33. "Du Ponceau on the Chinese System of Writing," *ibid.*, XLVIII (1839), 271–310.

34. *Knickerbocker Magazine*, IX (1837), 317; *New York Review*, III (1838), 457–460.

35. See, for example, "China and the Chinese," *Southern Literary Messenger*, VII (1841), 137–155.

36. *American Journal of Science and Arts*, XXXV (1839), 391–392.

37. *American Monthly Magazine and Critical Review*, II (1818), 443.

38. *Port Folio*, s. 5, VII (1819), 100–101.

39. *New York Observer* as reproduced in *Niles' Weekly Register*, XLIV (1833), 119.

40. John Nietz, *Old Textbooks* (Pittsburgh, 1961), p. 221. The fact that Professor Nietz saw the unfavorable characterization of the Chinese in nineteenth-century

geographies as a function of Guthrie's influence rather than the result of much broader and more complicated forces, further indicates the potential usefulness of this study.

41. *United States Chronicle*, Dec. 1, 1785, to March 9, 1786; Ralph Paine, *The Ships and Sailors of Old Salem* (New York, 1909) , p. 144.

42. Ruth Miller Elson, *Guardians of Tradition* (Lincoln, Nebr., 1964) , p. 162. Cf. Nietz, *Old Textbooks*, p. 221.

43. Jedidiah Morse, "The Present Situation of the World Contrasted with Our Own," *A Sermon Delivered by Morse at Charlestown, February 19, 1795. Being the Day Recommended by George Washington for Public Thanksgiving and Prayer* (Boston, 1795) , pp. 27–28.

44. Jedediah Morse, *The American Universal Geography* (Boston, 1812) , II, 483f. Cf. his *American Geography* (New Haven, 1784) .

45. Conrad Malte-Brun, *System of Geography* (Boston, 1828) , pp. 412–415.

46. Samuel G. Goodrich, *A System of Universal Geography* (2nd ed.; Boston, 1833) , pp. 905–906. For later works in which Goodrich became even more sinophobic, see *Peter Parley's Universal History on the Basis of Geography* (New York, 1845) , p. 116; *The World and Its Inhabitants* (Boston, 1845) , p. 240; *The Second Book of History Combined with Geography* (Boston, 1854) , p. 314; *A Natural Geography* (New York, 1856), p. 67; *The World as It Is, and as It Has Been; or a Comprehensive Geography and History* (New York, 1858) , p. 263; *The Tales of Peter Parley about Asia* (Phila., 1859) , pp. 53–58.

47. T. G. Bradford, *A Comprehensive Atlas* (Boston, 1835) , p. 126.

48. American Oriental Society, *Journal*, II (1851) , 183; Hugh Murray, *Encyclopedia of Geography* (Phila., 1837) , III, 409.

49. John A. Sahli, "An Analysis of Early American Geography Textbooks from 1784–1840" (unpub. Ph.D. diss., University of Pittsburg, 1941) , p. 150.

50. Edward Everett, *Orations and Speeches* (2nd ed.; Boston, 1850) , I, 422.

51. Thomas A. Bailey, *A Diplomatic History of the American People* (6th ed.; New York, 1958) , pp. 302–303.

52. John W. Foster, *American Diplomacy in the Orient* (Boston, 1904) , pp. 73–74. For a more recent diplomatic history that repeated this theme with no further details, see Alexander De Conde, *A History of American Foreign Policy* (New York, 1963) , p. 228.

53. "Adams' Lecture on the War with China," *Chinese Repository*, XI (1842), 274–289. This seems to be the only publication to publish the entire speech, although excerpts of it appeared in domestic newspapers. See, for example, *Weekly Intelligencer* (Washington, D.C.), Nov. 30, Dec. 4, 1841; *New World* (New York), IV (Jan. 1, 1842), 10–13.

54. Dennett, *Americans in Eastern Asia*, p. 108; Bailey, *Diplomatic History of the American People*, p. 302.

55. *Memoirs of John Quincy Adams*, ed. C. F. Adams (Phila., 1876) , XI, 31 (entry dated Dec. 3, 1841 in his diary) .

56. *New York Herald*, Jan. 30, 1841.

57. *Ibid.*, Nov. 24, 1840.

58. [New York] *Evening Post for the Country*, Nov. 24, 1840.

59. Paul R. Frothingham, *Edward Everett* (Boston, 1925) , p. 231. Because of his attacks on China, Everett withdrew from consideration for the job of leading a mission to China to secure a treaty after the war. It is interesting that Peter Parker recommended both Adams and Everett for this job.

60. Dennett, *Americans in Eastern Asia*, pp. 105–106; Samuel F. Bemis, *John Quincy Adams and the Union* (New York, 1956), p. 484. As a younger man Adams had evidently been an admirer of the Celestial Empire and even gave the Chinese credit for having developed the decimal system in his *Reports on Weights and Measures* in 1817. See *North American Review*, XIV (1822), 224. But the reports of European diplomats on missions to China, American traders, and Protestant missionaries as well as his own experience as secretary of state soured him on the Chinese over the next two decades.

61. *House Executive Documents*, no. 71, 26th Cong., 2nd Sess.

62. Dennett, *Americans in Eastern Asia*, 108.

63. See Parker's letters to *Niles' Weekly Register*, LX (1841), 50; to *Missionary Herald*, XXXVII (1841), 43; to his sisters, in Rev. George B. Stevens, D.D., *The Life, Letters, and Journals of the Rev. and Hon. Peter Parker, M.D.* (Boston, 1896), pp. 165–177.

64. Foster, *American Diplomacy in the Orient*, p. 73.

65. See R. B. Forbes, *Personal Reminiscences, with Recollections of China* (3rd ed.; Boston, 1892), pp. 149–151, 155; William Hunter, *The "Fan Kwae" at Canton Before Treaty Days, 1825–1844* (London, 1882), p. 115; Dennett, *Americans in Eastern Asia*, pp. 97–98.

66. Letter from Bull to Carrington, July 25, 1839, Carrington Family Papers, MSS, Rhode Island Historical Society.

67. Bull to Carrington, Jan. 11, 1840, *ibid*. See his letter of Nov. 24, 1839 for his first lukewarm support of the British.

68. Bull to Carrington, Jan. 28, 1840, *ibid*.

69. Bull to Carrington, June 24, 1840, *ibid*.

70. *Providence Journal*, Nov. 25, 1840.

71. Ping Chia Kuo, "Caleb Cushing and the Treaty of Wanghia, 1844," *Journal of Modern History*, V (1933), 34. Caleb Cushing did not fail to use this advice, aggressively maneuvering the U.S.S. *Brandywine* to force the Chinese to negotiate. See Dennett, *Americans in Eastern Asia*, pp. 151–152. Bailey's statement that Cushing's "most serious initial difficulties were of his own creation" also implies that he was eager to put this advice to use. See *A Diplomatic History of the American People* (4th ed.; New York, 1950), p. 326.

72. Augustine Heard, Jr., Diary, typescript, pp. 31–59 in Heard Collection, MSS, Baker Library, Harvard University.

73. Letters from W. H. Low to J. O. Low, Oct. 27, 1839, May 3, 1840, March 26, 1841, in Mercantile Papers, MSS, New York Public Library.

74. W. H. Low to J. O. Low, Jan. 2, 1841, Mercantile Papers, MSS; Whitman to Carrington, Nov. 21, 1840, and Ritchie to Carrington, Jan. 9, 1841, in Carrington Family Papers MSS; Augustine Heard to J. S. Armory, Sept. 27, 1841, Heard Collection, MSS; R. B. Forbes to Paul S. Forbes, April 2, 1839, Forbes Collection, MSS, Baker Library, Harvard University.

75. Letters from Martin to Carrington, Jan. 27 and April 15, 1840, Carrington Family Papers, MSS.

76. Hunter, *The "Fan Kwae" at Canton*, pp. 154, 143–144.

77. "Journal of Occurrences at Canton During the Cessation of Trade at Canton, May, 1839 [William C. Hunter]," MSS, typescript copy, pp. 10–11, Boston Athenaeum. Italics in original.

78. Frederick Wells Williams, *The Life and Letters of Samuel Wells Williams* (New York, 1889), p. 104.

79. *House Executive Documents*, no. 119, 26th Cong., 1st Sess., pp. 8 ff.

80. Hunter, *The "Fan Kwae" at Canton*, pp. 115–116, 144–145.

81. *House Executive Documents*, no. 119, 26th Cong., 1st Sess., pp. 21–22, 28.

82. Hsin-pao Chang, *Commissioner Lin and the Opium War* (Cambridge, Mass., 1964), p. 31.

83. *House Executive Documents*, no. 119, 26th Cong., 1st Sess., p. 24.

84. *Ibid.*, no. 40, pp. 2–3.

85. Dennett, *Americans in Eastern Asia*, pp. 103–104.

86. *Missionary Herald*, XXXVI (1840), pp. 115–116.

87. As quoted in his biography, W. E. Griffis, *A Maker of the New Orient* (New York, 1902), p. 71.

88. *Spirit of Missions*, VI (1841), 366.

89. Rev. J. B. Jeter, *A Memoir of Mrs. Henrietta Shuck, the First American Female Missionary to China* (Boston, 1846), p. 38.

90. *Missionary Herald*, XXXVII (1841), 43–44.

91. *Chinese Repository*, XI (1842), 289 note.

92. Stevens, *The Life, Letters and Journals of the Rev. and Hon. Peter Parker, M.D.*, p. 168.

93. *Ibid.*, pp. 220–224; *Niles' Weekly Register*, LX (1841), 50–51.

94. See, for example, *Missionary Herald*, XXXV (1839), 464; XXXVI (1840), 115, 317; XXXVII (1841), 43; XXXVIII (1842), 100; XXXIX (1843), 91; *Baptist Missionary Magazine*, XX (1840), 270–275; XXI (1841), 91, *Niles' Weekly Register*, LIX (1840), 19; *Daily National Intelligencer*, March 20, 1841.

95. *New York Herald*, Dec. 23, 1842.

96. American Sunday School Union, *The People of China* (Phila., 1844), p. 54.

97. Samuel Wells Williams, *The Middle Kingdom* (New York, 1848), II, 525.

98. *Baptist Misionary Magazine*, XX (1840), 274.

99. *Southern Literary Messenger*, XIX (1853), 626–627.

100. *Chinese Repository*, III (1834–35), 345, 360.

101. *Ibid.*, 352, 406; V (1836), 180.

102. As published in the *New York Times*, Oct. 9, 1855.

103. F. W. Williams, *Life and Letters of Samuel Wells Williams*, p. 268.

104. *The Friend. A Religious and Literary Journal*, XIII (1840), 360.

105. *Christian Examiner*, XXXII (1842), 281–319.

106. See [Philadelphia] *Pennsylvania Freeman*, May 7, July 23, 1840; March 17, 1841.

107. Francis Wharton, "China and the Chinese Peace," *Hunt's Merchants' Magazine*, VIII (1843), 205; "The Quarrel Between Great Britain and China," *Monthly Chronicle*, I (1840), 94–109; *Philadelphia North American*, Jan. 27, 1841; *National Intelligencer*, Jan. 22, 1842; [New York] *Morning Chronicle*, March 13, 1840; [New York] *Evening Star*, Jan. 24, 1840; *New-York American*, March 9, 1840.

108. *New Yorker*, IX (1840), 123.

109. *New York American*, March 9, 1840; Oct. 25, 1841.

110. *Niles' National Register*, LXI (1841), 130.

111. *Ibid.*

112. Cf. *New York Herald*, Nov. 24, 1840; Oct. 25, 1841; Dec. 23, 1842. *New-York Evening Post*, Nov. 24 and 26, 1840; Nov. 25, 1841.

113. *Providence Journal*, Jan. 15, 1841. Compare this with articles and editorials in *ibid.*, Nov. 25 and Dec. 28, 1840; Jan. 1, 5, and 11, 1841.

114. *Ibid.*, March 5, 1841. See *ibid.*, Jan. 23, 30 and Feb. 3, 6, 9, 1841, for critical reports of Chinese actions.

115. *Ibid.*, Dec. 6, 1842.

116. *Ibid.,* Dec. 28, 1842.

117. *Boston Atlas,* Jan. 23, 1841.

118. [Boston] *Columbian Centinel,* Jan. 11, 1840.

119. *New-York Journal of Commerce,* March 11, 1840.

120. *Morning Courier and New-York Enquirer,* Nov. 24, 1840.

121. *New York Commercial Advertiser,* Aug. 6, 1840.

122. *New York Sun,* Dec. 3, 1840.

123. *Ibid.,* Dec. 4, 1840.

124. *New-York Commercial Advertiser,* Aug. 6, 1840.

125. *Ibid.,* Jan. 21, 1841.

126. *Ibid.,* Oct. 25, 1841.

127. See *Ibid.,* April 14 and June 20, 1840; *The Evening Post,* Nov. 24, 1840; *New York Herald,* March 18, 1840; *Albany Argus,* May 14, Sept. 20, and Oct. 14, 1839 and March 18, 1840; *The Evening Star,* Jan. 24, 1840, for example, of how this news tended to make these editors sympathize with the English momentarily.

128. *Albany Argus,* April 16, 1839.

129. See *New York Sun,* March 31, April 9, and May 10, 1841, for excellent examples of this effect. See also *Morning Courier and New-York Enquirer,* Jan. 22, 1841; *New-York Commercial Advertiser,* Feb. 5, 1841.

130. *Daily National Intelligencer,* March 20, 1841.

131. *Northern Light,* I (1841), 28–31.

132. *New York American,* Nov. 26, 1841.

133. *The Evening Post,* Nov. 25, 1841; *New York Commercial Advertiser,* Nov. 25, 1841.

134. *New York Commercial Advertiser,* Nov. 19 and 26, 1840. Adams' admirers who disagreed with his speech on the Opium War attributed it to his "eccentricities." See *ibid.,* Nov. 25, 1841; *Albany Argus,* Nov. 27, 1841.

135. *Boston Evening Transcript,* Nov. 24, 1841.

136. *Boston Atlas,* Jan. 23, 1841; Dec. 1, 1840.

137. See, for example, *New York Herald,* Dec. 21, 1839 and Aug. 31, 1840; *New-York American,* May 5, 1841; *Monthly Chronicle,* II (1841), 425–428; *Boston Atlas,* Oct. 9, 1839; *New York Sun,* Nov. 30, 1840; *New York Commercial Advertiser,* May 5, 1840; *New York Morning Herald,* Sept. 14, 1840.

138. *Knickerbocker Magazine,* XVI (1840), 447–449.

139. *Boston Evening Transcript,* June 19, 1840. See also *New-York American,* Jan. 14 and March 12, 1840; *Norfolk Beacon,* March 5, 1840; *New York Journal of Commerce,* as reprinted in *Niles' National Register,* LIX (1840), 209.

140. *New York Herald,* March 17 and May 8, 1840; Jan. 23, 1841.

141. *Ibid.,* Jan. 29, 1841; *New World,* III (1841), 287 and V (1842), 381; *National Intelligencer,* Dec. 3, 1842.

142. *Monthly Chronicle,* II (1841), 471.

143. *New York Herald,* May 8, 1840; Dec. 8, 1841; Dec. 1, 1842. *American Penny Magazine,* I (1845), 13.

144. *Monthly Chronicle,* III (1842), 90.

145. *Brother Jonathan,* III (1842), 15.

146. *Niles' National Register,* LXIII (1842), 99.

147. *Boston Atlas,* May 3, 1841.

148. *Gentleman's Magazine,* XXIII (1753), 116–119; XXV (1755), 9 ff.

149. *New York Herald,* Oct. 25 and Dec. 22, 1841. Napoleon's alleged remark was discussed most recently by *Time,* Dec. 1, 1958, p. 21, in the latest revival of the

yellow peril fear. It seems unlikely that it was ever made, however. Napoleon only granted an audience to Captain Hall whose father was a classmate of his at Brienne. Hall reported the conversation, part of which dealt with China, with no mention of Bonaparte's yellow peril warning. Indeed, Napoleon was more fascinated with the pacifism of the Loo Choo Islanders. See Capt. Basil Hall, RN, FRS, *Narrative of a Voyage to Java, China and the Great Island of Loo Choo.* (London, 1840), pp. 79ff.

150. *Providence Evening Herald,* July 29, 1840.

151. *New York Herald,* Dec. 22, 1842.

152. *Hunts' Merchants' Magazine,* XII (1845), 44.

153. *New York Times,* April 30, 1852.

154. *North American Review,* LXXIX, (1854), 181.

155. *Graham's Magazine,* XLIII (1853), 359–360.

156. *New York Herald,* Oct. 15, 1855.

157. *Ibid.,* Oct. 18, 1855.

158. *Ibid.,* Sept. 13, 1855.

159. *Memoirs of John Quincy Adams,* XI, 227.

160. See *Catalogue of the Private Library of the Late Honorable Caleb Cushing* (Boston, 1879).

161. Bailey, *A Diplomatic History of the American People,* p. 327 n. 19.

6. THE MASS MEDIA ERA, 1850–1870

1. Paul Cohen, *China and Christianity* (Cambridge, 1963), 229–233.

2. For example, see *Goshen* [New York] *Democrat and Whig,* June 10, 17, 24; Aug. 5, 12; and Sept. 2, 1853. [Middletown, New York] *Banner of Liberty,* July 27, Aug. 9, and Dec. 3, 1853. [Flint, Mich.] *Genessee Whig,* Aug. 13, 1853. This reaction to the Taipings can be contrasted to the tepid editorial response to other revolutions in China during the nineteenth century. Revolts of the White Lotus Society (1796–1810), of the T'ien-li-chiao and of Chinese Moslems between 1810 and 1820 were sporadically mentioned only to document that China was not the well-ordered, peaceful, benign despotism conceived of by Jesuit missionaries. A serious Moslem revolt that began just as the Taipings were being suppressed and lasted until 1873 was acknowledged in the American press, but its site in Shensi and Kansu was too remote and its Moslem character failed to excite any fatuous hopes for a Protestant China.

3. For example, see the six-column article on Ward in China in [Washington, D.C.] *National Intelligencer,* Nov. 22, 1859.

4. *New York Times,* June 13, 1852. Cf. *ibid.,* June 10, 1852.

5. *New York Herald,* Dec. 1, 1852.

6. This was published in many newspapers. See *Rochester Daily American,* Nov. 10, 1853; [Boston] *Daily Evening Traveller,* Sept. 16, 1853.

7. See, for example, a letter from a Reverend Wright in China to his parents in Troy, New York, in the *Troy Whig,* Nov. 21, 1853; *Albany Argus,* Nov. 22, 1853; *Albany Evening Journal,* Nov. 22, 1853; *Rochester Daily American,* Nov. 22, 1853.

8. *National Intelligencer,* Sept. 10, 1853. For similar reports of misionaries, see *Daily Evening Traveller,* July 14, Aug. 18, and Sept. 16, 1853; *New York Herald,* Aug. 11, 1853; *New York Tribune,* Aug. 24, 1853; *New York Journal of Commerce,* Aug. 2, 1853; *Albany Evening Journal,* Aug. 25, 1853.

9. As reprinted in *The Great Sinim Mission* (London, 1853), p. 8.

10. See *Hunt's Merchants' Magazine*, XXXIII (1835), 275–282, for some letters from traders.

11. *Daily Evening Traveler*, Sept. 2, 1853.

12. "China and the Indies: Our Manifest Destiny in the East," *De Bow's Review*, XV (1853), 542. See pp. 541–572 for a good summary of the trader's position on the Taipings in 1853.

13. *Hunt's Merchants' Magazine*, XXXIII (1855), 272–282. For more trader comments on the rebellion, see *New York Herald*, June 3 and Dec. 12, 1854; *Albany Evening Journal*, July 12, 1853; *New York Times*, Oct. 6, 1854; *National Intelligencer*, Dec. 21, 1854; *Graham's Magazine*, XLIII (1853), 353–364; *New York Commercial Advertiser*, Aug. 25, 1854.

14. See Report of Daniel Spooner of Russell & Co. in *House Executive Documents* No. 123, 33rd Cong., 2nd Sess., p. 96; *North American Review*, LXXXIX (1854), 199–200.

15. *New York Herald*, Aug. 19, 1853.

16. *New York Tribune*, Aug. 24, 1853.

17. *Albany Evening Journal*, Aug. 13, 1853.

18. *Goshen Democrat and Whig*, June 24, 1853.

19. "Chinese Christianity," [Boston] *Daily Evening Transcript*, Aug. 20, 1853.

20. *Rochester Daily American*, Aug. 25, 1853; *National Intelligencer*, Sept. 10, 1853; *New York Times*, June 9 and Aug. 25, 1853; *Daily Evening Transcript*, Sept. 10, 1853. For a good summary of these doubts, see "The History of the Chinese Insurrection," *Littell's Living Age*, XXXIX (1853), 180–192.

21. Taylor's letters from China were as popular as those of missionaries and received wide coverage in the most obscure rural weeklies. See, for example, *Goshen Democrat and Whig*, June 24, 1853 and Oct. 27, 1854. For a summary of Taylor's views, see his *A Visit to India, China and Japan in the Year 1853* (London, 1855).

22. *Daily Evening Traveller*, Aug. 6, 1853.

23. *Daily Evening Transcript*, Sept. 10 and 13, 1853.

24. *Ibid.*, Sept. 13, 1853.

25. *Albany Evening Journal*, Aug. 25, 1853; *Daily Evening Traveller*, Aug. 11, 18, 29 and Sept. 2, 1853.

26. *New York Herald*, Sept. 17, 1854.

27. *Rochester Daily American*, Nov. 22, 1853.

28. *Presbyterian Magazine*, III (1853), 441.

29. *National Intelligencer*, Aug. 6, 1853.

30. *Ibid.*

31. "The Revolution in China," *Biblical Repertory*, n.s., XXVI (1854), 321–348.

32. *New York Herald*, Sept. 12, 1854; *New York Times*, Oct. 26, 1854.

33. *Daily Evening Traveller*, Sept. 15, 1854.

34. *National Intelligencer*, Dec. 28, 1854.

35. *New York Herald*, Sept. 17, 1854.

36. Tyler Dennett, *Americans in Eastern Asia* (New York, 1922), p. 234.

37. *New York Times*, Oct. 26, 1854.

38. See, for example, *New York Herald*, Sept. 16, 1854; *New York Times*, Sept. 14, 1854; *Albany Evening Journal*, Oct. 14, 1854; *Newburyport Herald*, Oct. 9, 1854; *Graham's Magazine*, XLVI (1855), 88–89, 234.

39. *Daily Evening Transcript*, Sept. 15, 1854.

40. *Daily Evening Traveller*, Nov. 3, 1854.

41. *New York Herald*, Sept. 17, 1854.

42. Dennett, *Americans in Eastern Asia*, pp. 206–224.

43. *New York Herald*, April 22, 1854.

44. *New York Times*, Oct. 25, 1854.

45. *Ibid.* See also Parker's letter to the *Daily Evening Traveller*, Oct. 21, 1854, and reprinted in the *New York Herald*, Oct. 25, 1854.

46. *Missionary Herald*, LVII (1861) , 88.

47. See letters in *New York Times*, Dec. 26, 1856; *Biblical Repertory*, n.s., XXVII (1855) , 687–689; *Missionary Herald*, LI (1855) , 9; American Oriental Society, *Journal*, VII (1857) , appendix, viii.

48. Russell H. Conwell, *Why and How* (Boston, 1871), p. 114.

49. W. A. P. Martin, *A Cycle of Cathay* (New York, 1896) , p. 141.

50. *Daily Evening Traveller*, Oct. 21, 1854.

51. See Buchanan's profile in *New York Herald*, Sept. 17, 1854.

52. See George C. Odell, *Annals of the New York Stage* (New York, 1927–1949) , IV, 503–504.

53. See *Congressional Record*, 47th Cong., 1st Sess., March 22, 1882, pp. 2168–2170.

54. *New York Herald*, Dec. 12, 1854. See also *National Intelligencer*, Dec. 28, 1854; *Graham's Magazine*, XLVI (1855) , 88–89.

55. *New York Times*, Jan. 23, 1857.

56. *Ibid.*, Feb. 2 and 14, 1857.

57. Even the missionaries were silent on this issue at this time. Samuel Wells Williams suggested in 1858 that legalization of opium was preferable to the bribery associated with the trade. See F. W. Williams, *Life and Letters of Samuel Wells Williams* (New York, 1899) , p. 292. Ten years later, however, he attacked the legalization of opium. See *ibid.*, p. 443.

58. *Daily Evening Transcript*, Jan. 20, 1857; *Daily Evening Traveller*, March 15, 1857; *Goshen Democrat and Whig*, Jan. 23, 1857; *New York Herald*, Jan. 18, 29, Feb. 2, April 16, 1857; *New York Times*, Jan. 19, 23, April 8, 1857; [Washington, D.C.] *National Era*, Jan. 29, March 19, April 9, 1857; *National Intelligencer*, Jan. 22, April 6, 1857. Even the *Christian Examiner*, one of China's few defenders among religious publications in the Opium War, switched to England's side in 1857. See "The Destiny of China," *ibid.*, LXIII (1857) , 200–210; "The Chinese," *ibid.*, LXV (1858) , 177–205.

59. *New York Times*, April 8, 1857.

60. *Ibid.*, Jan. 24, 1857.

61. *Daily Evening Traveller*, Jan. 23 and 26, 1857.

62. *Ibid.*, Jan. 19, 22, 31, and Feb. 13, 1857.

63. *Ibid.*, April 17, 1857.

64. *Albany Evening Journal*, Jan. 24, 1857.

65. *Ibid.*, Feb. 23, 1857.

66. *National Era*, June 11, 1857.

67. *New York Times*, Jan. 19, 1857.

68. *Ibid.*, Jan. 23 and April 4, 1857.

69. *Ibid.*, April 8, 1857.

70. *New York Herald*, Jan. 18, 1857.

71. *Ibid.*, April 1, 1857.

72. *Ibid.*, April 8, 1857.

73. *New York Times*, April 18, 1857.

74. *New York Herald,* April 8, 1857.

75. *New York Times,* April 8, 1857. See Dennett, *Americans in Eastern Asia,* pp. 300–302, for a description of Napier's negotiations. President Buchanan's refusal to commit more than moral support was undoubtedly out of practical considerations rather than due to any illusions about Sino-American relations. As secretary of state ten years earlier, Buchanan instructed our first commissioner to China, A. H. Everett, to "avoid giving offense to this excitable, ignorant, and jealous population." Letter dated Jan. 28, 1847, in James Buchanan, *Works,* ed. John Bassett Moore (Phila., 1911), VII, 202.

76. *New York Times,* June 6, 1857.

77. *Ibid.,* Jan. 23 and June 6, 1857.

78. *New York Herald,* June 22, 1857.

79. Dennett, *Americans in Eastern Asia,* pp. 280–291.

80. *New York Times,* Feb. 17, 1858.

81. *Ibid.,* Feb. 18, 1858.

82. *Ibid.,* March 13, 1858. See also *New York Herald,* Feb. 18, 19, and March 15, 1858, for similar comments.

83. *New York Times,* Aug. 11, 1858. See also issues of Aug. 10, 20, 21, 27, 1858, for Raymond's careful editorial iteration of this lesson.

84. See Dennett, *Americans in Eastern Asia,* pp. 333–340, for a description of this battle. Thomas A. Bailey has implied that the authenticity of Tatnall's alleged statement is doubtful. See his *Diplomatic History of the American People* (4th ed.; New York, 1950), p. 328 n. 2.

85. As cited in Dennett, *Americans in Eastern Asia,* p. 340, note.

86. Letter from Williams to F. W. Williams, Dec. 28, 1859, in F. W. Williams, *Life and Letters of Samuel Wells Williams,* p. 325.

87. Letter from Heard to his parents, June 22, 1859, in Heard Family Papers, MSS, Baker Library, Harvard University.

88. *National Intelligencer,* Sept. 29, 1859. See also *ibid.,* Oct. 8, 1859; *New York Times,* Oct. 1 and 5, 1859; *New York Herald,* Oct. 1, 1859, for similar editorial comment

89. *Springfield* [Mass.] *Republican,* Sept. 27, 1859.

90. *Albany Evening Journal,* Sept. 26, 1859.

91. *Littell's Living Age,* LXIII (1859), 444.

92. As reproduced in the *Daily Evening Transcript,* Sept. 30, 1859.

93. *Albany Evening Journal,* Sept. 29, 1859; *National Intelligencer,* Nov. 16, 1859.

94. As cited in *New York Times,* May 13, 1859.

95. For example, see editorials in *National Intelligencer,* Oct. 8, 1859; *New York Herald,* Dec. 13, 1859.

96. *Daily Evening Traveller,* Sept. 27, 1859.

97. *North American Review,* XC (1860), 125.

98. "The Destiny of China," *Christian Examiner,* LXIII (1857), 202–203.

99. *New York Herald,* Oct. 15, 1859.

100. *Ibid.,* Oct. 16, 1859; *New York Times,* Oct. 15, 1859.

101. *New York Herald,* Dec. 12, 1860.

102. *North American Review,* XC (1860), 158.

103. *New York Herald,* Dec. 21, 1860.

104. *New York Times,* Aug. 11, 1856.

105. *New York Herald,* Jan. 29, 1857.

106. *Ibid.,* April 1, 1857; *New York Times,* Nov. 17, 1857.

107. *Daily Evening Transcript*, Sept. 26, 1859.

108. *Christian Examiner*, LXIII (1857), 209–210.

109. *New York Times*, April 11 (supplement), 27, 1857; *New York Herald*, April 1, 1857; *Philadelphia Evening Bulletin*, April 4, 1857. This was not the first such accusation. It was reported in 1840 that they poisoned all the streams so that British admirals had to observe the Chinese through telescopes to find out where the Chinese drew their own water. See *New York Herald*, March 18, 1840. According to another report the Chinese attempted to sell the British poisoned tea, but it was pirated and sold to Chinese, many of whom died from it. See *Niles' National Register*, Nov. 28, 1840.

110. Entry of June 23, 1859, in George W. Heard, Jr., Diary, in Heard Family Papers, MSS, Baker Library, Harvard University.

111. See for example, *New York Herald*, Sept. 30, Oct. 22, 1859; *Littell's Living Age*, LIV (1857), 319.

112. *Littell's Living Age*, LXIII (1859), 448.

113. *New York Herald*, March 31 and Nov. 14, 1857; Jan. 10, 1858; Oct. 22, 1859. See also "Russian Agents in Peking," *New York Times*, Sept. 9, 1858.

114. See Richard Thompson, "The Yellow Peril, 1890–1925" (unpub. Ph.D. diss., University of Wisconsin, 1958), p. iv; Josiah Quincy, "China and Russia," *North American Review*, CLXXI (1900), 528–542; Ivanovich [pseud.], "Russo-Japanese War and the Yellow Peril," *Contemporary Review*, LXXXVI (1904), 162–177. The latter article goes back to 1870 and Bakunin's fears of an awakened China for the first expression of the yellow peril. By 1904, Field Marshall Wolseley narrowed "the combatants . . . at the great Battle of Armageddon" to China and the United States. *The Story of a Soldier's Life* (New York, 1904), II, 2. Count Gobineau also expressed yellow perilist fears in 1876 in his poem *Amadis*. It is an error to date the yellow peril, however. In all probability it was always part of the Western image of China going back at least to Genghiz Khan, although the Kaiser Wilhelm II officially gave the concept its name at the end of the nineteenth century.

115. *New York Herald*, March 29, 1857.

116. *New York Tribune*, June 14, 1853.

117. *Ibid.*, June 5, 1857. See also Marx's articles on China for Jan. 23, March 16, 25, 1857.

118. *New York Herald*, Sept. 30, 1859. See pp. 169–170, 174 for Bennett's reaction to Chinese immigration into the United States at this time.

119. *New York Times*, Jan. 31, Feb. 28, 1864.

120. See *ibid.*, Feb. 11, 18, March 29, Oct. 6, 1868; *New York Herald*, Feb. 18, 1868; *New York Sun*, Aug. 31, 1869, for examples of such editorials. One historian expressed surprise at the unrestrained optimism of E. L. Godkin in the *Nation* over this event, which was so out of character for him. But it was a common reaction among American editors at this time. See W. M. Armstrong, "Godkin and Chinese Labor. A Paradox in Nineteenth Century Liberalism," *American Journal of Economics and Sociology*, XXI (1962), 91–102.

121. *Daily Evening Transcript*, Feb. 27, 1868.

122. *New York Times*, March 29, 1868.

123. *Ibid.*, Oct. 6, 1868.

124. *New York Sun*, Sept. 4, 1869.

125. *New York Herald*, June 22, 1869.

126. *Ibid.*, Feb. 11, 1869. See also, *ibid.*, Dec. 13, 1869; *New York Sun*, Dec. 14, 1869. Bennett complained that "four-fifths" of the letters written by Americans in

China were opposed to the treaty which he attributed to a British influence. See *New York Herald*, June 22, 1869.

127. *New York Times*, Aug. 26, 1869; *New York Herald*, Feb. 11, 1869. See P. H. Clyde, "The Chinese Policy of J. Ross Browne, American Minister of Peking, 1868–1869," *Pacific Historical Review*, I (1932), 312–323.

128. *New York Herald*, Sept. 1, Nov. 11, Dec. 13, 1868.

129. See, for example, *ibid.*, Dec. 2, 1869; *New York Tribune*, Aug. 26, 1869; *New York Times*, Oct. 6, 1869; *New York Sun*, Dec. 14, 1869.

130. *New York Herald*, Sept. 25, 1869.

131. *Ibid.*, Feb. 11, 1869.

132. *Ibid.*, Feb. 11, April 28, 1869. See articles on "progress" in China in *New York Sun*, Sept. 3, 1869; *New York World*, July 22, 1868; *New York Times*, June 27, 1868. The latter was not consistent in this omission, however, and six months earlier included Christianity as part of the progress that would result from Burlingame's appointment. See *ibid.*, Feb. 18, 1868.

133. F. W. Williams, *The Life and Letters of Samuel Wells Williams*, pp. 291–292.

134. *New York Times*, Aug. 20, 1858.

135. Rev. John L. Nevius, *China and the Chinese* (New York, 1869), 357–359, 361–362.

136. *New York Observer*, June 25, 1868.

137. Bailey, *Diplomatic History of the American People*, p. 337.

138. For some good examples of editorial crow eating on the topic, see "A Death-Blow to Corrupt Doctrines," *New York Times*, Jan. 14, 1871; "Chinese Civilization," *New York Herald*, Oct. 7, 1870; "John Chinaman," *Auburn* [New York] *Daily Bulletin*, July 30, 1870.

139. *New York Times*, July 3, 1871.

140. *New York Herald*, Sept. 1, 1869.

141. *New York World*, Jan. 9, 1870.

142. *Auburn Daily Bulletin*, Aug. 23, 1870.

143. For some of the more inflammatory headlines and impassioned editorials, see: *New York Herald*, July 20, 29, 30, and Nov. 18, 19, 26, 1870; May 6, 1871. *New York Times*, Oct. 29, 30, and Nov. 1, 16, 19, 29, 1870. *Auburn Daily Bulletin*, July 27 and Aug. 27, 1870.

144. *New York Herald*, May 12, 29; June 26; Oct. 25, 1870.

145. *Ibid.*, Sept. 5, 1870, article reprinted from the *North China Daily News* and editorial comment.

146. See *New York Times*, Nov. 3, 1870, for the most extensive reproduction of these documents. Excerpts of them also appeared in *New York Tribune*, Aug. 22, 1870; *Salem* [Mass.] *Gazette*, Nov. 1, 1870.

147. *New York Times*, Sept. 17, 1870.

148. *New York Herald*, May 12, 1871; *New York Times*, Oct. 28, 1870.

149. The *New York Times* carefully rejected any relationship between the anti-Christian riots in China and the anti-Chinese ones in California, explaining that the Cantonese and Pekinese are as far apart as Norwegians and Italians. See *ibid.*, Sept. 17, 1870.

150. *New York Tribune*, Aug. 15 and 22, 1870.

151. *New York Times*, Jan. 1, 14, and April 27, 1871. See also "End of an Experiment," *Littell's Living Age*, CVI (1870), 501–503.

152. *New York Herald*, Oct. 2, 1870; May 2, 8, 10, 12, and 15, 1871.

153. *Ibid.*, Dec. 12, 1870.

154. *Ibid.*, Sept. 13, 1870.

155. *Albany Evening Journal*, Aug. 22 and 29, 1870.

156. *Salem Gazette*, Nov. 1, 1870.

157. *Daily Evening Traveller*, Aug. 22 and Oct. 30, 1870; *Springfield Republican*, Aug. 23, 1870; *New York World*, July 7, 1870; *New-York Evening Post*, Aug. 22, 1870; *Albany Evening Journal*, Aug. 29, 1870.

158. *Daily Evening Transcript*, Sept. 2, 1870.

159. *New York Tribune*, Aug. 8, 15, 1870.

160. *New York Herald*, Dec. 21, 1870.

161. *New York Times*, Dec. 31, 1870.

162. *New York Herald*, May 10, 1871.

163. *Ibid.*, April 24 and May 6, 8, 15, 1871; *New York Times*, Jan. 1 and 14, 1871.

164. *New York Times*, Jan. 1, 1871.

165. *Ibid.*, Jan. 14, 1871.

166. *New York Herald*, April 24 and May 2, 6, 15, 1871.

167. *Ibid.*, May 10, 1871.

168. For example, see *New York Times*, April 27, 1871; March 1, 1874; April 8 and June 10, 1875. *New York Herald*, Aug. 22, 1871.

169. *New York Times*, Feb. 28, 1874; March 26 and Aug. 28, 1875; May 23, 1878.

170. D. J. MacGowan, M.D., "On Chinese Poisons," *American Journal of Science and Arts*, s. 2, XXVI (1858), 25–31.

171. *New York Times*, May 26. 1883.

172. *Ibid.*, Oct. 8, 1872.

173. *Ibid.*, June 10, 1875.

174. *Auburn Daily Bulletin*, Aug. 16, 1870.

175. Hon. Edwin R. Meade, *The Chinese Question. A Paper Read at the Annual Meeting of the Social Science Association of America. Held at Saratoga, New York, Sept. 7, 1877* (New York, 1877), p. 12.

7. DOMESTIC ADAPTATIONS OF THE NEGATIVE STEREOTYPE, 1850–1882

1. *Brother Jonathan*, IV (1843), 388.

2. *Harbinger*, VI (1847), 35.

3. *American Quarterly Register*, II (1849), 150.

4. As cited in *Harbinger*, VIII (1848), 70.

5. *New York Herald*, April 14, 1859.

6. *Littell's Living Age*, LI (1856), 316.

7. Mrs. E. S. Barnaby, "A Visit to a Wealthy Chinaman. Extract from a Journal," *Ladies' Repository*, XXI (1861), 144. For similar comments see *Pathfinder*, I (1843), 163–164; *American Penny Magazine*, II (1846), 668; *Eclectic Magazine*, XV (1848), 222; *Knickerbocker Magazine*, XLV (1855), 872.

8. J. R. Bowman, *The Pacific Tourist* (New York, 1882–1883), p. 279.

9. *Scribner's Monthly*, XII (1876), 866.

10. *New American Cyclopedia: A Popular Dictionary of General Knowledge*, eds. George Ripley and Charles Dana (2nd ed.; New York, 1863), V, 108.

11. See, for example, *Harbinger*, IV (1847), 27; *New York Times*, Aug. 20, 1858;

Hunt's Merchants' Magazine XXXIX (1858), 440–443, and XLVII (1862), 522; *New York Express*, April 23, 1850.

12. *American Quarterly Register*, II (1849), 144–145.

13. See "Thomas de Quincy's China," *Eclectic Magazine*, XLI (1857), 65–75; "Williams's Account of China," *North American Review*, LXVII (1848), 265–291.

14. William Dowe, "Mantchows and Mings," *Graham's Magazine*, XLIII (1853), 353–364. See p. 354.

15. *Congressional Globe*, 41st Cong., 2nd Sess., Jan. 25, 1870, p. 752. The article was by Rev. W. A. P. Martin in *Harper's Magazine*, XXXIX (1869), 912.

16. *Congressional Globe*, 41st Cong., 3rd Sess., Jan. 7, 1871, p. 351.

17. "The Test of Civilization," *New York Times*, Oct. 8, 1872.

18. See, for example, *New York Herald*, Oct. 15, 1855. But this faint editorial grumbling quickly gave way to praise by 1857. See, for example, *Daily Evening Transcript*, Feb. 12, 1857.

19. Entry for Sept. 29, 1859, in G. W. Heard, Jr., Diary, typescript copy, Heard Family papers MSS, Baker Library, Harvard University.

20. *New York Times*, July 31, 1869.

21. *Ibid.*, July 29, 1869. See also a front page article contrasting these two Asiatic immigrants in *Poughkeepsie* [New York] *Daily Eagle*, July 3, 1869.

22. *New York Herald*, Aug. 14 and Sept. 3, 1872. For similar comments see the editorials and special articles in *ibid.*, Oct. 30, 1870; Jan. 1 and Dec. 28, 1871; May 18, Aug. 16, and Sept. 10, 12, 13, 1872; July 10, 1875. *New York Sun*, Dec. 27, 1873. *New York World*, June 13, 1877.

23. Ruth Miller Elson, *Guardians of Tradition* (Lincoln, Nebr., 1964), p. 165.

24. For example, see John Scoble, *Hill Coolies. A Brief Exposure of the Deplorable Conditions of the Hill Coolies in British Guiana and Mauritius and of the Nefarious Means by Which They Were Induced to Resort to These Colonies* (New York, 1840), 32 pp.

25. *Daily Evening Traveller*, July 14, 1853. See also *ibid.*, Aug. 20 and Sept. 12, 1853; Jan. 27 and March 23, 1857; May 12, 1858. *Daily Evening Transcript*, April 1, 1856; Jan. 23, 1857; May 12, 1858. *Newburyport Herald*, Oct. 2, 1854.

26. *Senate Executive Documents*, No. 105, 34th Cong., 1st Sess.

27. *Ibid.*, No. 99, p. 181. See also *House Executive Documents*, No. 443, 36th Cong., 1st Sess., pp. 8 ff; *Independent*, VIII (1856), 123; *National Era*, XI (1857), 127; *Christian Review*, XXVII (1862), 211–239, for some magazine protests against this "new slave trade."

28. Albert B. Hart (ed.), *The Commonwealth History of Massachusetts* (New York, 1930), IV, 157.

29. *Daily Evening Traveller*, Sept. 12, 1853.

30. Tyler Dennett, *Americans in Eastern Asia*, p. 536. See also John W. Foster, *American Diplomacy in the Orient* (New York, 1903), Chap. VIII.

31. See *New York Times*, March 17 and Aug. 16, 1869; *New York World*, Feb. 25, 27 and March 17, 1869; *New York Herald*, June 11 and Sept. 20, 1869. See also *House Executive Documents*, No. 105, 34th Cong., 1st Sess., pp. 152–154; No. 1, 42nd Cong. 2nd Sess., pp. 221–222; *Senate Executive Documents*, No. 30, 36th Cong., 1st Sess., p. 64.

32. *New York Herald*, Oct. 15, 1870.

33. *New York Tribune*, July 3, 1870.

34. *New York Herald*, July 27, 1870.

35. *Ibid.*, Oct. 13, 1870.

36. *Ibid.*, Oct. 14, 1870.

37. *New York Times,* Jan. 24, 1870.

38. *New York Herald,* July 28, 1869.

39. *De Bow's Review,* IV (1867), 151–152, 160.

40. *New York Herald,* July 29, 1870.

41. *Boston Daily Advertiser,* June 14, 1870.

42. Russell H. Conwell, *Why and How* (Boston, 1871), pp. 44, 180.

43. See for example, the editorial protest in the *New York Times,* July 31, 1869; "Our Labor System and the Chinese," *Scribner's Monthly,* II (1871), 61–70.

44. See, for example, *Daily Evening Traveller,* June 5, 1870; *Albany Evening Journal,* June 6, 1870; *Springfield Republican,* June 13, 1870; *Daily Evening Transcript,* June 25, 1870; Horace Greeley, *Political Economy* (Phila., 1869), p. 83.

45. *De Bow's Review,* s. 2, II (1866), 215–217; IV (1867), 362–364. Evidence collected in *Littell's Living Age,* CII (1869), 814; CVI (1870), 501–503.

46. *De Bow's Review,* s. 2, IV (1867), 363–364. Italics added.

47. Conwell, *Why and How,* pp. 140, 224–235.

48. *New York Times,* July 30, 1873; *Newburyport Daily Herald,* Jan. 21, 1870. The subject of Chinese female slavery in California was incessantly discussed by eastern editors. See *New York Times,* Feb. 25, March 2, 17, and July 30, 1869; June 14, 1872; Aug. 29, 1875; Feb. 11, 1879.

49. See, for example, Rep. Coghlan's speech, *Congressional Globe,* 42nd Cong., 2nd Sess., March 16, 1872, p. 1737; Sen. Sargent, *Congressional Record,* 44th Cong., 1st Sess., Mar. 1, 1876, p. 2853.

50. *Congressional Globe,* 41st Cong., 2nd Sess., July 4, 1870, pp. 5161–5162.

51. *Congressional Record,* 47th Cong., 1st Sess., March 22, 1882, p. 2169.

52. See speeches by Blaine, *Congressional Record,* 45th Cong., 3rd Sess., Feb. 14, 1879, pp. 1299–3000; Bayard, *ibid.,* 47th Cong., 1st Sess., March 8, 1882, p. 1717; de Uster, *ibid.,* March 18, 1882, p. 2030; Flower, *ibid.*

53. As quoted in *Scribner's Monthly,* XII (1876), 863.

54. *Congressional Record,* 43rd Cong., 2nd Sess., Dec. 7, 1874, pp. 3–4.

55. See William Stanton, *The Leopard's Spots* (Chicago, 1960), pp. 1–23, for a good discussion of this period.

56. *Boston Magazine,* Aug., 1784, and Oct., 1874.

57. Stanton, *The Leopard's Spots,* p. 9.

58. Edward Lurie, "Louis Agassiz and the Races of Man," *Isis,* XLV (1954), 229; Stanton, *The Leopard's Spots,* pp. 19–21.

59. Proclus, "On the Genius of the Chinese," *The Port Folio,* s. 3, V (1811), 342–356, 418–436.

60. Stanton, *The Leopard's Spots,* 25.

61. *American Quarterly Review,* XVII (1835), 103.

62. See Robert G. Latham, M.D., F.R.S., *The Natural History of the Varieties of Man* (London, 1850), pp. 17 ff.; William Carpenter, *Principles of Human Physiology* (2nd ed.; Phila.,1876), pp. 1004–1005; *Cyclopedia of Anatomy and Physiology* (London, 1849–52), p. 1330. This was popularly expressed in some geography texts and gazetteers. "In thickness of lips, flattened nose and expanded nostrils, they bear of considerable resemblance to the Negro," it was explained in *Lippincott's Complete Pronouncing Gazetteer, or Geographical Dictionary of the World* (Phila., 1857). Sir John Barrow, *Travels in China* (London, 1804), pp. 48–50, appears to have been the origin of this comparison between the Hottentot and Chinese which was picked up by ethnologists later in the century. One editor found the attempt

to link physically these two groups in an article in the May 1881 issue of the *Popular Science Review* to be "a fine example of the vague speculation indulged in under the name of anthropology." *New York Times*, May 15, 1881.

63. As cited in the *New Englander*, VIII (1850) , 544.

64. S. G. Morton, *Crania Americana* . . . (Phila., 1829) , pp. 3–9, 40, 290; *Brief Remarks on the Diversities of the Human Species* . . . . *Delivered Before the Pennsylvania Medical College* (Phila., 1842) , pp. 15, *passim*. See also the discussion of Morton in Stanton, *The Leopard's Spots*, pp. 27–35.

65. J. C. Nott and George Gliddon, *Indigenous Races of the Earth; Or New Chapters of Ethnological Inquiry* (Phila., 1857) , pp. 17, 236, 253–254.

66. J. C. Nott, *Two Lectures on the Connection Between Biblical and Physical History of Man* (New York, 1849) , pp. 17–18, 36.

67. See Louis Agassiz, "The Diversity of Origin of the Human Races," *Christian Examiner*, XLIX (1850) , 111–113.

68. *Ibid.*, pp. 134–135, 144.

69. John Higham, *Strangers in the Land* (New York, 1965) , p. 134; Stanton, *The Leopard's Spots*, p. 192.

70. Lurie, *Isis*, XLV (1954) , 234; Earl W. Count, "The Evolution of the Race Idea in Modern Western Culture During the Pre-Darwinian Nineteenth Century," *Transactions of the New York Academy of Science*, VIII (1946) , 139–165.

71. *American Journal of the Medical Sciences*, XXXIV (1857) , 468–470.

72. These private collections are catalogued in the New York Academy of Medicine.

73. Count, *Transactions of the New York Academy of Science*, VIII (1946) , 159.

74. Edward Saveth, "Race and Nationalism in American Historiography: The Late Nineteenth Century," *Political Science Quarterly*, LIV (1939) , 435. For an excellent example of this, see the statement by William Elder, M.D., *Questions of the Day* (New York, 1871) , in which this amateur political economist of some national reputation explained the biological basis to "societary life" which permitted civilization for the Caucasian but only "barbaric" social organization in Asia and a "savage" existence in Africa.

75. Theodore Parker, *The American Scholar* published in *Works* (Boston, 1907–1911) , VIII, 411–412.

76. J. C. Nott, "Instincts of Races," *New Orleans Medical and Surgical Journal*, XIX (1866) , 1–16.

77. "Race in Legislation and Political Economy," *Anthropological Review*, IV (1866) , 123.

78. "Race in History," *Anthropological Review*, III (1865) , 240. Such comments indicate a relationship between nineteenth-century romanticism and the unfavorable image of the Chinese, just as the earlier more favorable image was associated with rationalism—the "Noble Savage" displaced the "Noble Sage." Romanticism led to contempt for the mundane, reserved, stoic, if not "slavish" characteristics of the Chinese that kept him from the lofty cultural pinnacles reached by Greeks, Romans, and Europeans. As Dowe explained it, China's civilization was one "of beavers and bees" shaped by the "materialist and mundane philosophies" of Confucius, and "his industrial moralities." See *Graham's Magazine*, XLIII (1853) , 363. For this reason, the American Indian was also treated with greater respect by the polygenists than were the Chinese. See the comment of Agassiz, p. 156, above.

79. *Anthropological Review*, III, 247.

80. *Ibid.*, IV (1866) , 120, 133.

81. Gerritt Lansing, "Chinese Immigration: A Sociological Study," *Popular Science Monthly,* XX (1882), 721–735.

82. *New York World,* April 4, 1876.

83. See editorials in *New York Tribune,* Sept. 29, 1854; *New York Times,* Sept. 3, 1865; *New York Herald,* Oct. 7, 1869; *New York World,* July 1, 1870; *New York Sun,* July 9, 1870, for extreme racist fears concerning the Chinese. An English editor, William Hepworth Dixon of *Atheneum,* incorporated all these fears in his *New America* (Phila., 1867) which was also cited in newspapers.

84. See, for example, editorials in *New York Tribune,* Sept. 23, 1870; *New York Herald,* June 23, 1870; *New York Times,* July 7, 1870.

85. *Congressional Record,* 47th Cong., 1st Sess., Feb. 28, 1882, p. 1483; March 21, 1882, p. 2126; March 9, 1882, p. 1738.

86. *Congressional Globe,* 41st Cong., 2nd Sess., July 4, 1870, p. 5164.

87. *Ibid.,* p. 5177.

88. Lurie, *Isis,* XLV (1954), 233.

89. Stanton, *Leopard's Spots,* p. 65.

90. J. C. Nott, "Thoughts on Acclimation and Adaptation of Races to Climates," *American Journal of Medical Science,* XXXII (1855), 325.

91. Nott and Gliddon, *Indigenous Races,* p. 369; J. C. M. Boudin, "Études de pathologie comparée," *Annales d'hygiène,* XLII (1849), 38–79.

92. *Medical Repository,* III (1800), 290.

93. See the summary of this report in *American Journal of Medical Sciences,* XXVIII (1854), 182.

94. Thomas R. Colledge, M.D., *The Medical Missionary in China* (Phila., 1833), p. 8. See *Methodist Quarterly Review,* XXXII (1850), 596, and *Presbyterian Monthly,* II (1867), 230, for summaries of the effects of missionary reports of disease and death in China on the recruitment of new missionaries.

95. Arthur B. Stout, M.D., *Chinese Immigration and the Physiological Causes of the Decay of a Nation* (San Francisco, 1862), pp. 1–26.

96. Letter from Logan to Stout, March 1, 1871, in *First Biennial Report, State Board of Health in California* (Sacramento, 1870–1871), pp. 54–55.

97. Arthur B. Stout, "Report on Chinese Immigration," *ibid.,* p. 63.

98. *Transactions of the American Medical Association,* XXVII (1876), 106–107. Sim's speech was also published in Philadelphia and London as *Legislation and "Contagious Diseases,"* 16 pp. Dr. Joseph K. Barnes complained in 1873 that the approach to cholera was duplicating the earlier error of the medical profession in failing to see the relationship between sexual intercourse and the syphilitic virus. Contact with the "pre-existing cholera-virus" is also necessary to produce cholera. This virus was imported from Asia (largely "Hindoostan"), he concluded. See U.S. Surgeon General's Office, *The Cholera Epidemic of 1873* (Wash., D.C., 1875), p. 8.

99. *Transactions of the AMA,* XXVII (1876), 106.

100. *New York World,* June 5, 1876.

101. *New York Herald,* May 4, 1876. See also *Scribner's Monthly,* XII (1876), 742, for an expression of this fear.

102. *New York World,* June 23, 1870.

103. Mary P. Sawtelle, "The Foul Contagious Disease. A Phase of the Chinese Question. How the Chinese Women are Infusing a Poison into the Anglo-Saxon Blood," *Medico-Literary Journal,* I (Nov. 1878), 4–5.

104. *The Encyclopaedia Britannica* (4th ed.; London, 1810), VI, 42.

105. *New York Times,* Sept. 28, 1878.

106. *New York Herald,* Nov. 12, 1877.

107. Sawtelle, *Medico-Literary Journal,* I, 2.

108. See for example, *Lancet,* June 1, 1872; *American Journal of Syphilography and Dermatology,* III (1872), 274.

109. *American Journal of Syphilograpy and Dermatology,* IV (1873), 362.

110. "Leprosy in California," *New York Times,* July 20, 1881.

111. *New York Times,* March 6 and Dec. 22, 1880.

112. For example, E. R. Squibb, M.D., *Disinfectants* (New York, 1866); A. E. Sansom, *The Arrest and Prevention of Cholera, Being a Guide to the Antiseptic Treatment* (London, 1866); "On the Practice of Disinfection," *Chemical News,* Dec. 7, 1866.

113. *New York Herald,* Sept. 1, 1871.

114. *The American Annual Cyclopedia and Register of Important Events of the Year 1878,* n.s. III, 387–391. Even earlier Wilhelm Hugo von Ziemssen mentioned the germ theory of disease in his *Cyclopaedia of the Practice of Medicine* (New York, 1874–81), I, 374. This was a translation of an essay written by Ziemssen in 1874.

115. *New York Times,* May 6, 1875.

116. *Scribner's Monthly,* XV (1877–78), 480–493.

117. *New York Herald,* Aug. 2 and 12, 1871.

118. *New York Times,* Feb. 20 and March 1, 1877. An editorial in the *American Journal of the Medical Sciences,* LXXXI (1881), 527, indicates that members of the medical profession were generally uneasy over the crowded conditions, alleged filth, and unfamiliar germs in Chinatowns and predicted epidemics as a result.

119. *Congressional Record,* 47th Cong., 1st Sess., March 6, 1882, p. 1636.

120. *Ibid.,* 41st Cong., 2nd Sess., Jan. 25, 1870, p. 752.

121. *Ibid.,* 44th Cong., 1st Sess., July 6, 1876, p. 4419.

8. EAST COAST REACTION TO CHINESE IMMIGRATION, 1850–1882

1 J. Milton Mackie, "The Chinaman," *Putnam's Monthly Magazine,* IX (1857), 337–338.

2. Bayard Taylor, *A Visit to India, China, and Japan, in the Year 1853* (London, 1855), p. 354.

3. *North American Miscellany and Dollar Magazine,* n.s., I (1852), 272.

4. See editorials in *New York Times,* Oct. 5, 1852; *New York Herald,* April 26, 1852, and Dec. 12, 1853; [Wash., D.C.] *National Intelligencer,* May 20, 1852.

5. "The Coming of the Barbarian," *Nation,* X (1869), 45.

6. "The Chinese in California," *Milwaukee Sentinel,* as reprinted in *New York Times,* Sept. 27, 1852.

7. *New York Times,* Oct. 1, 1852.

8. *New York Herald,* April 26, 1852.

9. *Graham's Magazine,* XLV (1854), 486.

10. See *New York Tribune,* Sept. 29, 1854; *Newburyport Daily Herald,* Oct. 2, 1854; *New York Herald,* Oct. 2, 1854; *Rochester Daily American,* Aug. 26, 1854; *National Weekly Intelligencer,* Sept. 12, 1854; *Littell's Living Age,* XLIII (1854), 125.

11. [New York] *Morning Courier,* Sept. 26, 1854.

12. *New York Tribune,* Oct. 2, 1854. Bennett made a similar observation in the *New York Herald,* Oct. 9, 1853.

13. "Chinese Emigration to California," *New York Tribune,* Sept. 29, 1854.

14. *Ibid.*

15. While Governor Bigler made a sinophobic speech in California in 1852 and some queue cutting was reported as early as 1851, editors on the West Coast did not express much sinophobic sentiment before the spring of 1853. This was in response to Senator Tingley's bill in 1852 to enforce contracts made in China. Sandmeyer, however, believes that the most important source of criticism stemmed from the Chinatowns, on which a statewide committee made a sanitation report in 1854. See Elmer Sandmeyer, *The Anti-Chinese Movement in Californic* (Urbana, Ill., 1939), p. 36; Mary Coolidge, *Chinese Immigration* (New York, 1909), pp. 57–58; Rodman Paul, "The Origins of the Chinese Issue in California," *Mississippi Valley Historical Review,* XXV (1938), 181–196; Gunther Barth, *Bitter Strength* (Cambridge, Mass., 1964), pp. 136–143.

16. "The Growth of the United States Through Emigration—The Chinese," *New York Times,* Sept. 3, 1865.

17. See Horace Greeley, *Political Economy* (Phila., 1869), p. 83; *New York Herald,* Oct. 7, 1869; *New York Times,* June 7, 1868.

18. See *New York Tribune,* July 7 and Sept. 14, 1869; Jan. 28 and June 4, 23, 28, 1870.

19. *Daily Evening Traveller,* March 3, 1868.

20. *New York Times,* June 7, 1868.

21. *Albany Evening Journal,* July 5 and 9, 1870.

22. *Ibid.,* July 9, 1870.

23. "The Chinese in California," *New York Times,* Oct. 16 and 18, 1867.

24. Greeley, *Political Economy,* p. 83.

25. "Secondary Symptoms of Native Americanism," *New York Times,* Aug. 12, 1869; *New York Tribune,* Aug. 10, 1869.

26. "John Chinaman—What Shall We Do With Him?" *New York Times,* June 29, 1869.

27. [Boston] *Daily Evening Transcript,* Aug. 19, 1869.

28. *Albany Evening Journal,* July 21, 1869.

29. *New York Herald,* May 31, 1870.

30. "Sambo Versus John Chinaman—The California Republican," *New York Herald,* July 24, 1869.

31. *Ibid.,* Aug. 14, 1869.

32. *Ibid.,* July 14, 1869.

33. *Ibid.,* Aug. 3, 1869.

34. John R. Commons *et al.* (eds.), *Documentary History of American Industrial Society* (Cleveland, 1910–1911), IX, 80, 81–84. Italics added.

35. *New York Herald,* Nov. 25, 1869.

36. *New York Sun,* July 12, 1869.

37. See p. 152.

38. *New York World,* July 15, 1869.

39. *New York Times,* July 14, 1869. See also *ibid.,* July 16 and 24, 1869.

40. *New York Herald,* July 22, 1869.

41. *Ibid.,* Aug. 3, 1869.

42. *Ibid.,* Oct. 7, 1869.

43. *Ibid.,* Oct. 25, 1869.

44. *Hide and Leather Interest and Industrial Review* (New York), May 1869.

45. "What Shall be Done with John Chinaman," *New York Times,* March 3, 1870.

46. *New York Herald,* April 5, 1870.

47. See *Springfield Republican,* June 13, 1870; *Daily Evening Traveller,* June 13, 1870; *Daily Evening Transcript,* June 12, 1870.

48. See *New York World,* July 1 and Sept. 29, 1870; *New York Herald,* June 29, 30, July 1, and Aug. 9, 1870; *Auburn* [N.Y.] *Daily Bulletin,* June 27, 1870; *Boston Investigator,* July 6, 1870; *New York Times,* Aug. 13, 1870; *Workingman's Advocate,* July 2, 1870, for the sites of these meetings as well as descriptions of the lively protests.

49. *Boston Commonwealth,* June 25, 1870.

50. *New York Herald,* July 10, 1870.

51. *New York World,* July 10, 1870.

52. *New York Herald,* Sept. 23, 1870.

53. *Ibid.,* June 29 and 30, 1870.

54. *Ibid.,* July 1, 1870.

55. *New York World,* Sept. 29, 1870.

56. *New York Herald,* June 30, 1870.

57. See excerpts from his message in *New York Herald,* Aug. 9, 1870; *Workingman's Advocate,* Aug. 13, 1870; *New York World,* Aug. 8, 1870; *New York Times,* Aug. 6, 1870.

58. *New York World,* July 1, 1870. This infuriated the editor of Boston's *Daily Evening Transcript,* July 1, 1870.

59. *New York Times,* July 6, 1870.

60. *New York Herald,* Feb. 3, 1871.

61. *Congressional Globe,* 41st Cong., 3rd Sess., Jan 7, 1871, pp. 351–361. Mungen's sinophobic speeches were serialized in *Workingman's Advocate,* Feb. 11, 27, and March 18, 1870.

62. *Nation,* XI (1870), 20.

63. *National Standard,* July 25, 30, 1870. See also Wendell Phillips, *Speeches, Lectures, and Letters* (Boston, 1894), pp. 145–151.

64. Russell H. Conwell, *Why and How* (Boston, 1871), pp. 45, 48–49, 236–240.

65. *New York Herald,* Oct. 6, 1870.

66. See, for example, *Albany Evening Journal,* Nov. 1, 1870.

67. *Springfield Republican,* July 6, 1870.

68. *Daily Evening Traveller,* July 9, 1870.

69. *William Lloyd Garrison, the Story of His Life as Told by His Children* (New York, 1889), IV, 296–301; *New York Tribune,* Feb. 17, 24, and 27, 1879.

70. Letter from Bryant to Miss J. Dewey, Jan. 21, 1875, in Parke Godwin, *A Biography of William Cullen Bryant, with Extracts from His Private Correspondence* (New York, 1883), II, 360.

71. *Springfield Republican,* June 13, 1870.

72. *Albany Evening Journal,* June 24, 1869; June 23 and 24, 1870.

73. *Ibid.,* Nov. 1, 1870.

74. *Springfield Republican,* June 21 and 22, 1870.

75. *Daily Evening Transcript,* June 25, 1870.

76. *Ibid.,* July 14, 1870.

77. *New York Times,* March 3, 1870.

78. *Ibid.,* July 6, 1870.

79. *Ibid.,* July 1 and 7, 1870; *New York Star,* June 30, 1870.

80. *New York Tribune,* June 4, 1870.

81. *Ibid.,* June 23, 1870.

82. *New York Times*, July 1, 1870.

83. *New York Times*, July 1, 1870; *New York Tribune*, June 30, 1870.

84. *Ibid.*, Sept. 23, 1870. Thirty-five years earlier Greeley had used a related defense: "In China . . . there are no priests to incite assassinations—no riotous assemblies—no midnight murders. Compared with Ireland, it is a terrestrial paradise." *New Yorker*, II (1836) , 79. Many of the defensive articles on behalf of the Chinese were thinly disguised attacks on the Irish. See, for example, "China in Our Kitchens," *Atlantic Monthly*, XXIII (1869), 747–752; "Mary Ann and Chyng Loo," *Lippincott's Magazine*, VI (1870), 354–361; "The Asiatic Invasion," *Scribner's Monthly*, XIII (1876–77), 687–694; editorial in *New York Times*, Dec. 26, 1873. Protestant ministers often utilized this defense which infuriated Catholic editors. See "Preachers on the Rampage," *Catholic World*, XXVI (1878), 700–712.

85. *New York Tribune*, Aug. 27, 1870.

86. "The Coolie in Our Midst," *New York World*, June 28, 1870. This editorial ran three columns, and neatly encapsuled all the fears discussed in this chapter.

87. *Ibid.*, July 2, 1870.

88. *Ibid.*, June 30, 1870.

89. *New York Sun*, July 9, 1870; See Candace Stone, *Dana and the Sun* (New York, 1935), pp. 341–342, for a description of Dana's difficulty in reaching this decision.

90. *New York Herald*, June 16, 1870.

91. *Ibid.*, June 21 and 27, 1870.

92. *Ibid.*, June 23, 1870.

93. *Ibid.*, July 1, 1870.

94. *Ibid.*, July 15, 1870.

95. *Ibid.*, July 30 and Aug. 9, 1870.

96. *Ibid.*, Oct. 6, 1870.

97. *New York Times*, April 25, 1873.

98. *Ibid.*, May 20, 1873. See also E. W. Gilliam, "Chinese Immigration," *North American Review* CXLIII (1886), 26–34, for a good summary of these economic fears.

99. See R. I. Bunkhouse, "Lascars in Pennsylvania," *Pennsylvania History*, VII (1940), 20–30; Thomas La Fargue, "Some Early Chinese Visitors to the United States," *T'ien Hsia Monthly*, XI (1942), 128–139; Howard M. Chapin, "The Chinese Junk Ke Ying at Providence," Rhode Island Historical Society, *Collections*, XXVII (1934), 5–12.

100. "Chinamen in New-York," *New York Times*, Dec. 26, 1856. This leader was reported as "Quimbo Appo" in Louis Beck, *Chinatown* (New York, 1898), pp. 9–10.

101. "Chinese in New-York," *New York Times*, Dec. 26, 1873.

102. Sarah E. Henshaw, "California Housekeepers and Chinese Servants," *Scribner's Monthly*, XII (1876), 739.

103. Letter dated Nov. 27, 1879, in the Society's *Fifth Report* (New York, 1880) in New York Historical Society, New York, N.Y. This myth of a Chinese taste for sodomy with young boys appears frequently even in more scholarly works. Charles Le Tourneau in his *La psychologie ethnique* (Paris, 1901), p. 249, wrote: "En fait, l'amour contre nature est fort répandu en Chine. . . . C'est un genre de débauche, qui est admis et les jeunes hommes, faisant métier de mignons, ne se cachent pas plus que ne le font chez nous les femmes galantes de bas étage."

104. *Daily Evening Traveller*, July 1, 1870; *New York Herald*, June 30, 1870.

105. *Scribner's Monthly*, XII (1876), 741; *New York Herald*, April 3, 1876. See

also "The Gods of Wo Lee," *Atlantic,* XXV (1870) , 469–79. This last very friendly article conceded that the Chinese only go to Sunday school to learn English, but rejected the charge that they had any sexual designs on their female teachers.

106. *Brooklyn Eagle,* May 20, 1892. This was the celebrated Wing Lee marriage to his Sunday school teacher, Grace French, which caused "profound excitement," according to this editor. See *ibid.,* May 14, 1892. One headline proclaimed her "a mere girl" although she was 20 years old, but the reporter explained that she was so "girlish" that she was more like 14. See *ibid.,* May 21, 1892. For a similar case in Waynesboro, Georgia, see *New York Times,* June 11, 1883. Fearful that other white girls would be "caught in the toils of Chinese duplicity," townsmen ran the "rat-eaters" out and burned down their store. See also *ibid.,* May 28, 1883, editorial. One pro-Chinese immigration article suggested breeding Chinese women, "when more arrive," with white men for future workers in California's "semi-Asiatic climate, using the example of English planters and Kanaka women in Hawaii. But the author did not even consider Chinese men marrying white women as an alternate possibility. See *Lippincott's Magazine* (Phila.) , II (1868) , 36–41. For descriptions of some of the scandals that wracked New York churches on the issue of exposing white female teachers to adult Chinese male students, see *New York World,* March 28, 1892; *New York Times,* Dec. 29, 1891: "Why Girls Shouldn't Associate with Heathens in Sunday Schools," *Brooklyn Eagle,* Jan. 6, 1892.

107. Oscar Handlin, *The Americans* (Boston, 1963) , p. 304.

108. *New York World,* March 9 and 12, 1889.

109. *New York Tribune,* Oct. 2, 1903.

110. *Scribner's Monthly,* XVII (1878–1879) , 491.

111. *New York Times,* June 10, 1873; Feb. 16, 1874.

112. See *ibid.,* Dec. 6, 1874; March 5, 1875; July 15, 1877. *New York World,* April 10 and 16, 1876. *New York Herald,* April 15 and 16, 1882. See *New York Times,* Aug. 1, 1883, p. 8 for a good summary of these views.

113. *New York Herald,* April 3, 1876.

114. *New York Times,* Dec. 21, 1872. For another sarcastic editorial along the same lines, see "Converted Heathens," *ibid.,* June 16, 1874.

115. See, for example, *Irish Citizen,* July 9 and 16, 1870.

116. See the editorial description in the *New York Times,* Aug. 23, 1877. Polygamy was such a sensational charge that the simple appointment of Brigham Young's son to the U.S. Military Academy provoked the headline "Polygamy at West Point . . . Will the Boys Permit the Outrage?" *New York Herald,* June 5, 1871.

117. *New York World,* April 29, 1877.

118. *New York Times,* April 30, 1877, cf. *ibid.,* Oct. 2, 1874.

119. *Senate Reports,* No. 689, 44th Cong., 2nd Sess. For good summaries see Wen Hwan Ma, *American Policy Toward China as Revealed in the Debates of Congress* (Shanghai, [1916]) , pp. 63–66; Mary Coolidge, *Chinese Immigration* (New York, 1909) , pp. 97 ff. For a humorous attack on the committee, see Samuel E. Becker, *Humors of a Congressional Investigating Committee: A Review of the Report of the Joint Special Committee to Investigate Chinese Immigration* (Wash., D.C., 1877) , 36 pp.

120. *New York Times,* April 5, 1876. See *ibid.,* June 10, 1873 for last preceding doubts.

121. *New York Herald,* Oct. 1, 1876.

122. "The Asiatic Invasion," *Scribner's Monthly,* XIII (1876) , 687–694; *New York World,* April 4, 10, and 15, 1876; *New York Herald,* April 3 and May 4, 1876.

123. "The Mongol Problem," *New York World,* April 15, 1876.

124. *New York Herald,* June 8, 1876.

125. *New York Times,* Feb. 28, 1877.

126. "The Famine in China," *ibid.,* July 6, 1878.

127. *New York Herald,* Feb. 27, 1878.

128. *New York World,* June 20, 1870; *New York Times,* March 8, 1878.

129. *North American Review,* CXXVI (1878) , 516, 524, 526.

130. *Congressional Record,* 47th Cong., 1st Sess., April 17, 1882, p. 2973. Congressman Shelly of Alabama was touring the country and proposing in 1878 that the immigration be stopped and that those Chinese who could not return be put on a reservation like the Indians. *New York Times,* Feb. 4, 1878.

131. *New York Herald,* June 8, 1876.

132. *Congressional Record,* 45th Cong., 3rd Sess., Feb. 13, 1879, p. 1267.

133. Entry of Feb. 26, 1879, in C. R. Williams (ed.) , *Diary and Letters of Rutherford B. Hayes* (Columbus, Ohio, 1924) , III, 522. Hayes also had a great deal of proexclusion literature in his personal library at Fremont, Ohio, among which were reprints of John Boalt's lecture to the Berkeley Club, *The Chinese Question* (San Francisco, 1877) ; Edwin R. Meade's address to the Social Science Association of America, *The Chinese Question* (N.Y., 1877) ; Mrs. Mary Sawtelle's editorial in the Nov. 1878 issue of *Medico-Literary Journal* on "The Foul Contagious Disease: A Phase the Chinese Question—How Chinese Women are Infusing a Poison into the Anglo-Saxon Blood"; M. B. Star's inflamatory book, *The Coming Struggle; or What the People of the Pacific Coast Think of the Coolie Invasion* (San Francisco, 1873) ; and Russell Conwell, *Why and How* (Boston, 1871) .

134. F. W. Williams, *Life and Letters of Samuel Wells Williams* (New York, 1899) , p. 427.

135. *New York Times,* April 6, 1880.

136. *Ibid.*

9. CHINESE EXCLUSION IN HISTORICAL AND NATIONAL PERSPECTIVE

1. Ira B. Cross, *A History of the Labor Movement in California* (Berkeley, 1935) . See also Arthur Mann, "Samuel Gompers and the Irony of Racism," *Antioch Review,* XIII (1953) , 203–214.

2. Robert Seager, "Some Denominational Reactions to Chinese Immigration to California, 1856–1892," *Pacific Historical Review,* XXVIII (1959) , 49–66.

3. *Boston Commonwealth* as cited in John R. Commons *et al.,* (eds.) , *Documentary History of American Industrial Society,* (Cleveland, 1910–11) , IX, 84–85.

4. *Workingman's Advocate* (Chicago and Phila.) , June 25, 1870.

5. "A Warning Instance," *Workingman's Advocate,* July 17, 1869.

6. See *ibid.,* Sept. 4, 1869 and Feb. 12, 1870; George E. McNeil (ed.) , *The Labor Movement* (Boston, 1887) , Chap. XVI, for sinophobic statements by these labor leaders.

7. Commons, *Documentary History,* IX, 136–137; *Workingman's Advocate,* Dec. 11, 1869.

8. *Workingman's Advocate,* July 27, 1873; *Proceedings of the First Congress of the American International Workingman's Association* (New York, 1872) , 5 (photostatic copy held at Tamiment Institute Library, New York, N.Y.) . According to Norman Ware, "the Red International," or International Workingman's Associa-

tion representing American anarchism, gained a big following because of its strong anti-Chinese agitation. See his *Labor Movement in the United States, 1860–1895* (New York, 1929) , p. 310.

9. For example, see the editorials in the following: the *National Socialist,* May 18 and Aug. 31, 1878; March 8, 1879. The *Socialist,* June 1 and July 1, 1876; June 16, 1877; Feb. 10, 1878. For strong anti-Chinese editorials in other labor publications, see the *Labor Standard,* March 31 and April 7, 1878. *Paterson Labor Standard,* June 3, 1880 and Aug. 6, 1881. *National Labor Tribune,* April 29, May 27, and June 3, 1876; Oct. 28 and Nov. 23, 1878; March 1, 1879. The *Journal of United Labor,* Aug. 15, 1880. "The Chinese War," *Cigar Makers' Official Journal,* May and Aug., 1876; Jan. 15, 1878; May 10, 1880.

10. Joseph Buchanan, *The Story of a Labor Agitator* (New York, 1903) , p. 276.

11. *Workingman's Advocate,* Aug. 27, 1870. The description of the convention and the various anti-Chinese resolutions and amendments recorded in this issue make the national character of this sentiment among workers very clear. See also John R. Commons *et al., History of Labour in the United States* (New York, 1918–1935) , II, 149.

12. The *Socialist,* March 8, 1879.

13. As reproduced in John Swinton, *The New Issue: The Chinese-American Question* (New York, 1870) , p. 6.

14. Philip Taft, *The AF of L at the Time of Gompers* (New York, 1957) , p. 12.

15. *Workingman's Advocate,* March 28, 1874.

16. *Ibid.,* May 27, 1871; *National Socialist,* June 16, 1878.

17. *National Socialist,* August 31, 1878.

18. See *Meat vs. Rice* (AF of L, 1883), p. 31.

19. *Ibid.*

20. See, for example, *Workingman's Advocate,* Oct. 9, 1869; Oct. 11, 1873; May 6, 1876; Nov. 29, 1878.

21. *Ibid.,* Oct. 11, 1873.

22. *Ibid.,* May 10, 1873.

23. See pp. 183–184.

24. *Workingman's Advocate,* May 6, 1876.

25. *McGee's Illustrated Weekly,* II (1878) , 322. See also *Irish American,* April 15, 1882; *Irish World,* June 3, 1871; *Irish Citizen,* Sept. 4, 1869.

26. *McGee's Illustrated Weekly,* I (1877) , 406.

27. *Irish Citizen,* July 16, 1870.

28. *Ibid.,* July 9, 1870.

29. Mary S. Connaughton, *The Editorial Opinion of the Catholic Telegraph of Cincinnati on Contemporary Affairs and Politics, 1871–1921* (Washington, D.C., 1943) , p. 213.

30. *Nationalist Socialist,* May 11, 1878.

31. M. F. S., "The Labor Question," *American Catholic Quarterly Review,* III (1878) , 737–739.

32. John Gilmary Shea, "The Rapid Increase of the Dangerous Classes in the United States," *ibid.,* IV (1880) , 240–268.

33. Bryan Clinche, "The Chinese in America," *ibid.,* IX (1884) , 57–70.

34. Samuel Becker, *Humors of a Congressional Investigating Committee: Review of the Report of the Joint Special Committee to Investigate Chinese Immigration* (Washington, D.C., 1877) , 36 pp.

35. Edward C. Tolman, "Cognitive Maps in Rats and Men," *Behavior and Psychological Man* (Berkeley, 1961) , p. 262.

36. Frederick Rudolph, "Chinamen in Yankeedom: Anti-Unionism in Massa-chusetts in 1870," *American Historical Review*, LIII (1847), 19. Once again, the California thesis appears to have been an operational assumption for Rudolph. "Only in California did the question of Chinese labor remain a question of serious political importance," he asserts (p. 28), to explain why there was such strong editorial support for Sampson's action "with the exception of a comparatively miniscule labor press" (p. 18). In all fairness to Rudolph, however, he did state that by 1882 "the issue of Chinese immigration was a politically safe one," with both the worker and manufacturer favoring exclusion (pp. 28–29). If Rudolph meant this to be a national sentiment, as he seems to have, no one ever followed up this important and insightful generalization by systematically collecting the evidence necessary to support it or trace its evolution.

37. See pp. 180–181.

Bibliographical Note

In the hope that the notes will serve as an adequate guide to the primary and secondary sources used in this study, I would like to suggest a few additional bibliographical guides to these sources. Liu Kwang-Ching's *Americans and Chinese* (Cambridge, 1963) is by far the most valuable guide to both the published and unpublished writings of Americans who ventured to China in the late eighteenth and nineteenth centuries. Clayton H. Chu, *American Missionaries in China* (Cambridge, 1960), Valentin H. Rabe, *American Chinese Relations, 1784–1941* (Cambridge, 1960), and Louise M. Taylor, *Catalogue of Books on China in the Essex Institute* (Salem, 1926), provide useful guides to holdings in the Missionary Research Library at Union Theological Seminary, at Harvard University, and at the Essex Institute in Salem, Massachusetts, respectively. Yuan Tung-Li, *China in Western Literature* (New Haven, 1958), brings Henri Cordier's *Bibliotheca Sinica* (Paris, 1904–1908) up to date. Curtis W. Stucki, *American Doctoral Dissertations on Asia, 1933–1958* (Ithaca, 1959), provides a useful catalogue for this genre. Older but still useful guides to some of this literature include James W. Snyder, *A Bibliography for the Early American China Trade, 1784–1815* (New York, 1940); Robert E. Cowan and Boutwell Dunlap, *Bibliography of the Chinese Question in the United States* (San Francisco, 1909); *Catalogue of Publications of Protestant Missionaries in China* (Shanghai, 1876); George A. Clayton, *A Classified Index to the Chinese Literature of the Protestant Churches in China* (Hankow, 1918); and Arthur Probsthain, *Encyclopedia of Books on China* (London, 1927).

For nineteenth-century geography texts, Ruth Miller Elson's *Guardians of Tradition* (Lincoln, 1964) and John Nietz's *Old Textbooks* (Pittsburgh, 1961) provide useful bibliographies; but since the texts cited are so scattered the reader is advised to consult directly the impressive collections housed at the New York Historical Society, Teachers College and the University of Pittsburgh.

The newspapers and periodicals used in this study may be found in the following works: *American Newspapers, 1821–1936: A Union List of Files Available in the United States and Canada,* ed. Winifred Gregory (New York, 1937); *Union List of Serials in Libraries of the United States and Canada,* ed. Edna Brown Titus (3rd ed., New York, 1965), 5 vols.; and Clarence Brigham, *History and Bibliography of American Newspapers, 1690–1820* (Hamden, Conn., 1962). Unfortunately there is no adequate guide to Catholic and Irish serials, and the reader is advised to consult the catalogues at Catholic University, Holy Cross, and the Irish Historical Society in New York. A mimeographed list of American socialist and labor newspapers held by the Tamimant Institute in New York is available. The Surgeon General's Office has published a good index to medical sources and the card catalogue at the New York Academy of Medicine is also very helpful.

The most readable and valuable secondary works on European images of the Chinese include the following: William Appleton, *A Cycle of Cathay* (New York, 1951); Raymond Dawson, *The Chinese Chameleon* (London, 1967); J. F. Hudson, *China and Europe* (New York, 1939); Donald Lach, *Asia in the Making of Europe* (Chicago, 1965); Virgile Pinot, *La Chine et la formation de l'esprit philosophique en France* (Paris, 1932); and Adolph Reichwein, *China and Europe* (New York, 1925). Their frequent references to a host of excellent articles on this topic in professional journals form an efficient guide to these secondary sources, although S. Y. Teng's excellent article, "The Predispositions of Westerners in Treating Chinese History and Civilization," *Historian* XIX (1957), 307–327, has been generally overlooked.

Kenneth Latourette, "History of the Early Relations Between the United States and China," Connecticut Academy of Arts and Sciences, *Transactions,* XXII (1917), 1–209; Tyler Dennett, *Americans in Eastern Asia* (New York, 1922); and Foster Rhea Dulles, *China and America* (Princeton, 1946) remain the standard narratives on early Americans in China although all three are loaded with dubious, untested generalizations. Kuo Ping Chia's article "Canton and Salem: The Impact of Chinese Culture upon New England Life During the Post-Revolutionary Era," *New England Quarterly,* III (1930), 420–442, remains one of the best commentaries on this topic. Numerous works on American voyages to China— Eldon Griffin, *Clippers and Consuls,* 1845–1860 (Seattle, 1938); Agnes Hewes, *Two Oceans to Canton: The Story of the Old China Trade* (New York, 1944); Ralph Paine, *Ships Across the Sea* (Boston, 1920); C. E. Trow, *The Old Shipmasters and Salem* (New York, 1906) —are largely maritime histories. Some very good works exist from the Chinese perspective: Paul Cohen, *China and Christianity* (Cambridge, 1963); Chang Hsin-pao, *Commissioner Lin and the Opium War* (Cambridge, 1964); Earl Swisher, *China's Management of the American Barbarians* (New Haven, 1951); Merle Curti and John Stahler, "The Flowery Flag Devils: The American Image in China, 1840–1900," American Philosophical Society, *Proceedings,* XCVI (1952), 663–690; John K. Fairbank, "Tributary Trade and China's Relations with the West," *Far Eastern Quarterly,* I (1942), 129–149.

As stated earlier there are very few secondary works on Chinese immigration, and Mary Coolidge's *Chinese Immigration* (New York, 1909) remains the standard account from a national perspective. Gunther Barth's *Bitter Strength* (Cambridge, 1964) stops at 1870, over a decade short of exclusion; and except for the year 1870, it fails to examine the national reaction to Chinese immigration, however valuable as a reinterpretation of sinophobia in California. Rose Hum Lee, *The Chinese in the United States of America* (Hong Kong, 1960) is more of a contemporary sociological study than a historical account. W. M. Armstrong's "Godkin and Chinese Labor: A Paradox in Nineteenth Century Liberalism," *American Journal of Economics and Sociology,* XXI (1962), 91–102; Arthur Mann's "Samuel Gompers and the Irony of Racism," *Antioch Review,* XIII (1953), 203–214; and Frederick Rudolph, "Chinamen in Yankeedom: Anti-Unionism in Massachusetts in 1870," *American Historical Review,* LIII (1947), 1–29, are three of the rare attempts to examine the issue from a non-Western perspective, although both John Commons and Norman Ware suggested, decades before, that sinophobia played an important national role in the evolution of organized labor during the last third of the nineteenth century.

Index

Abeel, Rev. David: on Confucius, 63; on infanticide, 67; on the natural inquisitiveness of the Chinese, 69; view of Satan's role in China, 73; on the Opium War, 102; mentioned, 60, 161

Abel, Clark, 49, 50, 52, 54, 56, 80

Adams, John, 13

Adams, John Quincy: mentioned, 11; view on Chinese responsibility for the Opium War, 95, 97, 103; reaction to his lecture, 95–97, 101, 104, 107, 112, 226n*134;* later application of his thesis in response to Tientsin Massacre, 138; publication of lecture, 223n*53*

Addison, Joseph, 12

Agassiz, Louis, 155–156

Agriculture in China. *See* Chinese culture

Allport, Gordon, 206n*28*

American Board of Commissioners for Foreign Missions, 58, 73, 75

American Catholic Quarterly Review, 200–201

American Federation of Labor, 197

American Medical Association, 160–163 *passim*

American Sunday School Union, 63

Amherst mission to Peking: mentioned, 39, 53; description of, 48–49, 51; American response to books produced by, 87, 89, 92; role in evolution of yellow peril mythology, 110. *See also* Abel, Clark; Ellis, Sir Henry; Hall, Basil; M'Leod, John; Maxwell, Murray; Staunton, George T.

Amiot, Abbé Jean, 11, 12, 14

Anderson, Aeneas, 39–41, 42, 47, 52, 56

Anderson, Rev. Rufus, 73

Anglo-American relations in China: anglophobia presumed by historians, 18, 21, 23, 95; evidence of close, friendly ties in China, 23–24, 26, 55, 72, 210n*42;* American community in

China supports English in Anglo-Chinese wars, 97–103, 121–122, 124–127, 133

Anglophobia and American editorial reactions to Anglo-Chinese wars, 105–107, 122–125 *passim*

Anson, Lord, 11, 12, 13, 14, 50, 54

Anthropological Review, 156, 158

Antisepsis. *See* Chinese immigration

Appleton Nathaniel, 25, 33

Appleton, William, 11, 12, 43

Armstrong, W. M., 231n*120,* 246

Armstrong, Commodore, USN, 122

Arnold, Daniel, 30

Arrow incident, 113, 114, 121–122, 129, 131

Assimilation fears. *See* Chinese immigration

Auber, Peter, 23, 24

Bailey, Thomas A., 17, 95, 134–135

Ball, Rev. Dyer, 119

Banks, Hon. Nathaniel Prentiss, 176, 178

Barrow, Sir John: mentioned, 39, 55; influence of his book on China, 43, 47, 53, 54, 64, 67, 78, 80, 86, 87, 89; reputation among contemporaries, 43–44; views on China, 44–46, 50, 51, 52, 56

Barth, Gunther, 3, 7, 205

Bayard, Hon. Thomas, 153

Becker, Samuel, 201

Bemis, Samuel Flagg, 97

Bennett, James Gordon: on Wall St. press, 84; on Opium War, 96, 105, 109, 110–111; on Taipings, 115, 116, 119–121; on *Arrow* incident and Anglo-Chinese war, 124, 129–131 *passim;* on Russian influence and yellow peril, 131; on Chinese immigration, 169. See also *New York Herald*

Bennett, James Gordon, Jr.: split with missionaries, 133–134; on Tientsin